Income Distribution in Colombia

A Publication of the Economic Growth Center, Yale University

INCOME DISTRIBUTION IN COLOMBIA

ALBERT BERRY
and
MIGUEL URRUTIA

New Haven and London, Yale University Press, 1976

Copyright © 1976 by Yale University.
All rights reserved. This book may not be
reproduced, in whole or in part, in any form
(except by reviewers for the public press),
without written permission from the publishers.
Library of Congress catalog card number: 75-18164
International standard book number: 0-300-01874-6

Designed by Sally Sullivan
and set in Times Roman type.
Printed in the United States of America by
The Murray Printing Co., Westford, Mass.

Published in Great Britain, Europe, and Africa by
Yale University Press, Ltd., London.
Distributed in Latin America by Kaiman & Polon,
Inc., New York City; in Australasia by Book &
Film Services, Artarman, N.S.W., Australia;
in Japan by John Weatherhill, Inc., Tokyo.

Contents

List of Tables and Figures	vii
Foreword	xi
Preface	xiii
Acknowledgments	xvii

Part I *A Theoretical Framework: The Distribution Record in Colombia*   1

1. Broad Determinants of Changes in Income Distribution during the Process of Development   3
2. Income Distribution in the 1960s   27
   Appendix: Survey of Various Income-Distribution Estimates   47
3. The Distribution of Income in Agriculture: Determinants and Trends over Time   53
4. Changing Income Distribution under Development: 1930s–1960s   87
5. Changes in Regional Income Distribution over Recent Decades   124

Part II *The Effects of Economic Policy on Income Distribution*   147

6. Sectoral Policy and Income Distribution   149
7. Fiscal Policy and Income Distribution   153
8. Income Distribution and the Distribution of Education   175
9. The Financial Sector and Income Distribution   200
10. The Distributional Impact of Agricultural Policy   230
11. An Overview: Looking Ahead   252

Appendix Tables   265

Index   275

List of Tables and Figures

Tables

2.1	Income Distribution for the Economically Active Urban Population excluding Absentee Landlords, 1964	30
2.2	Income Distribution of Agricultural (excluding family helpers) and Nonagricultural Rural Labor Force, 1964	32
2.3	Average Income by Deciles of the Employed Labor Force in the Rural and Urban Sectors, 1964	34
2.4	Income Distribution for All of the Economically Active Population of Colombia, 1964	36
2.5	Coefficients of Income Concentration in Latin American Countries and Developed Countries	40
2.6	Gini Coefficients of Concentration, Urban and Rural Sectors, Six Countries	41
2.7	Distribution of Personal Pretax Income in the United Kingdom, 1967	42
2A.1	Comparison of Results of Various Studies of Income Distribution in Colombia	51
3.1	Personal Distribution of Income (national accounts concept) from Agriculture by Income Categories, 1960	54
3.2	Personal Distribution of Income from Colombian Agriculture by Deciles, 1960	55
3.3	Average Income of Producers by Farm Size, 1960	59
3.4	Distribution of Income among Wage Earners in Agriculture, 1960	59

3.5	Labor and Capital Shares by Deciles of the Personal Income Distribution in Agriculture	62
3.6	Index of Real Agricultural Wages, by Department and Climate and for Colombia as a Whole, 1935/37–64/67	66
3.7	Pure Labor Share as a Percentage of Agricultural Value Added, Selected Groups of Years	68
3.8	Tractorization over Time	78
3.9	Labor Income and Labor Share by Products	80
3.10	Tendency of Crops to be Grown on Small and Large Farms, 1960 and 1966	84
4.1	Changes in Average Income by Periods and by Occupational Categories	92
4.2	Real Wage Indices of Government Employees	98
4.3	Unskilled Construction Wages in Bogota Compared to Other Selected Wage Series	100
4.4	Selected Real Annual Wage Series	112
4.5	Income Distribution Comparisons, 1934–36, 1951, and 1964	114
4.6	Annual Percentage Income Change of Selected Occupational Groups Compared among Periods of Slow and Fast Overall Income Growth	120
4.7	Price Indices for Three Income Classes in Bogota	122
5.1	Regional Distribution of Income in Selected Countries	126
5.2	Income Differentials by Department, circa 1964	128
5.3	Average Income and Coefficient of Concentration by Region, Rural/Urban Factor, and Sex, 1970	131
5.4	Output Per Capita in Agriculture, Manufacturing, and Commerce by Department, 1953 and 1967	132
5.5	Relative Improvements in Housing Conditions by Department, 1938–51 and 1951–64	135
5.6	Indicators of Educational Advance by Department	137
5.7	Redistribution of Labor Force by Department, 1938 to 1951 to 1964	139
5.8	Occupational Structure Change by Department, 1951–64	140
7.1	Distribution of Personal Income before and after Taxes, 1966	155

List of Tables and Figures ix

7.2	Effective Rates of Taxation for Various Taxes by Income Brackets, 1966	157
7.3	Public Expenditures by Major Sector or Type, 1966	161
7.4	Distribution of Educational Expenditures by All Levels of Government among Deciles of the Population, 1966	163
7.5	Public Utility Rates for Bogota Homes, 1971	169
7.6	Current Expenditures of All Levels of Government, 1966	171
7.7	Distribution of Income after Taxes and All Transfers	172
8.1	Bogota, Income per Hour of Salaried and Independent Male Workers, 1963–66	182
8.2	Employed Persons in Bogota, by Income Group and Sex, April 1967	183
8.3	Concentration of Education and Income	189
8.4	Internal Rate of Return of Investment in Education, Men and Women, 1963–66	190
8.5	International Comparison of Rates of Return to Investment in Education	191
8.6	Relationship between Income and Educational Inequality	193
9.1	Outstanding Loans of the Banking System in November 1970	209
9.2	Classification by Gross Assets of the Users of Credit, November 1970	210
9.3	Gross Assets and Number of Taxpayers in Processed Tax Returns for 1967	211
9.4	Rates of Interest of Some Financial Assets of Families	212
9.5	Number and Size of Savings Deposits, 1963, 1966, 1969	214
9.6	Colombia: Net Assets by Sectors	216
9.7	Loan Applications Approved by the Mortgage Bank in 1970	219
9.8	Increases in Land Price per Hectare in Various Municipalities Compared with Cost-of-Living Increases in the Same Periods	224
10.1	Caja Agraria Credit/Value of Output, by Farm Size	235
10.2	Factor Productivity and Farm Size in Colombia, 1960	244
10.3	Land and Credit Achievements of INCORA	247

Figures

1.1	Labor Allocation between Modern and Traditional Sectors in a Labor-Surplus Economy	12
1.2	Effect on Income Distribution of the Shift of Labor Force from Agriculture to Nonagriculture	17
2.1	Lorenz Curve and the Coefficient of Concentration	38
2.2	Income Distribution in the Colombian Labor Force, 1964	45
3.1	Lorenz Curve of Personal Distribution of Income, Colombia, 1964	58
3.2	Size Distribution of Blue-Collar Labor Income and of Capital Income, 1960	61
4.1	Historical Trends in the Income Levels of Selected Occupational Groups from 1935	91
5.1	GDP per Capita and Decreases in the Share of Labor Force in Agriculture by Department, 1951–64	142
8.1	Lorenz Curves for Wage/Salary Income in Colombia and England	177
8.2	Lorenz Curves for Income of the Labor Force and Education of 20–24-Year-Old Population	186
8.3	Lorenz Curves for Rural Income and for Education of the 20–24-Year-Old Population Living in Rural Areas	187

Foreword

This volume is one in a series of studies supported by the Economic Growth Center, an activity of the Yale Department of Economics since 1961. The Center is a research organization with worldwide activities and interests. Its research interests are defined in terms of both method of approach and subject matter. In terms of method, the Center sponsors studies which are designed to test significant general hypotheses concerning the problem of economic growth and which draw on quantitative information from national economic accounts and other sources. In terms of subject matter, the Center's research interests include theoretical analysis of economic structure and growth, quantitative analysis of a national economy as an integral whole, comparative cross-sectional studies using data from a number of countries, and efforts to improve the techniques of national economic measurement. The research program includes field investigation of recent economic growth in twenty-five developing countries of Asia, Africa, and Latin America.

The Center administers, jointly with the Department of Economics, the Yale training program in International and Foreign Economic Administration. It presents a regular series of seminar and workshop meetings and includes among its publications both book-length studies and journal reprints by staff members, the latter circulated as Center Papers.

Lloyd G. Reynolds, Director

Preface

Colombia is now at a middle level of income relative to other developing countries. She is not poor in the way that India, Pakistan, and Haiti are. At the same time she has an extremely unequal income distribution, and this inequality is essentially the source of the absolute poverty found in the country. Extreme poverty is not necessary in a country with Colombia's average income; redistribution of only 7 or 8 percent of the national income would be adequate to double the income of the bottom quarter of the population. This amply justifies the study of income distribution in Colombia and makes improved distribution an important objective of economic policy.

Since distribution has received little analysis in Colombia, the empirical part of this study begins by presenting a benchmark estimate of income distribution corresponding to 1964. It then attempts to throw some light on the historical behavior of distribution over the last several decades. Data are at present inadequate for a scientific testing of the relation between apparent trends in distribution and the nature of the evolution of the economy, but it is possible at least to indicate which plausible or popular hypotheses are consistent with the data and which are not.

Effective policy for improving the distribution of income requires a good understanding of the determinants of inequality. Opinions as to which policies have potential are much more varied than one might guess. Many people believe that inequality of distribution reflects unequal distribution of talents; others feel that it reflects lack of organization of the laboring class and still others that it reflects the distribution of wealth. Some believe that the best way to rectify the inequality, at least in part, is through the government budget, that is, through tax, transfer, and government expenditure policy. Others feel that this is not a hopeful route, both for technical and political reasons, and that more basic remedies are needed. Still others think that government policies other than tax–expenditure management can help, such as the support of unions, the control of the prices of wage goods, and so on. As is mentioned in several chapters, there is a noticeable tendency in this area for intuition to be completely misleading—the policy which at first glance seems potentially effective often turns out to be of little use or even counterproductive. Accordingly, it is necessary to understand in as much detail as possible the role of various aspects of an economic and political structure in causing income inequality if the potential of a specific policy to alleviate it is to be accurately gauged. Colombian policymakers are now thinking increasingly in terms of income distribution—why it is so bad and what may be done about it. Their proposals and actions are of course constrained very much by the political and social context, but perhaps an equally strong constraint at present is lack of information and understanding of the sources of inequality and the effects of different policy decisions. We hope that this study will contribute toward a better understanding of the phenomenon.

Part I focuses on the measurement of income distribution in Colombia in the mid-1960s (chap. 2)—overall, urban, and rural—and on its historical trends, also by sectors. A theoretical discussion of the determinants of income distribution (chap. 1) is complemented by attempts to explain why the observed shifts in distribution over time have occurred overall (chap. 4), in agriculture (chap. 3), and by region (chap. 5).

In the second part of the book we discuss the effects of certain types of previous government policy on income distribution as we perceive them to have been and make some recommendations. The policy areas chosen are fiscal, educational, financial, and agricultural. Although we agree that fiscal policy can by no means be the sole weapon in the attempt to reduce inequalities, we believe it can play a substantial role and therefore deserves careful consideration (chap. 7). Of all types of public expenditure, education appears to have relatively great potential as a means of redistribution. Educational expenditures are large and can be directed fairly easily toward people at or near the bottom of the income distribution (chap. 8). We believe that the income distribution effects of both structure and past policy in the financial sector have been very negative but for reasons not well understood. We therefore place great importance on a more articulate and informed discussion of the distributional implications of financial policy (chap. 9). Agriculture, as we see in chapter 2, is a sector whose distribution appears to have been systematically worsening for the last forty years. It remains the largest sector in the economy and the one with the highest share of poor people. The importance of bearing in mind income distribution in the formulation of agricultural policy should be obvious (chap. 10).

It would be desirable to have comparable analyses of the distributional impact of trade policy, industrial organization, urban policies, and a number of other areas. In many, building up the needed data base is even more difficult than for the fields treated here.

Needless to say, firm conclusions cannot often be drawn about a phenomenon as imperfectly measured as distribution. The current study, although falling short of a satisfactory level of precision, does, we feel, leave little doubt that Colombia's distribution ranks among the most unequal. Direction of change is more open to question, but the likelihood is great that since the mid-1930s an initial period of worsening was followed by one of improvement at least in the urban, if not in the overall, distribution (chap. 4). In agriculture, however, the trend seems to have been consistently negative. Most disconcerting is the substantial evidence that government policy in several important areas has contributed to worsening distribution (or has offset potential improvement). This is evidently the case with credit policy and a number of aspects of tax–expenditure policy.

We hope this study will contribute to the airing of the issues in question, both in Colombia and more generally. It represents only a first step. Before research can provide satisfactory answers to the issues under discussion, both much better data and much more analysis will be needed.

Acknowledgments

Many people have read the present manuscript and made useful comments. We are particularly grateful to Gustav Ranis, Carlos Díaz Alejandro, and Jorge Katz for their comments, as well as to Clara Elsa de Sandoval, Ellen Hall, Alfonso Padilla, and Christina Lanfer for their skillful assistance in preparing many of the tables and computations.

Many institutions also supported us during the five years we worked on the research published here. We are particularly indebted to Banco de la Republica, Yale University, and the University of Western Ontario, which gave us time to work on this project, and to the Centro de Investigaciones para el Desarrollo (CID) of the Universidad Nacional and to the Ford Foundation, institutions that financed much of the research and without whose help this collaborative effort would have never been started.

PART I

A THEORETICAL FRAMEWORK: THE DISTRIBUTION RECORD IN COLOMBIA

1

Broad Determinants of Changes in Income Distribution during the Process of Development

In a typical economy the process of development brings with it an increase in output per capita and also changes in the distribution of income generated in the production process.[1] It is useful from a number of points of view to distinguish, as factors causing increases in output per capita, (1) increases in the capital/labor ratio, (2) increases in efficiency, including not only improvements in the production process in various sectors (technological change in the narrow sense of the term) but also a number of other effects often described as the residual and which include improvements in organization of production, changes in the structure of production toward sectors with higher productivity, and so forth.

1. We do not consider here the important question of how distribution can affect economic growth. Much attention is now being focused on it. Among the studies particularly relevant for Colombia is William F. Cline, *Potential Effects of Income Redistribution on Economic Growth: Latin American Cases* (New York: Praeger, 1972). No comparable study has been undertaken for Colombia to our knowledge. Several studies have concentrated on the relationship between income distribution and factor demands (e.g., Gustavo Jimenez, "The Capital, Labor and Import Content of Urban Consumption Patterns in Colombia," draft of Rice University M.A. thesis, 1972; Gregory Ballentine and Ronald Soligo, "Consumption and Earnings Patterns and Income Redistribution," paper presented at the Rice University Program of Development Studies Workshop on Income Distribution and its Role in Development, April 1, 1974).

Since our basic concerns in this study are to describe distribution trends and to discuss specific economic policies from a distributional point of view, we do not consider causal mechanisms leading from distribution to growth. Were our analysis sophisticated enough, it is true that focus on only one direction of causation in such a situation would lead to certain biases of interpretation. At this stage, our major problems of analysis are much more mundane.

At times, economies of scale are distinguished as a source of growth, implying that in their absence the increase in output associated with a given increase in the total quantity of factors would be less than that observed. But there is little evidence that economies of scale are significant at the level of the economy as a whole except when strong barriers to international trade exist. Otherwise, the inability to capture scale economies in the domestic economy can be overcome by producing for the world market. It is useful to have these determinants of the growth of output in mind because changes in the income distribution depend on the nature of the growth process.

Determinants of the Personal Income Distribution: Neoclassical System with Imperfections in Product Markets

Two concepts of income should be differentiated from the outset. Most theoretical analyses of income distribution consider only income generated directly in the production process of new goods and services. A form of income equally relevant for the recipient—although not for the economy as a whole—results from increases (or decreases) in the value of assets. In certain situations, such as when the real price of land and real estate tends to rise, the effect of this increase can be quite important for some people because it may constitute a substantial share of their total income. Most of the discussion that follows focuses on the determinants of income generated in the production process, but we refer occasionally to this capital gains income.

In order not to complicate the discussion unduly, we consider first determinants of changes in personal income distribution in a system with perfect markets except, possibly, for certain final goods. Assuming that factor markets are perfect, the personal income distribution before taxes and transfers depends on the distribution of factors, their prices, and the way in which product markets function.[2] With perfect markets, factor incomes equal factor marginal

---

2. Explanation of changes in the income distribution in terms of changes in the composition of production among sectors with different internal income distributions is instructive in some cases and for some purposes. An analysis of this type loses some of its interest if it is not explained why the different sectors

productivities; with imperfections in product markets, factor incomes are closely related (but not equal) to marginal productivities.[3] At the same time, the way in which changes in distribution occur over time can be expressed in terms of

1. Changes in the distribution of factors, that is, labor, human capital, and physical capital (reproducible or not reproducible);[4]

generate different income distributions and if it cannot be established how these sectoral income distributions change during the development process.

3. This neoclassical theory of distribution is powerful when factor and product markets are almost perfect, when factors are relatively homogeneous, and when given families tend to have only one factor. When markets are not almost perfect, distribution may be more closely related to who has monopoly power than to who owns factors of production. When factors are very heterogeneous, no simple vector of factor quantities and prices describes the distribution.

The marginal productivity theory of income distribution, our basic framework here, is at best only an approximation to reality, as emphasized by our various caveats and qualifications. But it has been challenged by other theories, among them those of Kalecki and Kaldor [M. Kalecki, "The Distribution of National Income," *AEA Readings in the Theory of Income Distribution* (Homewood, Ill.: R.D. Irwin, 1951), pp. 197–220, and N. Kaldor, "Alternative Theories of Distribution," *Review of Economic Studies* 23 (1956): 83–100]. Both of them, along with others, deny the equivalence of marginal productivity and factor remuneration, Kalecki arguing that the labor share is determined by the degree of monopoly and Kaldor that distribution depends on the ratio of investment to national income. [For a discussion of these theories and a good review of many aspects of distribution theory see Harry G. Johnson, *The Theory of Income Distribution* (London: Gray–Mills Publishing, 1973).] It is hardly to be questioned that existence of monopoly has its impact on distribution (we integrate it into the discussion below). Factor remunerations can also reflect the power of threat, often hypothesized in the context of high petroleum worker wages. Our position, however, is that the marginal productivity theory provides a useful starting point in the discussion of distribution in Colombia. It goes without saying that the complexities introduced by market imperfections must be allowed for.

4. The way in which factors are defined is somewhat arbitrary. The best way depends on the problem being analyzed. The three-factor division used here is a common one since for a number of purposes it is useful to consider the rate of return to investment in improved human capacity, commonly called "investment in human capital" in the literature.

The fact that some factors are owned by the government but that it does not charge for their services introduces a complication. (If it does institute a charge, the government can simply be treated like any other factor owner.) This implies that the complementary factors must have higher prices and the substitute factors lower ones than in the absence of this state intervention. Because the present and future factor remunerations are influenced by government investment, so is the wealth of factor owners. And since government investment is an important policy area, public capital should in many cases be treated separately.

2. Changes in the production function over time (technological change), which can change the marginal productivities of factors in a great number of ways; and

3. Changes in market imperfections over time, which can imply that factor remunerations do not change in the same way as their marginal productivities.

Schumpeter described how the process of technological change gives monopoly power to innovators and how this position is eroded with the passage of time. The rapidity of this erosion may sometimes be questioned, but the creation of new monopoly positions is clearly a permanent aspect of the growth process. It may be that the distribution of the asset monopoly power has more to do with changes in income distribution over time than do changes in the distribution of physical capital.

Market imperfections are also responsible for the fact that capital owned by different groups of people may have different rates of return.[5] Such differences may be an important determinant of changes in the distribution of income and of wealth over time.

The distribution of wealth should be analyzed jointly with the distribution of incomes since the former is at each point of time largely the result of previous income distributions and savings ratios. Distribution of wealth changes in response to variations in the relative prices of factors, in the distribution of monopoly power, and in rates of return on wealth held by different individuals or groups of individuals.

Returning to a more empirical plane, it may be noted that the process of growth in the majority of countries has been characterized by the following features.

1. An increase in the capital/labor ratio, which tends to lower the rate of return to capital and raise the wage rate, and which is likely to

---

The conditions under which the distribution worsens or improves over time in some models that emphasize changes in the distribution of capital are discussed in Joseph Stiglitz, "Distribution of Income and Wealth Among Individuals," *Econometrica* 37, no. 3 (July 1969): 382–97; and Guillermo Calvo, "Distribution of Income and Wealth Among Individuals: Some Examples of Long Range Inequality," mimeo, University of the Andes, Bogota, Nov. 1971.

5. Differences in risk are also presumably reflected in different rates of return, though in this case market imperfections are not the cause.

diminish the inequality of personal income distribution. In a simple model with homogeneous capital, homogeneous labor, and a complete separation between capitalists and laborers (i.e., workers have no capital and there are no changes over time in terms of who are capitalists and who are workers), an increase in the quantity of capital in the hands of each capitalist diminishes the income of the average capitalist relative to the worker if and when the elasticity of substitution between the factors is less than one. This condition is considered probable by the majority of analysts who have tried to estimate the elasticity of substitution,[6] although there remain doubts in this respect. If that elasticity is more than one, the increase in the capital/labor ratio would worsen the distribution, assuming always that the typical income of the capitalist is greater than that of the worker.

2. Labor-saving technological change,[7] which tends to maintain a high rate of return to capital and to lead to a decrease (at least in relative terms) of the wage rate. With this decrease in the marginal product of labor relative to that of capital, the income of the workers decreases relative to that of capitalists, and the personal income distribution worsens.

3. A higher average savings rate for people with higher incomes, which tends in general to increase inequality of income via concentration of wealth.

4. A higher rate of return to capital for people with higher incomes, which also tends to increase this inequality.[8]

The net effect of these factors is theoretically unpredictable until

6. Most empirical analyses have tended to find an elasticity of less than one or in the neighborhood of one (in which case the increasing capital/labor ratio would not tend per se to affect the distribution), and the assumption used here is based on such studies. However, it must be admitted that empirical analyses of factor substitution have been very problematic to date, and not too much confidence can be placed in their measuring what they are alleged to measure. So the increasing capital/labor ratio could be assumed only to probably diminish the inequality of distribution.

7. Technological change, which, given any specific factor combination, decreases the ratio of marginal productivity of labor to marginal productivity of capital.

8. Such a differential could be due to less risk averseness of the rich (in which case their higher nominal earnings would not necessarily imply higher net benefits per unit of capital), but capital market imperfections favoring the rich are perhaps the main explanatory factor.

the values of the relevant parameters are specified. Other factors can also be significant: for example, differences in the consumption baskets between the rich and the poor can imply that changes in the real distribution of income differ from changes in the monetary distribution. Demographic changes can also be important if family size varies to a significant degree with the income level, as has frequently been the case.[9]

Factors 3 and 4 mentioned above may not contribute as much to the explanation of changes in the distribution of human capital as of changes in the distribution of physical capital. It appears probable that as development proceeds, a smaller proportion of the new investment in human capital is purchased by families and the distribution of new human capital depends to a considerable degree on the educational policy of the government. A free educational system generally contributes to a more equal distribution of human capital. And differences in the return to human capital will depend more on the innate ability of individuals than on the level of human capital investment.

Although a neoclassical model without market imperfections constitutes a useful first step in the analysis of many problems, special consideration must frequently be given to those imperfections. We discuss below the way in which income distribution patterns differ from those of the neoclassical model with perfect markets when one particular imperfection—that characterizing the labor surplus economy—is present.[10]

The functional distribution between capital income and labor income will be treated first. This division is especially pertinent when physical capital is highly concentrated and the distribution of human capital is closely related to that of physical capital, that is, when the persons who do not have one tend also not to have the other. This situation commonly appears in developing countries. In such a case the functional distribution corresponds to the distribution of

9. These factors have been discussed by (among others) James E. Meade, *Efficiency, Equality and the Ownership of Capital* (London: George Allen and Unwin, 1964), and Herman Daly, "A Marxian Malthusian View of Poverty," Yale Economic Growth Center Discussion Paper no. 80, 1970.

10. Since the base for the comparisons is a model with perfect markets, factor 4 mentioned above as a determinant of changes in income distribution is not considered.

income between two groups of people who are quite distinct: one group that derives its income primarily from physical and human capital and another that sells only unskilled labor.[11] A second division, between income (from capital) of large-scale capitalists on the one hand and all income (whether from labor or capital) of everyone else, appears more pertinent in those countries characterized by widespread distribution of capital—frequently peasant economies with many small farms. In the early stages of development the second division is more pertinent because this situation is characteristic of the agricultural sector.

Distribution of Income over Time in a Neoclassical Economy

We turn first to the determination of changing income distribution in a neoclassical economy without market imperfections. Increases in output per member of the labor force result from increases in the capital/labor ratio and from technological change (in the broad sense of the term). Changes in distribution result from the relative savings rates of groups with different income levels and from the impact of capital accumulation and technological change on (1) relative prices of labor and capital and (2) relative prices of goods. The latter factor warrants attention since, as noted above, changes in income distribution expressed in nominal monetary units are not necessarily equal to changes in distribution of real income[12] if the relative prices of goods change.

When the source of increases in production is capital formation, the redistribution between capital and labor income expressed in monetary terms depends simply on the elasticity of substitution of the aggregate production function. With a Cobb–Douglas produc-

11. There is of course a continuum of persons in terms of the variable percentage of income derived from labor, but this complexity is not treated here, partly to maintain the analysis at a manageable level and partly because the more important results derived when only the two groups are considered can normally be generalized without difficulty to more complicated cases.

12. Defined here as "income expressed in nominal monetary terms and deflated by the price index of the basket of goods of the individual purchaser." We use the term "income expressed in nominal terms" not to exclude income in kind but to distinguish it from real income, which as just mentioned can change over time even though nominal income remains constant if relative prices of goods change.

tion function there will be no change in the shares of factors when capital deepening occurs although remuneration per unit of each factor does change. [The wage rises and the return to capital falls, but because K/L is rising, the total income going to each factor, WL for labor and NK for capital (where W is the wage rate and N the return to capital), can bear an unchanged relation to total income.] Nevertheless, as capital accumulates, relative prices will fall for those goods relatively intensive in capital and will increase for those relatively intensive in labor. Thus, a group whose consumption includes a disproportionately high share of capital-intensive goods will have an increase in real income greater than the increase in income expressed in nominal terms (assuming the general price level remains constant).

Hicks's neutral technological change[13] (another possible source of production increase) does not imply redistribution of nominal incomes so long as the production function is homogeneous of any degree. Under the same homogeneity condition labor-saving technological change will produce, other things being equal, a decrease in the labor share of total income. With capital-saving technological change, the result is the opposite. The situation becomes much more complicated if the production function is not homogeneous.

Changes in the Income Distribution over Time with a Labor-Surplus Situation

A condition apparently characteristic of the Colombian economy is the presence of some excess or surplus labor.[14] Technically this condition may be defined in terms of the existence, at least in part of the economy, of a difference between the marginal productivity of

---

13. That is, technological change that does not affect the marginal rate of substitution among the factors of production.
14. The distribution trends described in this section are essentially those outlined by Lewis in his original presentation of the labor-surplus model [W. Arthur Lewis, "Economic Development with Unlimited Supplies of Labor," *The Manchester School* 22 (May 1954): 139–92]. He focused on the relative constancy of the real wage under growth in the labor-surplus condition, the rising share of modern (capitalist) sector profits, and the quite probably negative redistributive effect of the inflation sometimes relied on to generate investment funds for modern sector growth.

labor and its reward.[15] The existence of labor surplus is in this technical sense an imperfection in the labor market. Normally it is possible to distinguish various sectors in one or more of which the salary is equal to marginal productivity of labor, whereas in others it is higher. This situation implies a nonoptimal distribution of resources and also a predictable evolution of income distribution over time.

In general terms the existence of labor surplus implies that during the first part of the development process—which in terms of the labor-surplus models is marked by a relative increase in the size of the modern sector of the economy at the expense of the traditional sector—a worsening of the income distribution is particularly probable [although under some sets of conditions it would not occur (see n. 21)]. Afterward, when the economy emerges from the labor-surplus condition (i.e., when there are no sectors in which the marginal product of labor remains below its income), the distribution is likely to improve.[16]

To exemplify distributional change over time under labor-surplus conditions, we present a relatively simple model in which the existence of excess labor determines a specific sort of change in income distribution over time.[17] The labor-surplus condition is represented in figure 1.1, where the total labor force is OO' and the marginal productivity curves of the traditional and modern sectors are represented by EL_1 and FL_2, respectively. The modern sector, in which the marginal productivity is equal to the wage (presumed to be fixed institutionally at the level OS_s[18]), employs a number of workers OL_0;

15. For a simple discussion of the labor-surplus model see John C. H. Fei and Gustav Ranis, "The Theory of Economic Development," *American Economic Review*, Sept. 1961. The original formulation of the model was by Lewis, "Economic Development."

16. More precisely, theory suggests that during the first stage cited a labor-surplus economy will suffer a more negative change in distribution than would characterize a neoclassical system with the same production conditions; in the second stage the opposite is true. Under certain conditions distribution would not worsen in absolute terms in the labor-surplus system, but the relative statement made here is a robust one.

17. For a more thorough discussion of changes in distribution in different labor-surplus models, see Albert Berry, "Relative Income Distribution Paths in Neoclassical and Labor Surplus Economies," mimeo, 1971.

18. In most labor-surplus theory it has been assumed, implicitly or explicitly, that there is a relationship between the individual's supply price to the modern sector and his income in the traditional sector. One specific hypothesis is that the

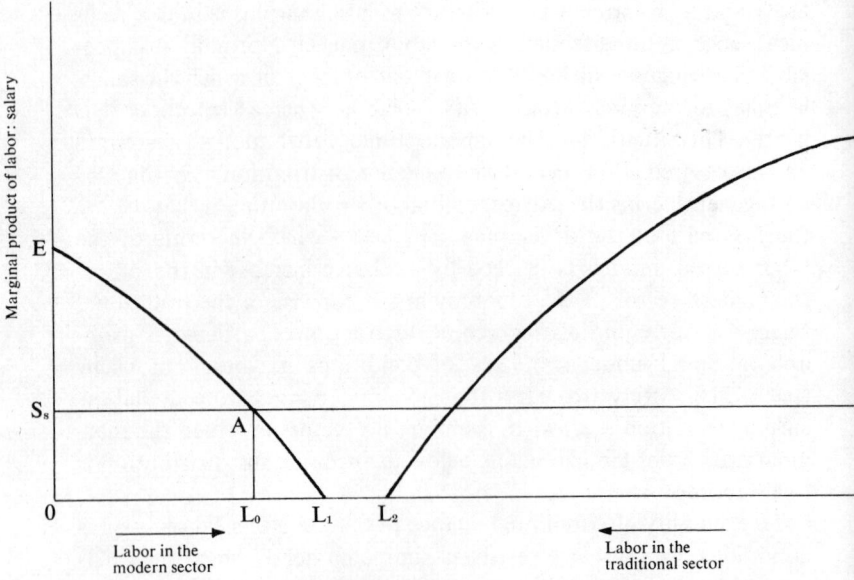

Fig. 1.1. Labor allocation between modern and traditional sectors in a labor-surplus economy.

the traditional sector absorbs the rest, that is, the quantity $L_0 0'$. If there is a large labor surplus (as in the case described) its marginal productivity can be zero (or even negative) in the traditional sector.

In this model static efficiency (the relation between actual output and potential output) and income distribution depend in part on the production functions in the economy (which determine the marginal productivity curves of the two sectors) and in part on the behavior patterns in the traditional sector. Given a wage of $0S_s$ in the modern sector, the static output loss in the economy represented by figure 1 would be AL_1L_0. Obviously, the loss depends on the elasticity of the marginal product of labor curve in the modern sector. If this curve is very elastic at wages below the institutionally set rate and there is a large surplus of labor, the static loss can become very substantial.

Two institutional situations have been most frequently postulated to explain the existence of some individuals receiving an income

---

supply price to the modern sector is equal to the average income of the traditional sector.

greater than their marginal productivity in the traditional sector. If, as is rather typical in the agricultural sector, the economic unit is a family consisting of several workers, then as long as average income is sufficiently high so that all can survive, it is unlikely that the family will not provide income to each member even if not all the workers available are really needed to achieve maximum possible output. A model based on this hypothesis may be called a "family case."

It has also been postulated that in an agricultural community with feudal characteristics the landowner may feel a sense of responsibility to employ more workers than he needs to maximize profits. We refer to this as a noblesse oblige case. In order not to extend the discussion unduly and in order to focus on what appears more realistic for Colombia, we here consider only the family case.

We also limit the discussion to the division between (1) the income of the capitalists in the modern sector[19] and (2) the total income of the traditional sector plus the labor income of the modern sector. As was mentioned above, the way in which the distribution of income between capital and labor changes in the development process is of interest when it may be assumed that families tend to obtain all, or almost all, their income from only one of the two factors of production. This is a reasonable assumption in modern sectors, where capitalists and laborers usually form well-defined separate groups. It is less applicable to the traditional sector of small-scale farmers who, although they do not operate large amounts of land, do own what they cultivate and thus have both types of income (originating in capital and in labor). In that situation the breakdown between capital and labor does not correspond to the distribution between two groups of families at the two ends of the overall income distribution. The breakdown considered here is therefore more pertinent. It may be assumed that the higher the income of the traditional sector and of the workers of the modern sector, the better is the family or personal distribution of income.

---

19. Note that the modern (i.e., capitalist) sector includes commercial or capitalist agriculture and that the traditional sector includes a great deal of family commerce, manufacturing, services, and so forth. Transfer of workers from the traditional to the modern sector is not therefore identical to rural–urban migration.

The process of growth in the model under discussion is characterized by the gradual shifting to the right of the marginal product of labor curve in the modern sector as a result of the accumulation of capital (and possibly also technological change) in that sector. In some versions of the theory the wage in the modern sector does not rise until the labor surplus is ended. In other versions it is assumed that the wage is related to average income in the traditional sector and therefore rises before the labor-surplus state ends.

In the case where the wage does not increase in the presence of surplus labor, it is almost assured that during this stage the share of national income received by the group consisting of the traditional sector and the modern sector workers will decline, while the share received by modern sector capitalists rises. When the labor surplus ends, the wage increases, possibly rapidly, which probably implies the end of the downward trend in the share received by the proletariat and the small-scale farmers.

The decrease in the share of this group while a labor surplus exists can be seen if we assume the simple case where salary in the modern sector remains constant. Absolute increase in income of the proletariat–small-farmer group is equal to or less than the increase in modern sector wage income associated with the increase in employment of that sector—equal when the marginal productivity of labor in the traditional sector is zero and less when that productivity is positive. The labor share of modern sector income tends to diminish (given the constant wage) as long as the average productivity of labor rises in that sector, a likely situation since the contrary would imply capital-saving technological change.[20] At the same time the weight of the traditional sector—in which the share of the worker/traditional sector group is 100 percent—diminishes, implying a

20. Capital-saving technological change would seem desirable from both social and private points of view, given a low and constant wage for an unlimited supply of labor. Were most technological advance locally generated, it might be capital saving. Fei and Ranis ("The Theory of Economic Development," chap. 4) argue that the K/L ratio declined over a lengthy period in Japan's industrial sector—while the country was still characterized by surplus labor. They contend that a large share of the growth of industrial output could be attributed to capital-saving technological change. In most currently developing countries borrowing of foreign technology, without much local adaptation, seems to have been a significant factor in generating a continuous rise in modern sector labor productivity. Colombia is such a country.

downward trend in this group's share of total income. For this decrease not to occur the technological change would have to be substantially capital-saving in order to more than offset the negative effect just explained.

Even when the wage of workers in the modern sector rises during the labor-surplus stage, maintaining equality with average income in the traditional sector, it is very probable (but not certain) that there will be a downward trend in the share of total income for the non-modern capitalist group. The result depends in part on the production functions. In the majority of cases, which will be found between the two extremes mentioned, it is probable that the share of this group decreases during the labor-surplus stage.[21]

When the labor-surplus condition ends, the modern sector salary must increase and it is quite probable that the labor share in the modern sector will increase because now the capital/labor ratio in that sector will tend to rise. This factor pushes the labor share up if the elasticity of substitution between the factors is less than one. Now the negative effect of the decrease in size of the traditional sector will also be less because its weight has been reduced.

The Effect of Changes in the Sectoral Distribution of the Economically Active Population

In the context of the trend of the income distribution it is interesting to analyze changes in the sectoral distribution of the labor force since (1) it is possible that the sectoral production functions differ among the different sectors, with the result that intrasectoral distributions would be different, even given the same average capital stock per person, and (2) it is possible that factor market conditions are different (for example, the tendency to monopoly). Thus an an-

---

21. Lewis and others have hypothesized a gap between the wage level in the modern sector and earnings in the traditional sector. If this differential reflects a real income differential, the shift of these relatively low-income people from the traditional to the modern sector, and the resultant increases in their incomes, may contribute to an improvement in distribution, at least in certain respects. We have not emphasized this possibility here, because the differential in Colombia appears to be relatively small (compared, for example, to some African countries). It could easily be due to cost-of-living differences and to net nonmonetary advantages of rural living.

alysis of change in the sectoral structure may complement the aggregate analysis (at the level of the economy as a whole) and permit more detailed understanding of the process of income distribution change.

One proponent of relating income distribution to the sectoral distribution of the labor force is Simon Kuznets,[22] who focuses especially on the effects of the transfer of people from the agricultural sector to other sectors, a transfer which he considers to be the major structural change in the process of economic development. In the early stages of the development process this transfer does not involve a decrease in the total active population in agriculture but rather in the percentage of the labor force in that sector. In later stages the absolute number of persons employed decreases as the emigration removes more people than are added through natural growth. Because this process involves not only a change in sector of occupation but also in place of residence (from country to city and town) it would not be surprising if it produced changes in the income distribution.[23] The fact that the average and modal income in agriculture is generally well below that in nonagricultural sectors implies that overall distribution will depend on the portion of the total labor force in each of these sectors. When the total number of workers is more or less equal in the two sectors[24] and they have similar distributions, the migration of persons from the modal range of the agricultural distribution into the modal range of the nonagricultural distribution would not affect the overall variance much (although the result also depends in some degree on the precise form of the distribution), but it would affect the degree of skewness. When the two sectors do not have similar sizes, the migration would affect the variance of the overall distribution.

22. See Simon Kuznets, "Quantitative Aspects of the Economic Growth of Nations: Distribution of Income by Size," *Economic Development and Cultural Change* 11, 2, pt. 2 (Jan. 1963): 1–79.

23. When an increase in nominal income accompanies a change in life style as great as that between rural and urban areas, it cannot be taken for granted that an increase in welfare is occurring. Much evidence on the reluctance of people to make this move suggests caution. What we discuss here is therefore an aspect of the development process that may generate a specific pattern of measured income distribution over time. It is by no means clear in this particular case that the trend of welfare distribution is the same.

24. For a more precise statement of this relationship, see n. 25.

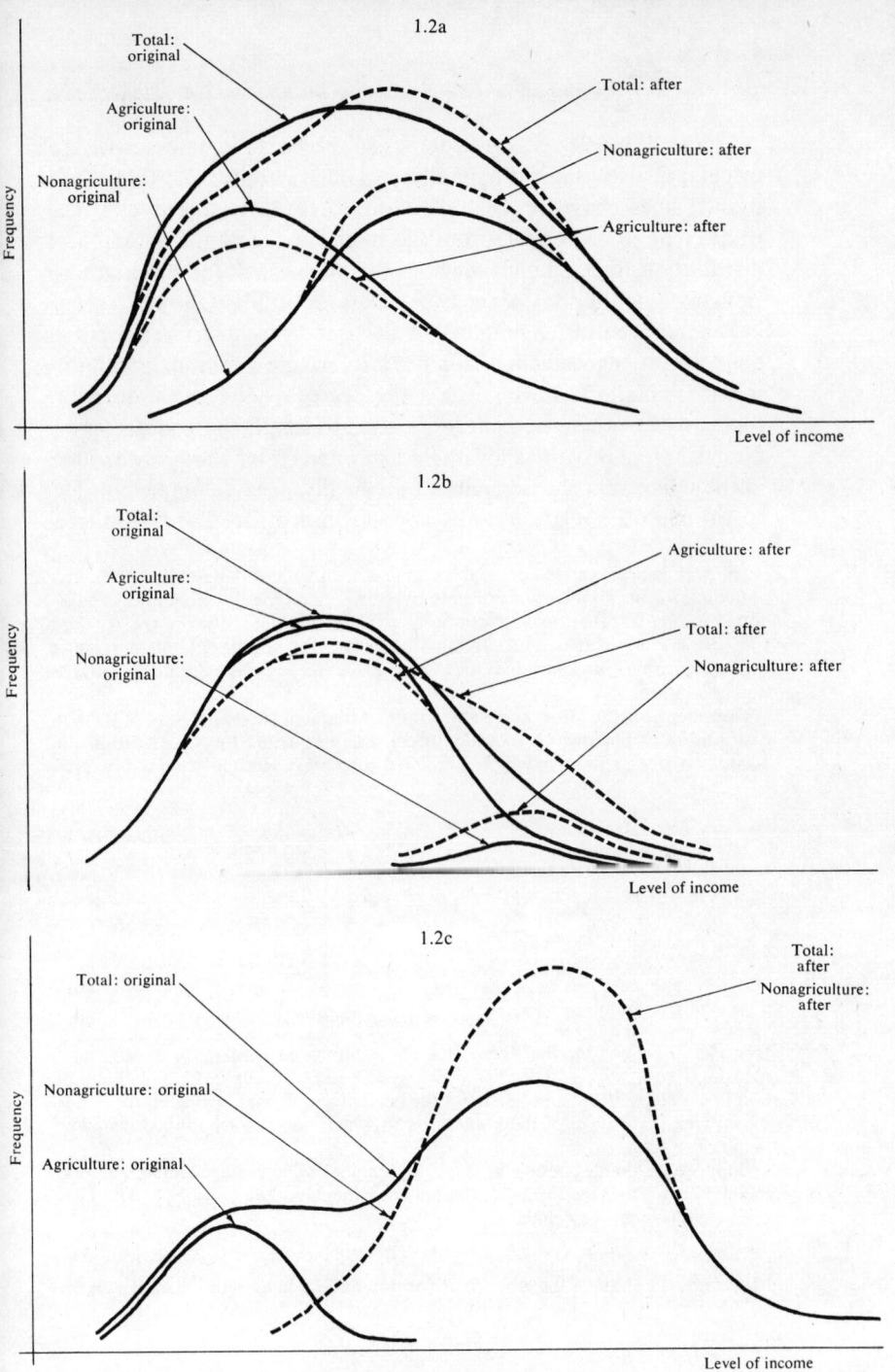

Fig. 1.2. Effect on income distribution of the shift of labor force from agriculture to nonagriculture.

Figure 1.2 presents this comparison. The solid lines show the original distribution for agriculture, nonagriculture, and total. The dashed lines show the corresponding three distributions after the transfer of some persons from the modal range of the agricultural distribution to the modal range of the nonagricultural distribution. In figure 1.2a the sizes of the two sectors are similar, and the level of income concentration implicit in the frequency distribution curve does not change much. In figure 1.2b, where the nonagricultural sector is small, it is evident that the degree of concentration rises. In figure 2c, where agriculture is already small, the concentration diminishes; in order to show this effect with greater clarity we assume in the figure that the agricultural sector disappears completely.[25]

Although the relationship is not shown in figure 2, it is also true

---

25. An algebraic exposition of the simple case in which all agricultural incomes are equal to one another and constant over time, nonagriculture incomes are also equal to one another and constant over time, but the latter are greater than the former, may be helpful. In such a system, development (and increase in average income) is associated with the transfer of persons from agriculture to nonagriculture.

Consider now the Gini coefficient, the most frequent single measure of the size distribution of income. Graphically, it can be represented by $A/(A + B)$ in the accompanying diagram, in which cumulated percentage of population is measured

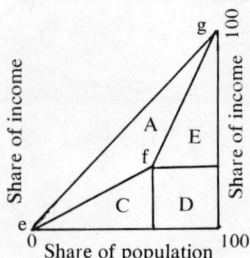

from left to right on the horizontal axis, cumulated percentage of income is measured vertically, and $B = C + D + E$. The Lorenz curve (here made up of two linear segments ef and fg) shows the percentage of total income in the hands of a given percentage of the population in which persons are ranked from low incomes to high.

Suppose we define average agricultural income as y_a, average nonagricultural income as y_n, and the fixed relation between them as $D = y_n/y_a > 1$. The Gini coefficient (G) can be defined as

$$G = 1 - p_a S_a - 2S_a(1 - p_a) - (1 - p_a)(1 - S_a), \qquad (1')$$

where p_a is the share of the labor force (or population) in agriculture, and S_a is the

that a proportionate emigration from all parts of the agricultural distribution, which is then distributed proportionately to the already share of income that they earn. (Note that $G = 1 - 2C - 2D - 2E$.)

$$\therefore G = p_a - S_a. \tag{2'}$$

Now
$$S_a = \frac{y_a p_a}{y_a p_a + y_n p_n}$$
$$= y_a p_a / y_a p_a + D y_a - D y_a p_a. \tag{3'}$$

Substituting equation (3') in (2') yields

$$G = \frac{(1 - p_a) p_a (D - 1)}{D - p_a (D - 1)}$$

Consider now how G changes as the share of population in the labor force changes.

$$\frac{dG}{dp_a} = \frac{2p_a(1 - D) - (1 - D)}{p_a(1 - D) + D} - \frac{p_a^2(1 - D)^2 - p_a(1 - D)^2}{[p_a(1 - D) + D]^2},$$

which simplifies to

$$\frac{p_a^2(1 - D)^2 + 2p_a D(1 - D) - D(1 - D)}{(H)^2}, \tag{4'}$$

where $H = p_a(1 - D) + D$.

The sign of this derivative is the sign of its numerator, which may be simplified to

$$p_a^2(1 - D)^2 + 2p_a(D)(1 - D) - D(1 - D). \tag{5'}$$

This quadratic function in p_a has both real and positive roots. With $p_a = 0$, it is positive; with $p_a = 1$, it is negative, indicating that one root occurs between these two values of p_a. Thus as the share of the labor force in agriculture declines from 100 percent (p_a falls from 1 toward 0), dG/dp_a is at first negative so that the Gini coefficient rises; later dG/dp_a becomes positive so that the Gini coefficient falls.

Since the roots of equation (5') are $(-D \pm \sqrt{D})/(1 - D)$, it is apparent that the root lying between 0 and 1 [i.e., $R = (-D \pm \sqrt{D})/(1 - D)$] lies closer to 1 the lower D is. ($dR/dD = (1 + D - 4D\sqrt{D} - 2\sqrt{D}/H^2$; the numerator of this fraction is negative because $D > 1$.) In other words the transition from the distribution-worsening phase of development to the distribution-improving phase occurs sooner (with a smaller share of the population in nonagriculture) when the differential between agricultural and nonagricultural incomes is small.

For a differential of 2:1, the transition would occur with about 60 percent of the population in agriculture; with a 3:1 differential, it would occur with about 65 percent of the people in agriculture. As the differential approaches 0, the transition occurs closer and closer to the point at which one-half the population is in agriculture.

The above propositions presumably hold with little variation when, instead of all incomes being the same in each of the two sectors, each has a distribution but around different means. Results would not change at all if per capita income in each sector was rising at the same rate.

existing distribution in the nonagricultural sector, tends not to change the variance of the overall distribution if the sizes of the sectors are similar. If the sector of in-migration is smaller, the variance of the total distribution is increased and in the opposite case it decreases.

These conclusions are of some explanatory value, but in fact there is no reason to suppose that the migrants are representative of the universes from which they come and to which they go. To have a complete theory of the effects of the structural change on distribution, it is necessary to know the migrants' rank in the income distribution of the sector from which they come and their rank in the distribution of the sector to which they go. To date, little light seems to have been thrown on this empirical question. One theory is that rural–urban migration is based primarily on a push effect: the rural dwellers prefer to remain in the country until circumstances force them to migrate to the city. If this is the case, one would suppose that the migrants are individuals from the lower ranges of the agricultural income distribution. Even if they receive the lowest urban incomes, the overall distribution of income could have improved in the process. On the other hand, if the people from the upper part of the agricultural distribution were to migrate to the cities and arrive in the upper part of the urban distribution, the total distribution would worsen.

In Colombia it seems at least as probable that the migration has been a result of the economic attractions of the nonagricultural sector because people appear to migrate from all segments of the rural distribution. In that event it is likely that migration tends to worsen the overall distribution at first (when the relative size of the nonagricultural sector is small) and to improve it afterward (when the nonagricultural sector is already large).

There remains another problem in this type of analysis. The implicit assumption that the wave of migration has no effect either on those who remain in the agricultural sector or on those already in the nonagricultural sector is probably false. It would be more acceptable to assume that the migration raises the incomes of those who remain in agriculture and lowers the incomes of those already in the urban sector. This tendency itself should have a positive effect on overall distribution, and thus the total effect of migration is likely to be positive except when the effect discussed in the previous paragraph more than offsets this factor.

The Effect of the Import-Substitution Process

The policy of import substitution has been in Colombia, and in many other countries, an important aspect of the development process.[26] The policy of protecting certain industries normally has at least two important effects: (1) to increase the payment of the scarce factor—in this case capital—and to lower the payment of the abundant factor, labor;[27] (2) to generate monopoly profits. Presumably both effects increase the concentration of income through their impact on the return to capital. This suggests the hypothesis that during the period of most rapid import substitution in Colombia (i.e., more or less since World War II and until the middle of the 1950s), this process had the effect of worsening the distribution of income. If the import substitution corresponds in general to the first phase of industrial development, there is an additional reason to expect that in the early phases of development the distribution of income will worsen.

Market Imperfections

Any economy tends to have market imperfections and although, as was noted above, a neoclassical model with perfect markets is useful as a stepping stone, it is necessary in the analysis of many problems to consider imperfections. Until now we have assumed one specific imperfection: that which defines the labor-surplus situation. Next we treat the problem of imperfections in a more general sense.

Given that the development process tends to bring integration and broadening of markets, improvement in communications and transportation, and so on, there would appear to be strong forces

---

26. This is not to say that the process has necessarily contributed positively to development in all cases.
27. This effect was analyzed first by the Swedish economists Heckscher and Ohlin. It is probable that in a country such as Colombia the more capital intensive an industry is, the more protection it will require to survive. Generalized protection increases the demand for capital.

working to diminish these imperfections and distortions. And if development eventually favors a more equal distribution of income and of sociopolitical power, this also could imply a decrease in personalism (a tendency to employ friends even when they cannot perform the job as well as someone else).

But there are factors operating in the opposite direction. Development involves an increase in the relative importance of the industrial sector, which generally tends to be characterized by more market imperfections (both of goods and of factors) than does the agricultural sector.[28] At the same time it brings increases in firm size in almost all sectors—a phenomenon probably associated with a decrease in competition. On the other hand the service sector, which probably has few monopolies, grows rapidly during the development process. Technological change is continuously creating new monopoly positions and destroying others so that it is not possible to conclude whether its effect on the average level of monopoly is positive or negative.

The presence of all these phenomena obviously implies that a very detailed empirical analysis would be necessary in order to establish a theory pretending to describe the implications of changes in market imperfections on income distribution.

Changes in the Distribution of Wealth

Much can be learned about the mechanisms that determine changes in income distribution by analyzing the functional distribution between capital and labor—an analysis frequently referred to in the previous discussion. However, it is also true that capital can have varying degrees of concentration and that this concentration is a significant determinant of the distribution of personal or family income. Thus the distribution of income at a given moment depends greatly on the distribution of physical and human capital,[29] and

---

28. This would be at least a reasonably accurate description for developed countries where many producers sell each agricultural product and only a few produce each industrial product. Organizations restricting the market increase the level of monopoly in agriculture, but this probably still remains below the level that characterizes industry in the majority of countries.

29. Human capital may be defined as the factor that explains the difference between the total remuneration of human effort and the remuneration of pure

trends in the distribution of wealth over time are very important in determining trends in income distribution. In an extreme case, where capital is the only source of income, changes in the distribution of capital and of income over time would depend entirely on the relation between income level and savings or reinvestment rate. If the savings rate with respect to income were the same for people at all income levels, the distribution of both capital and income would remain the same as long as there was no systematic relationship between the rate of return to capital invested and the level of wealth.[30] If the savings rate were greater for people with higher income levels, the distribution would become more unequal over time.[31] Some authors are less than convinced of the generality of this relationship but no one argues that the savings rate as a proportion of labor income is greater than that of capital income, especially if the average capital income is well above average labor income. The more different the savings rates and the higher the rate of return to capital, the more rapid would be the increase in inequality. And if the savings rate is also a positive function of the wealth of investors (as would appear to be the typical case) the tendency toward increasing concentration of income would be still stronger.[32]

The presence of labor income and the tendency for its relative price vis-à-vis the rate of return to capital to rise during the develop-

---

labor, the latter term being arbitrarily defined as the payment of a person in whom little or no expenditure has been made to increase his productivity.

30. With a perfect capital market such differences would not exist except when they were due to monopoly positions. It is possible that the capital market would be perfect and the goods market not.

31. Empirical studies in various countries suggest that the savings rate out of labor income is very low or zero and that almost all savings come from capital income. See, for example, Irving Kravis and I. Fried, "Entrepreneurial Income, Savings, and Investment," *American Economic Review* 47 (June 1957): 269–301; and Simon Kuznets, *Share of Upper Income Groups in Income and Savings* (New York: National Bureau of Economic Research, 1953). However, this interpretation is probably somewhat oversimplified.

32. For an excellent discussion of this phenomenon and related aspects see Meade, *Efficiency, Equality and the Ownership of Capital.* Although the empirical evidence is very limited on this question, Meade (p. 27) presents data for the United Kingdom that imply that in 1959 the rate of return on the 42 percent of total personal wealth possessed by the richest 1 percent of the population was twice the rate of return on the remaining 58 percent of wealth held by the rest of the population.

ment process suggest that whatever secular tendency may exist to-toward concentration of capital can be offset to a good degree. At the same time the increase in the relative price of labor does not necessarily bring with it an improvement in distribution if it must counteract the two negative influences previously mentioned. Also, it must be noted that an increase in the relative price of pure labor is not inevitable, since if pure labor is a substitute for human capital and human capital increases more rapidly than fixed capital, the price of pure labor could fall.

The Demographic Aspect

Another factor influencing changes in the distribution of capital is the relative family size of rich and poor people. Usually the poor have larger families,[33] which serves (other things being equal) to increase the concentration of capital and to depress the wage rate in relation to the rate of return to capital, thus worsening the distribution of income.[34]

Conventional Wisdom on Distribution Trends during Development

The most widely accepted generalization about distribution trends as development proceeds is that it first worsens, then improves. Kuznets provided empirical evidence for this pattern in his "Quantitative Aspects" (see n. 22). Lewis described it (or at least the worsening phase) as the natural evolution in a labor-surplus context as growth was propelled by the increasing profits of modern sector

---

33. At least this is the evidence for Colombia. In the 1965 national health survey [Ministerio de Salud y ASCOFAME (Asociacion Colombiana de Facultades de Medicina), *Hechos Demograficos*] the recorded age-specific birth rates implied a birth rate more than twice as high for families with incomes less than 3,600 pesos per year than for families with incomes greater than 30,000 pesos. Completed family size would differ less (because of higher infant mortality in poor families), perhaps by 1.6:1. Such data relate fertility to annual income rather than longer-period income and are accordingly subject to certain well-known biases. But the evidence for a genuine long-run negative relationship between income and family size is strong. (See, for example, the discussion in Kuznets's study cited in n. 34.)

34. For a discussion of this relationship see Simon Kuznets, "Income-Related Differences in Natural Increase: Bearing on Growth and Distribution of Income," Yale Economic Growth Center Discussion Paper no. 162, Jan. 1972.

capitalists. Myrdal argued that regional distribution worsens in the early stages of growth.[35] Recent studies (e.g., Adelman and Morris[36] and Weisskoff[37]) have lent further support to the so-called U-shaped pattern. The total evidence, it must be admitted, is hardly convincing even now, owing to data problems of one sort or another. In particularly short supply are detailed over-time studies for individual countries.

Summary and Prelude

Theoretically there is no way of knowing which factors are most important as determinants of changes in distribution; this is an empirical question. Broadly speaking, it may be assumed in the Colombian case that the basic elements are (1) changes in the distribution of physical and human capital, which result in part from savings rates and rates of return to capital that vary positively with the income level. These two differences help to maintain a high level of concentration, but other aspects (e.g., public education) operate in the opposite direction; (2) a downward tendency in the rate of return to capital, possibly in absolute terms and definitely in relation to the wage rate; (3) the nature of technological change, a factor that almost certainly has a negative effect in terms of the income of pure labor (its effect on the distribution between physical and human capital is not clear); (4) changes in the significance and distribution of monopoly rents, including those that result from import substitution; (5) changes in the distribution of the population between rural and urban areas (at the moment, with the majority of the population in the cities, this transfer tends to improve the distribution); (6) a larger family size for poor people, which increases the concentration of income and of capital. In chapters 3 and 4 we attempt to relate the apparent trends in distribution to some of the phenomena mentioned here; in many cases the data do not permit testing of

35. Gunnar Myrdal, *Economic Theory and Under-Developed Regions* (London: Gerald Duckworth, 1957).
36. Irma Adelman and Cynthia Taft Morris, *Economic Growth and Social Equity in Developing Countries* (Stanford, Calif.: Stanford University Press, 1973).
37. Richard Weisskoff, "Income Distribution and Economic Growth in Puerto Rico, Argentina and Mexico," *Review of Income and Wealth* 16, no. 4 (Dec. 1970): 303–32.

interesting hypotheses. There is a suggestion that the U-pattern has held in Colombia, but it is possible also that something more complicated has occurred. A long period of little or no apparent increase in unskilled wage rates is consistent with the predictions of the labor-surplus model, but not only with them. Distribution worsened during the import-substitution phase (1945–mid-1950s), as theory would suggest. But it would be presumptuous to argue that any of the "consistencies" (on which we comment later) between the predictions of one theory or another and the data constitutes a proof. Our analysis of the data leaves us with some interesting hypotheses and much more work to be done.

2

Income Distribution in the 1960s

Estimates of Income Distribution

A good index of the lack of interest of Colombian policymakers in the problems of distribution is the lack of research in this area until quite recently. There has been no effort on the part of government departments either to determine the levels of income concentration or to evaluate the impact of major economic policy decisions on income distribution. In fact, until 1967 income distribution was studied exclusively by foreign experts and technical missions.[1]

Since 1967 new data have become available from various sources making possible an income distribution estimate for 1964 which is more detailed and, we believe, more reliable than previous ones. Although a detailed methodology for these calculations can be found elsewhere,[2] it is useful here to review quickly the data sources and

---

1. For a description of previous efforts to measure income distribution in Colombia, refer to Miguel Urrutia, "Reseña de los Estudios de Distribucion de Ingresos en Colombia," *Revista del Banco de la Republica* 43, no. 508 (Feb. 1970): 180–91. The first studies on income distribution were carried out by the World Bank in 1951, the United Nations Economic Commission for Latin America (ECLA) in 1957, the Lebret Mission in 1958, Milton C. Taylor in 1967, and the Musgrave Commission in 1969.

2. Albert Berry and Alfonso Padilla, "La Distribucion de Ingresos Provenientes de la Agricultura en Colombia—1960," Universidad Nacional, Centro de Investigaciones Para el Desarrollo, "Documentos de Trabajo," Jan./March 1970, no. 1 (Bogota: Universidad Nacional, 1970); Miguel Urrutia and Clara Elsa de Sandoval, "La Distribucion de Ingresos entre los Perceptores de Ingresos en Colombia—1964," *Revista del Banco de la Republica* 43, no. 513 (July 1970); 987–1006; Urrutia and Sandoval, "La Distribucion de Ingresos Urbana para Colombia en 1964," *Revista del Banco de la Republica* 62, no. 503 (Sept. 1969): 1,277–89.

the methods used for computing the urban and rural distribution of income.

Data Used in Calculating the 1964 Income Distribution

The urban income data used here come from unemployment surveys conducted in various urban areas by CEDE (Centro de Estudios sobre Desarrollo Economico) from 1967 to 1969. Although these areas included 48 percent of the urban population in 1964, the distribution utilized for small towns came from a locality that may not be typical of all towns of that size. But more importantly, since all the urban data come from household surveys, they have many of the weaknesses one has come to expect from survey data on incomes. Thus, although there is evidence that the income data for salaried workers are reasonably accurate, it is probable that the income of high-level independent workers and businessmen is underestimated. Although some corrections were made to compensate for this, the final distribution may still have such a bias.[3]

The major source of information for the rural distribution is the agricultural census of 1960. Estimates of production per hectare of different crops from 1966 surveys plus land distribution data by land use from the census were used to calculate the income distribution of farm operators, which, together with wage data of agricultural laborers, was utilized to produce a distribution for the agricultural sector. The 1964 population census was the principal source of data on the agricultural labor force by job category (wage worker vs. operator) and by region. Survey data were used as a base for estimating the income distribution among the members of the rural nonagricultural labor force.

As can be seen, the data base for the distributions involved a wide-ranging variety of sources. It should be pointed out, however, that the final results check well with national income aggregates and that

---

3. The survey data did not contain the income of the urban unemployed. All these people were placed arbitrarily in the two bottom deciles although obviously some of them may have had higher income, especially if they were educated unemployed. This methodology would tend to exaggerate income concentration and therefore might compensate for some of the underreporting in the highest brackets. Another problem with the survey is the short period for which there are recorded data.

such income data from the surveys as could be checked with other sources seemed to be of relatively good quality.[4]

In summary, despite the obvious limitations of the fundamental data, it is likely that the set of income distribution tables presented in this chapter reflects Colombian reality fairly accurately. The reader interested in the methodological details involved in generating these distributions should refer to the publications mentioned in note 2 above.

Urban Distribution of Income

Table 2.1 summarizes the urban distribution of income in Colombia. The absentee landlords who live in the cities but derive most of their income from their rural properties have been left out of this distribution. Otherwise the data cover all the labor force living in cities and small towns. Since in Colombia some small villages are considered urban areas because they are the administrative center of a municipality, this distribution may include workers who in other countries would be classified as semirural laborers.

As will be readily noticed, the degree of income concentration in the urban areas is substantial. One and one-half percent of the labor force controls about 15 percent of total income, the top two deciles control 60 percent of the income, and the poorest 30 percent of the work force earns only about 4.5 percent of all income.

This degree of concentration has surprised observers of the Colombian scene, mostly because of the generalized impression that in Colombia there are not the great family fortunes that appear to be common in neighboring countries. This is to some extent true. In any case the real problem is the extremely low income of the majority of the population.

Using the DANE (Departamento Administrativo Nacional de Estadistica, or National Statistical Institute) figures for 1970, when the exchange rate appeared to be at a more realistic level than in

---

4. The distribution we obtained for 1964 is similar to the one that the National Statistical Institute (DANE) derived from a national sample survey carried out in 1970. The appendix to this chapter gives a short summary comparing our income distribution estimate to other estimates made in Colombia.

Table 2.1
Income Distribution for the Economically Active Urban Population excluding Absentee Landlords, 1964

Annual Income (Thousands of 1964 pesos)	Economically Active Urban Population	Total Income (Thousands of pesos)	Percentage of Population	Percentage of Income	Accumulated Percentage of Population	Accumulated Percentage of Income
0– 1.1	294,848	162,166	12.69	0.65	12.69	0.65
1.1– 2.2	278,351	459,279	11.98	1.34	24.67	2.49
2.2– 3.4	7,203	20,168	0.31	0.08	24.98	2.57
3.4– 4.5	122,679	484,582	5.28	1.94	30.26	4.51
4.5– 6.0	250,702	1,316,186	10.70	5.27	41.05	9.78
6.0– 6.7	234,903	1,491,634	10.11	5.97	51.16	15.75
6.7– 7.8	206,556	1,497,531	8.89	5.99	60.05	21.74
7.8– 9.0	110,365	927,066	4.75	3.71	64.80	25.45
9.0– 10.1	126,630	1,209,316	5.45	4.84	70.25	30.29
10.1– 11.2	78,766	838,858	3.39	3.36	73.64	33.65
11.2– 13.5	131,974	1,629,879	5.68	6.52	79.32	40.17
13.5– 15.7	116,638	1,702,915	5.02	6.81	84.34	46.98
15.7– 17.9	73,189	1,229,575	3.15	4.92	87.49	51.90
17.9– 20.2	30,205	575,405	1.30	2.30	88.79	54.20
20.2– 22.4	24,861	529,539	1.07	2.12	89.86	56.32
22.4– 28.0	82,251	2,072,725	3.54	8.29	93.40	64.61
28.0– 33.6	24,164	744,251	1.04	2.98	94.44	67.59
33.6– 39.2	36,478	1,327,799	1.57	5.31	96.01	72.90
39.2– 44.8	12,314	517,188	0.53	2.07	96.54	74.97
44.8– 50.5	22,770	1,084,990	0.98	4.34	97.52	79.31
50.5– 56.0	8,597	1,457,790	0.37	1.83	97.89	81.14
56.0– 67.3	15,103	931,100	0.65	3.73	98.54	84.87
67.3– 78.5	12,082	880,779	0.52	3.52	99.06	88.39
78.5– 89.7	5,808	488,453	0.25	1.95	99.31	90.34
89.7–100.9	4,414	420,654	0.19	1.68	99.50	92.02
100.9–112.1	1,394	148,461	0.06	0.59	99.56	92.61
112.1–134.5	5,809	716,250	0.25	2.87	99.81	95.48
134.5–157.0	697	101,588	0.03	0.41	99.84	95.89
157.0–224.2	2,788	531,393	0.12	2.13	99.96	98.02
224.2–673.0	697	312,674	0.03	1.25	99.99	99.27
673.0–897.0	232	182,120	0.01	0.73	100.00	100.00
Totals	2,323,468	24,992,314	100.0	100.0		

1964,⁵ it seems that only the top two deciles of the income distribution earned more than 100 U.S. dollars a month, and only the top 5 percent of the urban labor force earned more than about 300 U.S. dollars a month. These statistics show that the real problem in Colombia may not be the absolute number of very high incomes but the extremely low levels of living of the great majority of the population.

In the rural areas the concentration of income at the top is worse. This can be observed in table 2.2, where the top 1.5 percent of the labor force is shown to have 27 percent of the income instead of the 15 percent in urban areas, and the top two deciles are shown to have 65 percent of the income instead of 60 percent. Nevertheless, because of the lack of overt unemployment, the bottom 30 percent of the rural labor force earns about 8.5 percent of all rural income whereas the bottom three deciles of the urban workers earned only about 4.5 percent of urban income.⁶ However, it must be borne in mind that the rural distribution excludes unpaid family workers in agriculture, whereas all the urban unemployed are assigned arbitrarily to the first two deciles. If the unpaid family workers had been included, the rural distribution would have been more unequal, and the lower deciles would probably not have earned a greater proportion of income than that earned by the comparable deciles of the urban distribution.

The absolute level of rural income, however, is in general lower than that found in the urban areas. Thus 58 percent of the rural population had less than 3,400 pesos a year, whereas only 25 percent of the urban population had an income under this figure.⁷ At the top the situation is similar. The richest 1.5 percent of the urban labor

---

5. In 1964 the official exchange rate was 10 pesos per dollar (the principal selling rate of dollars).

6. Note that the estimates of income in agriculture—making up most of the rural labor force—include agricultural income in kind (in principle at least). As discussed further in chap. 3 the estimation of incomes from agriculture is based on output statistics, including data on crops such as plantains that are primarily home consumed. However, these crops have the least accurate of all statistics so error may be considerable. Nonagriculture income in kind, e.g., artisan manufacturing, of the agricultural labor force is not included.

Overall, we cannot claim a high level of accuracy for our estimate of the rural income distribution, but we suspect it is substantially superior to other estimates (e.g., DANE's of 1970) and that it compares favorably to most estimates made in other less developed countries.

7. In 1964 the exchange rate was about 10 pesos per dollar, as noted above.

Table 2.2
Income Distribution of Agricultural (excluding family helpers) and Nonagricultural Rural Labor Force, 1964

Annual Income (Thousands of 1964 pesos)	Percentage of Agricultural Labor Force	Persons in Agriculture	Total Income of Agricultural Sector (Thousands of pesos)	Agricultural and Nonagricultural Rural Labor Force	Total Income of Rural Labor Force (Thousands of pesos)	Percentage of Income in Each Interval	Percentage of Rural Labor Force	Percentage of Accumulated Labor Force	Percentage of Accumulated Income
0.0–0.9	0.093	1,952	878	104,668	36,812	0.24	4.22	4.22	.24
0.9–1.1	0.180	3,778	3,778	20,734	19,886	0.13	0.84	5.06	.37
1.1–1.3	0.690	14,483	17,380	14,483	17,380	0.11	0.58	5.64	.48
1.3–1.5	1.750	36,732	51,425	82,150	119,552	0.77	3.31	8.95	1.25
1.5–1.7	2.508	52,642	84,227	52,642	84,227	0.54	2.12	11.07	1.79
1.7–1.9	3.569	74,911	134,849	74,911	134,849	0.87	3.02	14.09	2.66
1.9–2.1	5.476	114,938	229,876	114,938	229,876	1.47	4.63	18.72	4.13
2.1–2.2	6.395	134,228	288,598	166,374	360,918	2.32	6.70	25.42	6.45
2.2–2.4	6.465	136,117	313,069	136,117	313,069	2.01	5.48	30.90	8.46
2.4–2.6	6.989	146,697	366,742	146,697	366,742	2.35	5.91	36.81	10.81
2.6–2.8	7.371	154,713	417,725	198,866	539,146	3.46	8.01	44.82	14.27
2.8–3.0	6.146	129,001	374,103	129,001	374,103	2.40	5.20	50.02	16.67
3.0–3.2	5.208	109,313	338,870	109,313	338,870	2.18	4.40	54.42	18.85
3.2–3.4	4.617	96,908	319,796	96,908	319,796	2.05	3.90	58.32	20.90
3.4–3.5	3.796	79,676	274,882	79,676	274,882	1.76	3.21	61.53	22.66
3.5–3.7	2.587	54,300	195,480	54,300	195,480	1.25	2.19	63.72	23.91
3.7–4.1	3.821	80,201	312,784	80,201	312,784	2.01	3.23	66.95	25.92
4.1–4.5	2.463	51,697	222,297	160,217	710,637	4.56	6.45	73.40	30.48
4.5–4.3	2.069	43,427	201,935	43,427	201,935	1.30	1.75	75.15	31.78
4.8–5.2	1.872	39,292	196,460	39,292	196,460	1.26	1.58	76.73	33.04
5.2–5.6	1.675	35,157	189,848	35,157	189,848	1.22	1.42	78.15	34.26
5.6–6.0	1.478	31,022	179,928	31,022	179,928	1.15	1.25	79.40	35.41

6.0–	6.3	1.330	27,916	171,683	27,916	171,683	1.10	1.12	80.52	36.51
6.3–	6.7	1.182	24,810	161,265	24,810	161,265	1.04	1.30	81.52	37.55
6.7–	7.1	1.084	22,753	156,996	22,753	156,996	1.01	0.92	82.44	38.56
7.1–	7.4	0.985	20,675	149,894	20,675	149,894	0.96	0.83	83.27	39.52
7.4–	8.4	2.217	46,534	367,619	74,345	590,107	3.79	3.00	86.27	43.31
8.4–	9.3	1.817	38,768	343,097	38,768	343,097	2.20	1.56	87.83	45.51
9.3–	10.2	1.506	31,610	308,197	31,610	308,197	1.98	1.27	89.10	47.49
10.2–	11.2	1.344	28,210	301,847	28,210	301,847	1.94	1.14	90.24	49.43
11.2–	12.1	1.308	27,454	319,839	27,454	319,839	2.05	1.11	91.35	51.48
12.1–	13.0	1.162	24,390	306,094	24,390	306,094	1.96	0.98	92.33	53.44
13.0–	14.0	0.845	17,736	239,436	17,736	239,436	1.54	0.71	93.04	54.98
14.0–	14.9	0.721	15,133	218,672	15,133	218,672	1.40	0.61	93.65	56.38
14.9–	16.7	1.243	26,090	412,222	31,959	500,257	3.21	1.29	94.94	59.59
16.7–	18.6	0.793	16,645	293,784	16,645	203,784	1.89	0.68	95.62	61.48
18.6–	20.5	0.584	12,258	239,644	12,258	239,644	1.54	0.49	96.11	63.02
20.5–	22.3	0.543	11,397	243,896	11,397	243,896	1.56	0.46	96.57	64.58
22.3–	24.2	0.478	10,033	233,267	10,033	233,267	1.50	0.40	96.97	66.08
24.2–	26.0	0.448	9,403	236,015	9,403	236,015	1.52	0.38	97.35	67.60
26.0–	27.9	0.370	7,766	209,294	7,766	209,294	1.34	0.31	97.66	68.94
27.0–	32.6	0.592	12,426	375,886	12,426	375,886	2.41	0.50	98.16	71.35
32.6–	37.2	0.340	7,136	249,046	7,136	249,046	1.60	0.29	98.45	72.95
37.2–	55.8	0.721	15,133	703,684	15,133	703,684	4.52	0.61	99.06	77.47
55.8–	74.4	0.360	7,556	491,396	7,556	491,896	3.16	0.30	99.36	80.63
74.4–	93.0	0.180	3,778	316,219	3,778	316,219	2.03	0.15	99.51	82.66
93.0–186.0		0.289	6,066	846,207	6,066	846,207	5.43	0.24	99.75	88.09
186.0–279.0		0.119	2,498	580,785	2,498	580,785	3.73	0.10	99.85	91.82
279.0–372.0		0.103	2,162	703,731	2,162	703,731	4.52	0.09	99.94	96.34
372.0 and more		0.068	1,427	570,320	1,427	570,320	3.66	0.06	100.0	100.00
Total		100.00	2,098,948	14,465,448	2,482,537	15,578,259	100.0	100.0		

Table 2.3
Average Income by Deciles of the Employed Labor Force in the
Rural and Urban Sectors, 1964

Decile	Agricultural and Nonagricultural Rural Employed Labor Force		Urban Employed Labor Force	
	Percentage of Total Income	Average Income per Employed Person per Year (Pesos)	Percentage of Total Income	Average Income per Employed Person (Pesos)
1	1.40	380	0.9	1,140
2	3.10	1,940	3.3	4,200
3	3.60	2,260	4.3	5,470
4	3.90	2,450	5.0	6,360
5	4.50	2,620	5.5	7,000
6	5.50	3,450	7.0	8,910
7	6.00	3,760	8.0	10,180
8	8.00	5,020	11.0	14,000
9	13.00	8,160	14.5	18,450
10	51.00	32,000	40.5	51,530

force had incomes above P67,300 in 1964, while the top 1.5 percent of the rural labor force surpassed only the level of P37,200.

In summary, the distribution among rural dwellers plus agriculturalists living in the city is worse than the distribution among urban dwellers excluding agriculturalists living in the city.[8] Furthermore, at the same relative position in the income scale, the urban dweller clearly has a higher nominal income and appears in general to be better off. Table 2.3 compares the urban and rural distributions, with the unemployed excluded from the former. For the purpose of welfare comparisons the income of this group tends to understate their situation. The table reveals the extent to which poverty and inequality in Colombia are a rural phenomenon.

8. The evidence from other countries is mixed in this respect, and comparisons are difficult because it is not always clear how various groups are treated. Weisskoff has found that in Puerto Rico and Mexico the distribution of income within the agricultural sectors is more equal than within the nonagricultural sector, whereas the opposite is true in Argentina and the United States. (See Richard Weisskoff, "Income Distribution and Economic Growth in Puerto Rico, Argentina and Mexico," Yale University Economic Growth Center Discussion Paper no. 93.) In Colombia the rural distribution generated by sample surveys is more equal than the urban, but this is due to the fact that the big landlords appear in the urban sample. Finally, although the rural (including farmers living in the city) Gini coefficient is higher than the urban (excluding farmers living in the city), because the two Lorenz curves cross, an unambiguous ranking of concentration is not really possible.

Since the rural distribution is based mainly on agricultural production data by size of farm, most income in kind should be included and total income not seriously underestimated. Nevertheless, while table 2.3 shows how much better the urban dweller lives and helps to explain the very rapid rate of migration from the countryside, it could be argued that the difference in welfare is not so large as that indicated by the income data, owing primarily to price differentials that make living in rural areas less expensive than in the urban areas.

Very little can be said concerning these price differentials since there are virtually no data on rural prices. Although it can be presumed that the food grown on the farm and the surrounding areas will be cheaper in the countryside, in Colombia there is some degree of regional specialization, and there is evidence that such traded food is more expensive in local markets than in the cities. In other words, food that is not grown locally is distributed with greater cost to the villages than to the major cities. Therefore the cost of a *balanced* diet in the countryside may not be less than in the cities. Most manufactured goods are more expensive the farther one is from the city.

Although people spend much less on housing in the countryside, it is of much lower quality than in the cities. In fact, the size of a dwelling and the materials used are often inferior to that found in urban slums. Moreover, there are no services. If the man-hours dedicated to fetching water are priced, water services are much more expensive in the countryside. The same is true of health and education services. It is therefore not at all clear that the typical basket of goods and services purchased by a poor family is less expensive in the rural than in the urban areas.[9]

If average prices are similar, the type of income difference shown in table 2.3 does much to explain urban population growth rates of more than 6 percent in the recent past. Growing unemployment might have been expected to provide some brake to rural–urban migration, especially because from the early 1960s to 1967 unemploy-

9. The basket purchased by a poor urban family is almost certainly cheaper in the city since the rural price of some components is very high, e.g., education beyond grade 2, which has in most rural areas had an infinite or very high price (a child would have to be sent to the town to go beyond grade 2). The basket purchased by a poor rural family may well be cheaper in the rural area. Which family gets the most utility per peso would then be indeterminate.

Table 2.4
Income Distribution for All of the Economically Active Population of Colombia, 1964

Annual Income (Thousands of 1964 pesos)	Total Economically Active Population	Total Estimated Income (Thousands of pesos)	Percentage of Population	Percentage of Income	Percentage of Accumulated Population	Percentage of Accumulated Income
0– 1.1	420,250	218,894	8.75	0.54	8.75	0.54
1.1– 2.2	783,849	1,406,072	16.31	3.47	25.06	4.01
2.2– 3.4	824,105	2,271,894	17.15	5.60	42.21	9.61
3.4– 4.5	497,073	1,978,365	10.34	4.88	52.55	14.49
4.5– 6.0	399,600	2,034,357	8.32	5.14	60.87	19.63
6.0– 6.7	287,629	1,824,582	5.99	4.50	66.86	24.13
6.7– 7.8	249,984	1,804,421	5.20	4.45	72.06	28.58
7.8– 9.0	223,478	1,860,270	4.65	4.58	76.71	33.16
9.0– 10.0	158,240	1,517,513	3.29	3.74	80.00	36.90
10.0– 11.2	106,975	1,140,705	2.23	2.81	82.23	39.71
11.2– 13.5	183,819	2,255,812	3.83	5.56	86.06	45.27
13.5– 15.7	149,507	2,161,023	3.11	5.33	89.17	50.60
15.7– 17.9	121,793	2,023,616	2.53	4.99	91.70	55.59
17.9– 20.2	42,463	815,049	0.88	2.01	92.58	57.60
20.2– 22.4	36,258	773,435	0.75	1.91	93.33	59.51
22.4– 28.0	109,453	2,751,301	2.28	6.78	95.61	66.29
28.0– 33.6	36,590	1,120,137	0.76	2.76	96.37	69.05
33.6– 39.2	43,614	1,576,845	0.91	3.89	97.28	72.94
39.2– 56.0	58,814	2,763,652	1.22	6.81	98.50	79.75
56.0– 93.0	44,327	3,108,447	0.92	7.66	99.42	87.41
93.0–186.0	18,380	2,233,160	0.38	5.50	99.80	92.91
186.0–673.0	9,572	2,698,903	0.19	6.65	99.99	99.56
673.0–897.0	232	182,120	0.005	0.44	100.0	100.0
Total	4,806,005	40,570,573	100.0	100.0		

Note: Pensioners and rentiers are not included, and the data are for pretax income. Income in kind of domestic servants is included and given the methodology used for calculating rural income, most rural income in kind is also included. Family helpers, who earn no income, were not included in the labor force, and their income is therefore assigned to the family head. Finally, the nonrural income of landowners was not included in total income due to difficulties in identifying such income. This, together with the common tendency of rich informants to undervalue their income in survey responses, tends to underestimate income concentration.

ment in Bogota and other large cities crept up from about 8–10 percent to 14–15 percent. But from 1967 on this tendency has been reversed and in 1972 unemployment seems to be at about the level of the early 1960s. Under these circumstances migration has continued at a rapid rate. The possible impact of this migration on the global income distribution was discussed in chapter 1.

It may be useful at this point to look at the global income distribution, described in table 2.4. It will be noticed that the top 1.5 percent of the labor force has 20 percent of all income, while the figure was 15 percent for the urban population and 27 percent for the rural sector. Thus although less unequal than the rural distribution, the global income distribution for Colombia still shows a substantial degree of concentration.

In order to be able to compare the degree of concentration implicit in table 2.4 with that of other countries, it is useful to calculate concentration ratios. Although there are various measures of concentration, all of them more or less imperfect, we employ the Gini coefficient, both because it is well known and because its wide use facilitates comparisons between the distribution of income in Colombia and that in other countries.

The Gini Concentration Ratio

This short section on the meaning of the Gini concentration ratio and the method for calculating it is intended for the nontechnical reader. The Gini concentration ratio is a simple summary measure of dispersion; it measures the extent to which a distribution described by a Lorenz curve differs from the diagonal in a Lorenz diagram—which reflects perfect equality. The coefficient is given by the area between the distribution curve and the diagonal, divided by the area that denotes maximum inequality (i.e., the whole triangle under the diagonal).

In figure 2.1 the coefficient of concentration (R) is equal to area A/(area A + area B). The X axis measures the cumulative proportion of the population in a universe, and the Y axis the cumulative proportion of total income. The population is ranked by income level beginning with the lowest incomes. Each point on the curve shows the amount of total income belonging to a given proportion of a

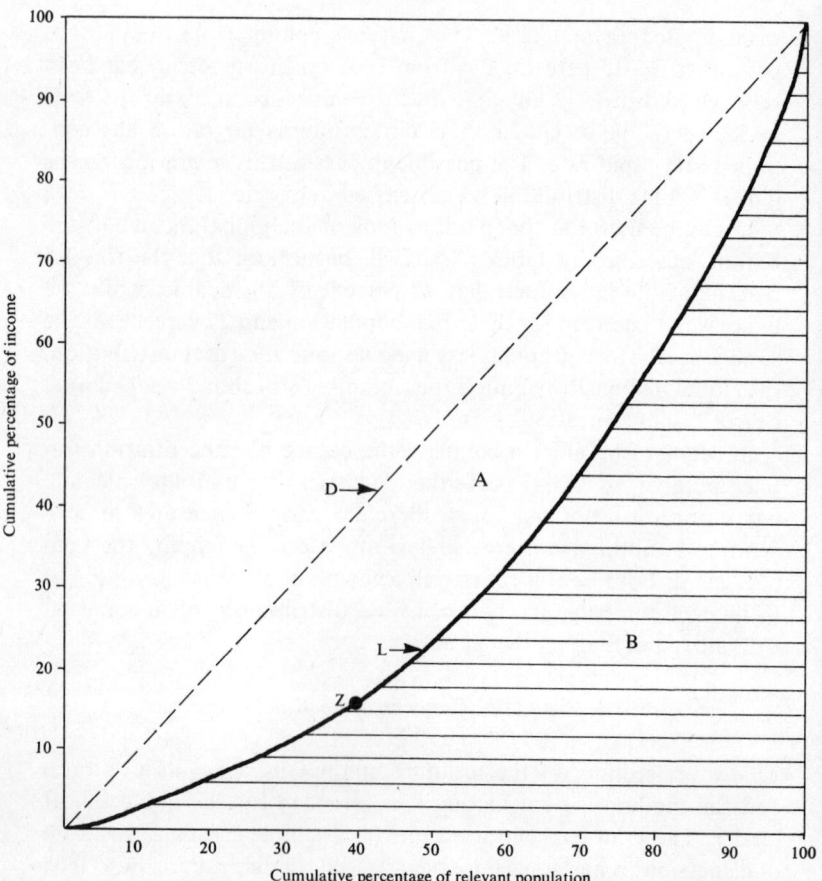

Fig. 2.1. Lorenz curve and the coefficient of concentration. D, the diagonal; L, the Lorenz curve; A and B, areas demarcated by the Lorenz curve.

population. Point Z, for example, shows that the poorest 40 percent of the population has only about 17 percent of all income.

As is evident from figure 2.1, the smaller R is, the closer the distribution approaches theoretical equality. (Everyone has the same income.) On the other hand, as R approaches 1, we approach the situation of perfect inequality.

A close approximation of R, the Gini coefficient of concentration, is given by the following formula:

$$R = \sum_k (P_{(k-1)} Q_k - P_k Q_{(k-1)}) \frac{1}{10{,}000},$$

where Q_k is the percentage of income in interval K, P_k the accumulated percentage of population at interval K, and K the intervals (percentiles, deciles, or whatever).

The application of the Gini ratio to summarize the distribution presents several difficulties. First, because two different Lorenz curves may intersect, it follows that significantly different distributions may yield identical Gini ratios. Second, the Gini ratio is insensitive to shifts of a small percentage of total income from one group to another; yet such shifts may represent large income variations for the lower-income classes. Third, the boundaries of perfect inequality and equality are so extreme that meaningful changes in the level of inequality may correspond to small changes in the Gini ratio, making it therefore somewhat difficult to interpret.

Although other measures of inequality such as the Kuznets ratio, the coefficient of variation, or the standard deviation of the logs of income have useful properties for some studies, in this book we shall use only the better-known Gini coefficient in order to keep the discussion as simple as possible. This coefficient, plus the distribution of income by deciles, is usually sufficient for most comparisons based on imperfect data such as ours.

International Comparisons of Income Distribution

Few underdeveloped countries have good statistics on income distribution, so it is very difficult to make meaningful comparisons. For example, ECLA (UN Economic Commission for Latin America) has published coefficients of concentration for some countries, and even a Gini coefficient of concentration for Latin America, but clearly most of the basic data used do not warrant taking these estimates very seriously.

Table 2.5 presents some of the pertinent estimates.[10] As will be

---

10. As far as we are able to ascertain, the only income distribution studies in Latin America that have been complete enough to give some assurance of reliability are those quoted from Argentina, Brazil, Chile, Mexico, and Puerto Rico. Work has been in progress on Peru but was not available when this book went to press. There are now many estimates of income distribution in developing nations,

readily seen, the degree of concentration in Colombia is high even by the standards of underdeveloped countries. It is interesting to note, however, that in general concentration in Latin America is also high; the Colombian situation is therefore in a certain sense not very surprising. An obvious question to ask is whether the high degree of inequality found in Latin America is typical for countries starting on

Table 2.5
Coefficients of Income Concentration in Latin American Countries and Developed Countries

Country	Data Description		R
Colombia (a)	Active workers	1964	0.57
Brazil (b)	Active workers	1960	0.52
(c)	Active workers	1960	0.62
(b)	Active workers	1970	0.63
Puerto Rico (d)	Active workers	1960	0.55
Argentina (c)	Active workers	1961	0.49
(c)	Families	1961	0.43
Chile (c)	Families	1968	0.46
Mexico (c)	Families	1963	0.53
Venezuela (c)	Families	1962	0.48
El Salvador (e)	N.a.	1965	0.54
Costa Rica (e)	N.a.	1965	0.52
Latin America (e)	N.a.	1965	0.57
United States (c)	Families	1964	0.35
United Kingdom (c)	Families	1965	0.33

Sources: (a) From table 2.4.
(b) Albert Fishlow, "Brazilian Size Distribution of Income," *The American Economic Review* 62, no. 2 (May 1972): 391–402, tables 1, 5.
(c) William R. Cline, *Potential Effects of Income Redistribution on Economic Growth* (New York: Praeger, 1972), p. 111.
(d) Fuat M. Andic, *Distribution of Family Incomes in Puerto Rico* (Rio Piedras, Puerto Rico: Institute of Caribbean Studies, 1964), p. 145.
(e) CEPAL, *Notas sobre la Economia y el Desarrollo de America Latina*, no. 46, May 16, 1970. It appears that the distributions used by CEPAL are for the income of economically active persons and are therefore comparable with the Colombian data.

but the quality of the underlying data is often of such a nature as to make the usefulness of the distribution estimates doubtful. The World Bank has collected all the statistics obtainable but has not yet made a list of those that seem of good quality. See H. Chenery, M. Ahluwalia, C. Bell, J. Duloy, and R. Jolly, *Redistribution with Growth: An Approach to Policy* [Washington, D. C.: International Bank for Reconstruction and Development (IBRD), 1974].

the path of economic development or whether there are common historical causes for income concentration on the continent.

Although the discussions in later chapters on land tenure and the possible effect on distribution of the typical import-substitution pattern of development common in Latin America may help to give a partial answer to this question, the lack of distribution data from other developing countries and of reliable historical data from the advanced ones implies that much more country-by-country empirical research must be done before genuine answers can be given to this extremely important question.

Returning to Colombia, table 2.6 confirms that the most serious problem remains that of inequality and poverty in the rural areas. Although the methodology used for calculating rural income distribution is subject to error in either direction, independent data, particularly from the 1970 DANE household survey,[11] suggest that

Table 2.6
Gini Coefficients of Concentration, Urban and Rural Sectors, Six Countries

Country	Gini Coefficient	
	Urban	Rural
Argentina	.461[a]	.496[b]
Brazil	.629[a]	.458[b,c]
		.448[b,d]
Chile	.440	.393
Colombia	.553	.570[e]
Mexico	.512	.462
Venezuela	.427	.440

Source: William R. Cline, *Potential Effects of Income Redistribution on Economic Growth* (New York: Praeger, 1972), p. 113. For Brazil, the Fishlow and Longoni estimates may be superior, since they are based on more detailed data.

[a]Nonagricultural.
[b]Agricultural
[c]Unadjusted.
[d]Adjusted for unpaid family workers and income in kind.
[e]Includes agriculturalists living in urban areas.

---

11. The DANE distribution, which owing to various sample and other weaknesses probably underestimates rural income concentration, produced a Gini coefficient of 0.47 (see the discussion in the appendix to this chapter). This coefficient would make income concentration in rural Colombia similar to that in other Latin American countries. However, it is virtually certain that the DANE figure is low and that the true level of concentration is between 0.47 and 0.57.

rural distribution is not likely to be very much more equitable than that which produced the Gini coefficient of table 2.6. In that case the much higher concentration in rural Colombia than in other Latin American countries is surprising.

Although apparently less relevant, it is still useful to compare the Colombian income distribution with that of a developed country. Since even in the developed world there is growing concern about relative incomes and income inequality, often translated into rather wide-ranging political changes (the 1973 French election is instructive in this respect), it is not rash to presume that the much greater inequality prevalent in countries such as Colombia will soon be translated into an ever-greater dissatisfaction with the political and economic structure that produces it. For this reason it is interesting to see how much worse the Colombian distribution is than that of a developed nation. Table 2.7 shows a personal pretax income distribution (comparable to that of table 2.4) for the United Kingdom.

As is readily apparent from a comparison of the two tables, the U.K. distribution is consistently better. The lowest fourth of the

Table 2.7
Distribution of Personal Pretax Income in the United Kingdom, 1967

Income before Taxes (Pounds)	Number of Persons	Income before Taxes (Pounds)	Cumulative Percentage of Persons	Cumulative Percentage of Income
50– 250	2,338	493	8.4	1.7
250– 300	940	256	11.8	2.6
300– 400	1,912	662	18.7	4.9
400– 500	2,104	940	26.3	8.2
500– 600	2,068	1,131	33.7	12.2
600– 700	1,904	1,232	40.6	16.6
700– 800	1,729	1,292	46.8	21.2
800– 1,000	3,435	3,071	59.2	32.1
1,000– 1,500	6,741	8,251	83.4	61.4
1,500– 2,000	2,769	4,721	93.4	78.2
2,000– 3,000	1,298	3,061	98.1	89.1
3,000– 5,000	370	1,369	99.4	94.0
5,000–10,000	150	1,000	99.9	97.5
10,000–20,000	35	467	(99.98)	99.2
20,000 and more	7	233	100	100

Source: Central Statistical Office, *National Income and Expenditure: 1969* (London: Her Majesty's Stationary Office, 1969), table 23.

labor force has 8 percent of the income instead of 4 percent, whereas at the other end of the scale the top 7 percent only receives 22 percent of all income against the 40 percent in Colombia. The top 0.6 percent of the labor force in the United Kindom also has half the relative income of the Colombians, that is, 6 percent as against 12.6 percent. It appears therefore that in general the poor in Colombia receive a proportion of total income that is half the proportion received by a similar group of U.K. citizens and that the rich receive twice as great a proportion.

In this rather restricted sense, the above comparison leads to the dramatic conclusion that inequality of income (before taxes) is twice as bad in Colombia as in a country such as the United Kingdom. Further, in the United Kingdom taxes improve the distribution significantly, whereas in Colombia the pretax distribution is similar to the posttax distribution.

Individual and Family Income Distributions

As can be seen in table 2.5 for the case of Argentina, income distribution varies according to the definitions of both income and the income receiving unit. For example, as Table 2.5 shows, very frequently the distribution of family income is less unequal than that of individual income earners.

An income distribution is thus influenced by the definition of the unit receiving income. If interest is concentrated on purchasing-power differentials, the logical unit to choose would be the family since this unit best measures income requirements and since consumption is carried out by and for the family. On the other hand, if the purpose is to measure the capacity for income generation of persons with different levels of education, age, and even family status, the logical unit is the individual income earner. However, if the latter unit is used for calculating an income distribution, it should also be expected that such a distribution will change through time with changes in the age and sex composition of the labor force as long as the relationships of such factors as age and sex with income continue to hold.

The distribution of individual incomes is usually less equitable than that of families, mainly because when the family unit is adopted, a number of income recipients are included in each unit, thus increasing the income of the average unit and reducing the weight of low-income earners, many of whom are secondary earners within the family. (The same is true of part-time workers, who usually have low incomes and are also secondary earners within the family.)

Although it would be desirable to have both individual and family distributions for Colombia, the data base did not permit the calculation of the latter. As noted, the distribution of table 2.4 is that of economically active persons (see note to the table).

Although the methodology employed in calculating the rural income distribution did not allow estimation of an overall family income distribution, some distribution data for urban family units are available. Surprisingly, but rather fortunately, such data show that in Colombia the income distributions for families and for individuals in the labor force are similar. For example in Medellin[12] the Gini coefficients are 0.53 and 0.52 respectively, and for Manizales 0.56 and 0.57. Thus the urban distribution presented here probably reflects well the degree of concentration of both family and individual incomes.

The definition of income also affects the distribution. The most common definitions are (1) personal income, that is, all income generated in a given period except that which does not reach individuals in that period, such as the savings of corporations; and (2) disposable income, that is, personal income after taxes.

It is to be expected that personal income will be less unequally distributed than national income because it excludes nondistributed profits of corporations, which in general belong to the upper-income groups.

12. As can be seen, different cities have different degrees of concentration. The data from surveys carried out in 7 major cities were used to calculate the income distribution of the population living in those areas. In addition, data were available for 5 smaller cities typical of the general category of small towns and intermediate cities. Together the cities covered included 48 percent of Colombia's urban population. Income was distributed among the other half of the urban population by applying each existing distribution to similar towns not covered in the survey but which resembled the cities covered in size, percentage of houses with more than 4 people per room, and labor productivity in industry. But even if these indices have no definite relationship to income concentration, the concentration ratios are not so different between cities and therefore the estimating procedure does not make too much difference. The Gini coefficient ranges from 0.53 to 0.62, but 6 out of 8 cities have coefficients between 0.55 and 0.61.

Income Distribution in the 1960s

Capital gains income, although potentially quite important to individuals, is very difficult to measure. Theoretically, capital gains can be measured on a yearly basis, but they are not in fact realized yearly and are therefore not measured in most income surveys. However, they constitute a significant proportion of the total income of high-income groups. A distribution including capital gains would therefore reveal more concentration than the usual personal distribution of income. In Colombia it was impossible to calculate capital gains because in addition to the usual difficulties, the lack of a capital gains tax leaves the investigator with no statistics on this type of income.

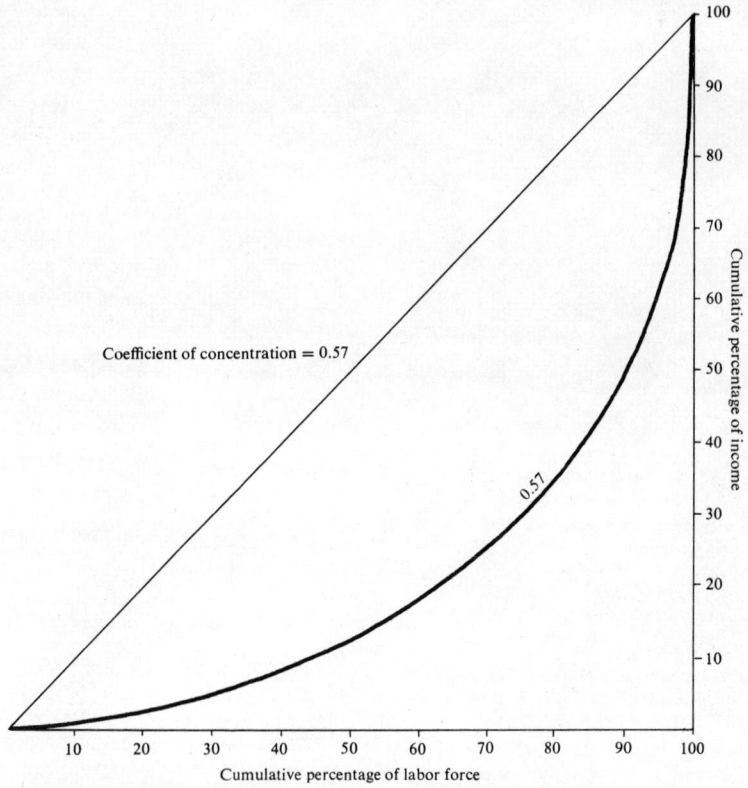

Fig. 2.2. Income distribution in the Colombian labor force, 1964.

This chapter presents what we believe to be the best income distribution estimates for Colombia.[13] Table 2.4 and figure 2.2 summarize the distributions. International comparisons show that income in Colombia is very concentrated, even by the standards of Latin America. In the following chapters the determinants of this concentration are discussed, and an attempt is made to describe what has happened to income dispersion over time in Colombia.

13. The discussion of the methodology used to make the estimates is kept to a minimum because it is assumed that the reader interested in these details can consult the journal articles published in Colombia that describe in great detail the methodological and data problems involved. The appendix to this chapter surveys the income distribution estimates that exist for Colombia.

Appendix

Survey of Various Income-Distribution Estimates

Before 1967 various foreign economic missions to Colombia tried to estimate the distribution of income, but most of these attempts limited themselves to quantifying income per capita differentials by economic sectors. The first discussion of income distribution in Colombia was that presented in the World Bank study of the Colombian economy in 1949.[1] Using scattered data, such as one or two rural surveys and some income tax and wage statistics, the mission estimated the number of people with high, medium, and low incomes. However, the sources for this estimate are so deficient that the resulting distribution can only be considered an important first step in the study of an important subject.

The second estimate of income distribution is that of ECLA in 1954–55. This study includes information on the upper 5 percent of the distribution from tax data and average incomes by industrial sector[2] and therefore does not really give an income distribution. A third foreign mission headed by C. J. Lebret studied distributional problems in the late 1950s.[3] Although the mission did not produce an estimate different from that of ECLA or Planeacion, it did carry out surveys in various parts of the country to obtain social indicators such as standards of housing, education, and health.

1. Banco Internacional de Reconstruccion y Fomento, *Programa de Fomento para Colombia* (Bogota: Banco de la Republica, 1951).
2. CEPAL (Comision Economica Para America Latina), *Analisis y Proyecciones del Desarrollo Economica: El Desarrollo Economico de Colombia* (Mexico City: Naciones Unidas, 1957).
3. Mision Economica y Humanismo, *Estudio sobre las Condiciones de Desarrollo de Colombia* (Bogota: Aedita, 1958).

Probably the first complete income distribution provided for Colombia from which income by deciles can be derived was carried out by still another foreign mission in 1961, headed by Milton Taylor.[4] This estimate is based on income tax data, information on salaries from national accounts, and the income distribution of blue-collar and white-collar workers obtained in a 1953 family budget survey. Also, the income of people in services and commerce was found by combining the labor force in those sectors with the workers employed in manufacturing industry surveyed in 1953. The assumptions used to estimate rural income are arbitrary and the basic rural wage data are of low quality. Since it has been shown that the 1953 budget survey is not representative and tends to exclude low-wage urban workers (as indicated by the relatively low average weight of food expenditures of the families surveyed), the Taylor figures probably underestimate urban income dispersion because they undervalue the importance of low-income urban workers. In summary, this estimate does not seem reliable and cannot be usefully compared with later estimates using better basic data. Since the Taylor estimate gives a significantly more equitable distribution than the more complete later estimates and since the methodology employed would seem to bias the results in that direction, it should not be used jointly with the more recent estimates to measure changes through time in income dispersion.

In 1968 still another mission, this time headed by Richard Musgrave, estimated an income distribution for 1964. This effort (undertaken by Charles McLure, a member of the mission) was also largely based on income tax data, national income information, and some income statistics from survey data and rural wages.[5] The distribution estimated is significantly more concentrated than that found by Taylor. The study seems superior from a methodological/data point of view. The McLure estimate for 1964 utilizes a methodology generally similar to that of Taylor but with better data, including the 1964 census results on the population distribution by

---

4. Milton C. Taylor et al., *Estudio Fiscal de Colombia* (Washington, D.C.: Pan American Union, 1957).

5. Charles E. McLure, "The Incidence of Taxation in Colombia," in Richard Musgrave and Malcolm Gillis, *Fiscal Reform for Colombia* (Cambridge, Mass.: Harvard Law School, 1971).

sector and some more recent survey data. The McLure estimate for 1964 coincides generally with the Urrutia-Berry tables described in detail in this chapter. It provides an interesting check (the two refer to the same year) on the latter, independently estimated distribution, which is based on urban surveys, the data from the 1960 agricultural census, and a rural survey for nonfarm income.

Another published income distribution estimate for the same period is that of the Ministry of Public Health, which in 1965–66 carried out an extensive survey of the health situation, including a question on income.[6] Unfortunately, the question was very general, the income intervals were large, and the highest, open-ended interval included a substantial proportion of the population. As a result the total income of the population as estimated by the Ministry of Health is much lower than that derived from national accounts. For example, for the city of Bogota, the ministry data when blown up account for only 61 percent of the total income estimated from the CEDE unemployment sample, which in turn somewhat underestimates total income. It appears therefore that the ministry data are very deficient and cannot be useful for income distribution studies.

Two additional income distribution studies have been based on the large household sample made by DANE in 1970. This sample was very ambitious and included questions on employment and labor force status, family expenditures (budget study), and incomes. The design of the urban sample seems to have been quite good, so the resulting urban distribution is probably of high quality. There are doubts, however, about the representativity of the rural part of the sample. It appears that the rural areas surrounding the large cities make up a significant part of the rural sample, and these areas are clearly not typical. Furthermore, whereas over 40 percent of the nation's population is believed to have been rural as of 1970, only 38 percent of the sampled population was rural. It thus seems that the DANE sample did not capture the poorest rural families, who in general will be found in areas located far from the principal urban centers. This would tend to bias the resultant income distribution toward greater equity than exists in reality.

The results of the DANE survey, first published by Polibio Cor-

6. *Estudio de Recursos Humanos para la Salud y Educacion Media en Colombia* (Bogota: Aedita, 1958).

doba,[7] show less concentration than does the Urrutia–Berry distribution: the Gini coefficient of concentration is 0.53 as opposed to the 0.57 of the latter study. Nevertheless, the urban distribution is quite similar to that reported by Urrutia–Berry. On the other hand, the concentration coefficient for the rural sector is much lower in the DANE distribution (0.42 against 0.57). This difference is partly definitional. The DANE data do not include the high-income farmers who live in towns, whereas the Urrutia–Berry distribution includes those landowners in the rural distribution. Second, the DANE survey is not representative for the rural areas; a disproportionately small number of the poorest farmers in marginal areas seem to have entered the sample. For the latter reason reservations are in order with respect to the rural part of the DANE distribution. And both factors imply that no comparison should be made between the 1964 and 1970 published distributions, since the statistical bases for them are so different. However, it is of interest to observe that the 1970 and 1964 urban distributions yield similar results, that is, the type of concentration described in the Urrutia–Berry distribution is consistent with the independent evidence of the DANE survey.

Charles McLure has recently adjusted his earlier 1964 estimate using the 1970 DANE survey results.[8] He too obtains an urban distribution similar to that of Urrutia–Berry, although the latter is slightly more unequal. The rural distribution is less unequal than that of Urrutia–Berry, but McLure finds this logical, particularly because the DANE survey does not include in the rural sector the landowners who live in towns and because the DANE information refers to households instead of economically active persons. McLure concludes that "the Taylor group found that the bottom two-thirds of individuals received roughly 28 percent of income and the top 10 percent of individuals received slightly less than 42 percent of income. This is difficult to reconcile with the present study in that the Taylor group also used individuals as the basis of its estimate. Finally, Urrutia's estimates are quite consistent with those reported here and

7. Polibio Cordoba, Clara Elsa de Sandoval, and Mario L. Rodriguez, "La Distribucion de Ingresos en Colombia," *Boletin Mensual de Estadistica* no. 237 (Apr. 1971): 55–95.

8. Charles E. McLure, "The Incidence of Colombian Taxes, 1970" (Houston, Tex.: Rice University Program of Development Studies Discussion Paper 41, 1973).

in the author's [McLure's] previous study."[9] In summary, the McLure, Urrutia–Berry, and DANE studies all show similar distributions of income and therefore reinforce the validity of the Urrutia–Berry estimates, but they cannot be used to show marginal changes in income distribution in the short period 1964–70, because it is hard to tell which differences are due to inadequate data and which differences may reflect real underlying trends. Table 2A.1 illustrates some of the differences in four of the distributions discussed.[10]

Table 2A.1
Comparison of Results of Various Studies of Income Distribution in Colombia

Author		Percentage of Income Received by		Basis of Estimate
		Lowest Two-thirds	Top 10 Percent	
Taylor	1961	28	42	Individuals
McLure	1964	27	50	Individuals
Urrutia	1964	24	48	Individuals
McLure	1970	25	44	Households

Source: Charles E. McLure Jr. *The Incidence of Colombian Taxes, 1970* (Houston, Tex.: Rice University Program of Development Studies, paper 41, 1973).

To complete this survey, we should mention the urban distribution estimated by Rafael Prieto from the ECIEL (Estudios Conjuntos de Integracion Economica Latinoamericana) family budget study in the four largest Colombian cities.[11] This is probably the best income survey carried out in Colombia, but it has a series of shortcomings. The interviews and questionnaires were of high quality, but the research was designed as a family budget study to obtain income elasticities for consumer goods. For that reason a stratified sample was used, with high-income individuals overrepresented. In order to blow up this sample to estimate an income distribution it was necessary to assign weights to the three major categories of consuming units (high, middle, and low income). These weights were derived from the Taylor distribution and were corrected by impres-

9. Ibid., pp. 11–12.
10. For a more complete survey of the income distribution studies carried out in Colombia and summary tables of the distributions discussed above, see Urrutia, "Reseña de los Estudios."
11. Rafael Prieto, *Estructura del Gasto y Distribucion del Ingreso Familiar en Cuatro Ciudades Colombianas*, 1967–68, pt. 1 (Bogota: CEDE, 1971).

sionistic evidence concerning the incomes of people, by barrios, in the cities covered. Since the Taylor distribution underestimates concentration, the weights used to obtain an income distribution from the actual sample data probably lead to an underestimation of concentration. In fact, as expected, the Gini coefficient in the Prieto study for the four cities is 0.47 against the urban coefficient of 0.55 found in the Urrutia–Berry distribution.

In addition to the problems that may exist in the coefficients used to transform the stratified sample, the Prieto data refer to the income of families over a three-month period. This methodology would be expected to produce a lower degree of concentration than Urrutia–Berry, because family income may be less concentrated than individual income and because there should be less dispersion in quarterly income than in weekly income, which is the basis of the Urrutia estimates for the urban sector. In Colombia this would certainly be the case because unemployment is of short duration and weighs heavily in the Urrutia results, whereas it would have a lesser impact on the lower deciles in the Prieto data.

In summary, the Prieto data may give a better representation of the permanent income distribution and can be very useful for in-depth study of the distribution problems of the large urban centers, but owing to the methodology used to transform the stratified sample into a global distribution, the published distribution is likely to underestimate the true degree of concentration.

3

The Distribution of Income in Agriculture: Determinants and Trends over Time

This chapter presents in greater detail than the previous one our estimate of the distribution of income in the agricultural sector at the beginning of the 1960s (when about one-half of the active population was involved in agriculture), with a view to determining its relation to the distribution of land and other forms of wealth. It also attempts to trace and explain the changes that have occurred in the agricultural income distribution over time, leading into chapter 4, which undertakes this task for the economy as a whole. Chapter 10 offers evidence on the relative static efficiency of different-sized farms with the intention of ascertaining whether the goals of growth in agricultural output and better distribution are complementary or competitive; in the same chapter some tentative policy conclusions are discussed as well. The present chapter limits itself to measurement and some interpretation of the distribution and its changes over time.

As background, it is helpful to summarize some of the important characteristics of the agricultural sector in Colombia. First, land is quite unequally distributed, in terms both of ownership and operation.[1] Second, great inequality exists in the distribution of income generated in agriculture. Third, there is evidence of some form of surplus labor, especially in the highly populated Andean regions, where quite small farms (*minifundios*) are very common. And fourth, there are such systematic relationships between size of farm and type

1. It appears that about 10 percent of agricultural families exploit 75 percent of the land (measuring land by its value instead of area); the ownership of land seems to be somewhat more concentrated than its operation.

of product as to suggest that farms of different sizes vary considerably in the factor proportions they use and in factor productivities.[2] For example, it is clear that small farms produce more per hectare and large farms more per worker.

Personal Distribution of Income Generated in Agriculture: 1960

The figures presented here (tables 3.1 and 3.2) refer to 1960[3] and give an income distribution for the labor force in agriculture,[4] specifically a distribution of income generated in agriculture and defined by what we may call the national accounts concept. Although available information limits us to this concept, some data are also given on

Table 3.1
Personal Distribution of Income (national accounts concept) from Agriculture, by Income Categories, 1960
(Basic estimate)

Annual Income (Thousands of 1960 pesos)	Percentage of People in Category	Percentage of Income accruing to People in Category	Cumulated Percentage of People	Cumulated Percentage of Income
0–1	8.87	1.93	8.87	1.93
1–1.5	29.76	9.73	38.72	11.67
1.5–2.0	21.77	9.71	60.50	21.38
2.0–3.0	14.00	8.60	74.50	30.07
3.0–5.0	10.56	10.36	85.05	40.43
5.0–10.0	9.82	17.78	94.87	58.20
10.0–20.0	3.44	12.06	99.31	70.27
20.0–100.0	1.41	14.47	99.72	84.73
100.0–200.0	21	8.19	99.93	92.92
200.0 and more	.07	7.08	100.00	100.00

Sources and Methodology: The data are adjusted slightly from those presented in Albert Berry, "The Distribution of Agriculturally Based Income in Colombia, 1960," mimeo, 1970. The appendix to that study, with the figures underlying these estimates and the details of the methodology, is available from the author.

---

2. The basic reasons for differing factor proportions among farm sizes may be different factor prices, nonhomogeneous production functions, and so on. Varying output composition is likely to signal some such underlying factors.

3. Some individual pieces of information correspond to other years, but the general methodology is aimed at estimating the distribution for 1960.

4. Family workers who did not receive salaries are excluded. Such workers make up about 15 percent of the agricultural labor force.

Table 3.2

Personal Distribution of Income from Colombian Agriculture by Deciles (Basic estimate and alternatives), 1960

Decile	Basic Estimate		Low Estimate of Bottom Deciles Income		Low Estimates of Upper-Decile Income		
	Percentage of Income	Cumulative Percentage of Income	Percentage of Income	Cumulative Percentage of Income	(a)	(b)	(c)
	(1)	(2)	(3)	(4)			
1	2.24	2.24	1.18	1.18			
2	2.87	5.11	2.38	3.56			
3	3.34	8.45					
4	3.73	12.18					
5	4.21	16.39					
6	4.68	21.07					
7	5.78	26.85					
8	7.90	34.75					
9	12.77	47.52					
10	52.48	100.00			49.48	46.32	43.08

Sources and Methodology: The basic estimate is an adjusted version of the one presented in Albert Berry and Alfonso Padilla, "La Distribucion de Ingresos Provenientes de la Agricultura en Colombia—1960," Universidad Nacional, Centro de Investigaciones Para el Desarrollo, *Documentos de Trabajo*, Jan./March 1970, no. 1 (Bogota: Universidad Nacional, 1970), Appendix table A-1. The lower estimate for the bottom two deciles [cols. (3) and (4)] is designed to be downward biased with respect to each doubtful assumption that was made. It assumed in particular that the workers with the lowest wages work fewer days per year than anyone else and do not own or operate any land.

The three estimates designed to give various types of lower limits for the upper-decile share involve the following assumptions:

(a) There was no dispersion of incomes for farmers in a given farm size category. Our estimation technique involved calculating the average income accruing to farmers in a given size group, then assuming a certain dispersion around this mean; the share of the upper decile is an increasing function of the amount of dispersion assumed. To assume no dispersion is clearly unrealistic, so, with respect to this aspect of the methodology, estimate (a) is clearly downward biased.

(b) cf. (a) but also assumes salary payments to blue-collar workers twice as high as in the basic estimate. It seems almost sure that with such an assumption another downward bias is created in the upper decile share.

(c) Here it is further assumed that the basic estimate overstated value added in the large farms by 10 percent. Because the 1966 data we used on relative yields by farm size showed higher yields of many crops for larger than for small farms, if the former had risen relative to the latter in the period 1960–66 (which is possible) the basic estimate might have had an upward bias from this source. Note that this could well mean that the 1966 distribution would be more like the basic estimate.

the distribution of wealth in land (probably the major source of capital appreciation), and some conjectures are made about the way in which inclusion of capital gains income would affect the income distribution.

Tables 3.1 and 3.2 present in slightly different form estimates of the personal distribution of income excluding family workers. Such estimates are naturally fraught with statistical problems, but the methodology used permits some firm conclusions:

1. The great majority of the agricultural labor force had an income from agriculture of less than 5,000 1960 pesos a year (or about $700) and the bottom half had less than 3,000 1960 pesos (or $430);[5]

2. The upper 15 percent had about 60 percent of income (say 55–65 percent) and the bottom 85 percent therefore had about 35–45 percent.[6]

It must be emphasized that tables 3.1 and 3.2 present the estimated distribution of income generated in agriculture, not the distribution of all income (from agriculture and other sources) of persons involved in agriculture or the rural distribution. Impressionistic evidence suggests that income received in other sectors may be a particularly high share of total income for some people in the upper end of the agricultural income distribution (i.e., the absentee landlords and the partially absentee commercial farmers). Further, capital gains (not included in the tables), although difficult to guess, may be very significant.[7] Although not many people in the bottom part of the

---

5. Since the figures refer to income of economically active persons, translation into income per capita terms (including dependent persons) would require division of each figure roughly by 3. Thus, the income per capita in families constituting the bottom half of the distribution was probably about 1,000 1960 pesos per person ($145), assuming that family size was the same for this group as for all families together.

6. The methodology used gives less precise results for the upper and lower tails of the distribution. For the poorest group the uncertainty is the result of not knowing in detail which small operators also work on other farms, how much they work, and what their salaries are. The estimates are also made difficult by a lack of information on the distribution of value added and on certain input costs by size of farm.

7. Of persons with income from agriculture those in the top decile probably have about 75 percent of all the land, the only asset capable of continuously producing reasonably high capital gains. Unfortunately, not enough information

distribution of "income from agriculture" are absentee, the pressure of very low agricultural incomes does force them to search for income from other sources.[8] Thus the data for these two groups (especially the first) may underestimate significantly the total income of persons whose principal source of income is agriculture.

As indicated in table 3.2, the bottom decile could have between 1.2 percent (an estimate based on the most pessimistic assumptions) and 3 percent of agricultural income. The bottom two deciles could have between 3.6 and about 6 percent (always excluding nonagricultural income). For the top decile, 50–55 percent appears to be the probable range; it is unlikely that less than 45 percent could be appropriated by this group. If income from capital gains is included, it is improbable that the top decile would receive less than 50 percent.

Our basic estimate of distribution is illustrated by the Lorenz curve in figure 3.1. The corresponding Gini coefficient of concentration is 0.58.

Determinants of the Variance of Agricultural Income

At a first level of discussion, the explanation for the inequality in agricultural incomes is the unequal distribution of land. Average income of persons with large farms is much greater than that of persons with small farms (see table 3.3). Although the relationship is

---

is available to give a satisfactory feel for the rate of land appreciation in the country as a whole. For 1960 we have estimated the value of land in possession of persons defined as being tied to the agricultural sector at approximately 23 billion pesos. If land increased in real value at 5 percent a year, this would add another 20.7 percent to the incomes of the top decile and would imply a share for this group in total income (including capital gains) of 55.6 percent, beginning with our basic estimate of 52.5 percent for their share of national-accounts-type income. If the true rate of appreciation were 3 percent, their income would rise by 12.5 percent and their share would be 54.1 percent. The surprising aspect of these calculations is that when the distribution is as unequal as in the present case, the inclusion of capital gains does not affect it a great deal. Because a 5 percent annual increase is almost surely an upper limit for the real value of land in Colombia, it is improbable that the share of the top decile depends very much on such gains.

8. The results of a study of the Suarez River basin were consistent with this. See Marco Reyes, Rafael Prieto, and Bill Hanneson, *Estudio Agroeconomico de la Hoya del Rio Suarez* (Bogota: CEDE, Universidad de los Andes y CAR, 1965). On the other hand the figures for municipalities not so close to regions with important nonagricultural activities show a much smaller share of income obtained outside agriculture.

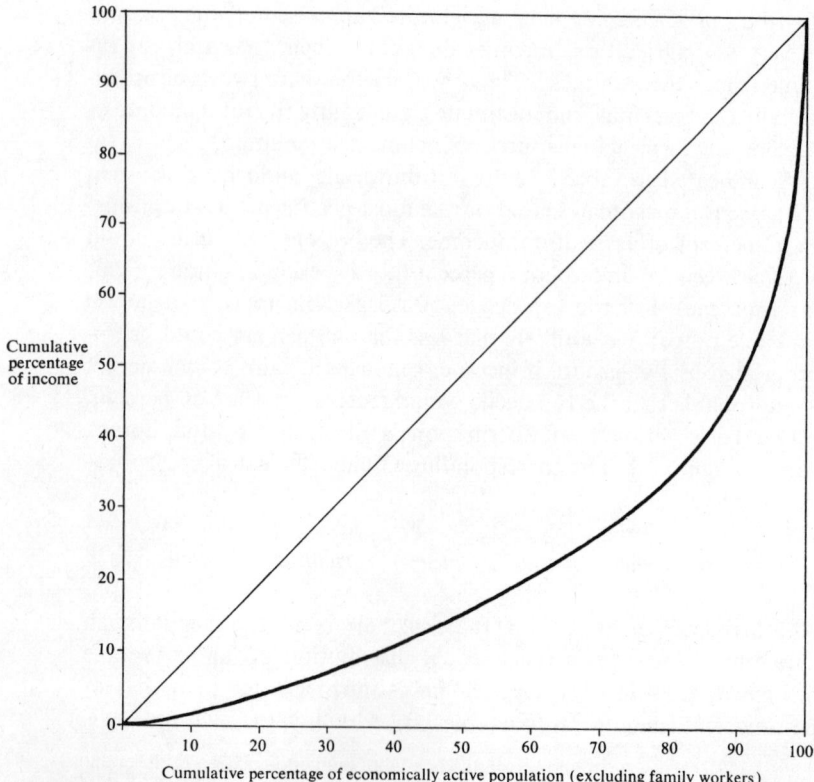

Fig. 3.1. Lorenz curve of personal distribution of income, Colombia, 1964.

more random on a farm-by-farm level than the simple presentation of size category averages may suggest, it is nevertheless a dominant one. As we will see below, the bulk of the incomes of the largest producers is due to their role as owners of land and capital, and not to their role as suppliers of labor. Although the distribution of income among paid workers covers a substantial range (in considerable degree due to wage differentials among the different regions of the country), it does not contribute much to the overall dispersion of income distribution, since all these incomes are found in the lower part of that distribution. Table 3.4 shows the distribution of the approximately 1 million wage earners according to their income in 1960.[9]

9. The majority of families have at least a small plot for their own use. This figure corresponds approximately to the number of paid man years.

Table 3.3
Average Income of Producers by Farm Size, 1960
(1960 pesos)

Farm Size (Hectares)	Average Income	Number of Producers
1–2	1,300	191,350
2–3	1,900	117,000
3–4	2,320	92,000
4–5	2,640	58,200
5–10	3,670	169,150
10–20	5,580	114,200
20–30	6,750	44,050
30–40	8,340	26,500
40–50	10,203	16,240
50–100	12,800	40,000
100–200	23,800	22,300
200–500	41,140	13,700
500–1,000	102,500	4,140
1,000–2,000	189,800	1,975
2,000 and more	527,700	790
Total	6,145	911,595

Source: A. Berry, *The Development of the Agricultural Sector in Colombia*, forthcoming, Appendix table A-2, revised to take account of new information.

Table 3.4
Distribution of Income among Wage Earners in Agriculture, 1960

Category Number	Average Annual Income of Category (1960 pesos)	Percentage of Workers	Cumulative Percentage of Workers
1	600	1.3	1.3
2	715	2.0	3.3
3	835	4.6	7.9
4	950	3.0	10.9
5	1,070	10.5	21.4
6	1,190	8.3	29.7
7	1,310	25.7	55.4
8	1,430	5.5	60.9
9	1,550	15.8	76.7
10	1,670	3.9	80.6
11	1,787	8.5	89.1
12	1,900	1.8	90.9
13	2,025	5.7	96.6
14	2,290	3.4	100.0

Source: Based on wage statistics collected in each municipio by DANE and published in its *Boletin Mensual de Estadistica*. The details of the calculation are presented in Berry and Padilla, "Distribucion de Ingresos Provenientes," Appendix table A-5. It was assumed that each worker was occupied 250 days per year.

The average incomes of various groups are revealing. Laborers earned an average of about 1,400 pesos per year; the earnings of operators of very small farms (less than 2 hectares) were in this same range and even up to 5 hectares they were very low. Colombia's "small farmers" may be thought of roughly as the group with 5–20 hectares and with average income of about 4,500 pesos. Although hardly living in luxury, these nearly 200,000 farmers are relatively well off. The upper 10 percent of agricultural families are those with 20 hectares and more. There is still a wide range of incomes in this category, which probably includes almost all the few white-collar workers in agriculture as well as the producers.

If the market for factors were perfect (so that all units of a given factor earned the same), differences in personal or family incomes would depend only on differences in factors owned. Therefore, with information on factor distribution and factor prices it would be possible to indicate how much of income distribution skewness was related to the skewness of distribution of each factor. Although the assumption of perfect factor markets is untenable and no information exists on the distribution of human capital, this exercise is still of some interest as a first step.

It is possible that human capital is distributed more or less proportionally to physical capital. Lumping land into the factor capital we may express overall income variance as a function of the variances of income from capital and from labor, the covariance of the income from the two, and the share of total income going to each factor. Special interest attaches to the question of whether unequal distribution of capital is the main determinant of income distribution skewness or whether it depends more on such unmeasured elements as the innate ability of the farmer or the amount of work done.

Figure 3.2 gives estimates of the size distribution of (blue collar) labor income and that of capital income (estimated as value added minus labor income). The former is much less skewed than the latter and its variance is much less than that of all income. Part of these differences may be artificial—a result of our assumption that all workers in a given municipality (*municipio*) had the same wage.[10]

---

10. This assumption, i.e., the basing of the estimates primarily on average wages of different municipalities, not wages of individuals, tends to underestimate the variance. In fact, however, since geography is the main cause of the variation

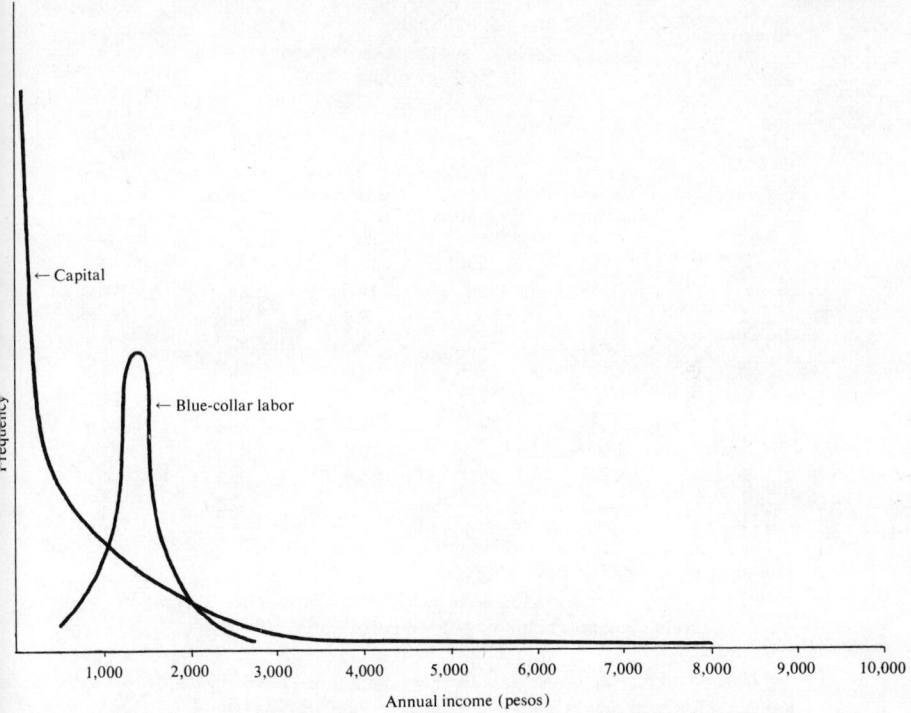

Fig. 3.2. Size distribution of blue-collar labor income and of capital income, 1960.

Table 3.4 suggests that only about 20 percent of hired blue-collar workers earned less than 1,000 pesos (the lower limit of category 5 would be about 1,000 pesos) or more than 1,850; the average was 1,400 and the ratio of the standard deviation to the mean was 0.26. Average income from all factors was about 3,800 pesos and the ratio of the standard deviation to the mean was 0.35. Estimates of the functional distribution within each decile (table 3.5) reinforce the conclusion, evident also in figure 3.2, that it is income from capital that gives the overall distribution its skewness. The Gini coefficient

and rural labor is relatively homogeneous, this bias may not be severe. Variance is probably overestimated in another respect due to a positive correlation between wages and the cost of living. Variance of all labor incomes is underestimated due to exclusion of white-collar workers of all types.

Table 3.5
Labor and Capital Shares by Deciles of the
Personal Income Distribution
in Agriculture

Decile	Average Income (National accounts concept)	Hired Labor Share	Imputed Pure Labor Share[a]	Hired Labor Share plus Imputed Pure Labor Share	Capital Share (Including human capital income of operators)
1	865	72.3	13.9	86.2	13.8
2	1,108	70.2	14.9	85.1	14.9
3	1,290	80.8	9.6	90.4	9.6
4	1,441	80.6	9.7	90.3	9.7
5	1,626	81.9	9.0	90.9	9.1
6	1,807	57.7	21.1	78.8	21.2
7	2,232	30.3	34.8	65.1	34.9
8	3,060	7.5	40.4	47.9	52.1
9	4,940	10.7	25.3	35.9	64.1
10	20,270	6.8	5.7	12.5	87.5
Total	3,830	23.2	14.4	37.6	62.4

Source: Calculations by the authors.

Note: The assumption used for these calculations is that the income of small-scale producers with income less than 2,800 pesos was attributable equally to labor and capital.

[a] Calculated as the number of unpaid workers times 1,400 divided by the value added on farms in the respective size category. This includes the pure labor component of the income of self-employed white-collar workers, professionals, and so on.

of the distribution of labor income presented in table 3.4 is 0.14. If capital were no more unequally distributed than labor income, the Gini coefficient for total income would be only moderately higher. The much higher overall coefficient of 0.58 therefore seems to be determined primarily by the distribution of capital.[11]

11. As suggested in n. 10, the Gini coefficient for labor incomes is probably greater than 0.14, perhaps considerably. But our methodology (classifying farms by size instead of by income) implies an underestimation of the variance of captial and total incomes as well, so the conclusion that labor income shows much less variance and skewness than capital income is not in doubt.

ECIEL urban family budget data reveal that the Gini coefficients for labor income alone are not much lower than those for total income. But urban labor is much more heterogeneous than rural blue-collar labor, and the labor share is higher in the urban than the rural economy. Note finally that the data presented

The Distribution of Income in Agriculture

Table 3.5 provides an estimate of the relative importance of capital and labor in the income of each decile of agricultural income earners, along with a division between payments to hired labor and imputed income of pure labor of the self-employed. A fairly plausible approximation of returns to pure labor—where we try to exclude the payment to human capital—is the average wage per agricultural worker (defined in relation to the number of days actually worked). In 1960 this figure appeared to be about 1,400 pesos per year;[12] applied to all the active population in agriculture, it implied a pure labor share of about 36 percent.[13] Although the figures are only best estimates, consideration of different assumptions from those used suggest that the general character of the functional distribution by deciles is not highly sensitive to changes of assumption. The conclusions that emerge clearly are the following.

1. Approximately the bottom half of income earners receive by far the largest part of their income as paid blue-collar workers on other farms. It seems unlikely that any of the first five deciles earn much less than 75 percent of their income in this way; the rest comes from production on land the farmer operates. Paid blue-collar income remains significant in the sixth and seventh deciles but essentially does not enter the top three.

---

here refer to the agricultural sector, not the rural sector as a whole; labor incomes for the latter would probably exhibit greater variance than those for the former.

12. If the average figure of 1,400 pesos includes some people with a reasonable amount of human capital, one should perhaps define the pure labor share as somewhat less than this. The concept of a pure labor share is in one sense a contradiction of terms since if all learning is included as human capital the share could be zero or negative. However, it is useful if there is a level of learning and ability that almost everyone can achieve fairly quickly on the job without outside instruction. For the present case the concept meets the generally reasonable criteria of corresponding to people with almost no formal education and to a large group of the agricultural population.

13. Because this calculation is appropriate only if returns to labor are the same whether the wage is paid or imputed, the possible existence of market imperfections or other obstacles to this condition's being met makes the figure difficult to interpret. (The fact that 1,400 pesos is not the wage received by all paid workers does not create a problem at this point; the pure labor share estimate of 36 percent would be incorrect only if the average imputed labor income were not equal to the average paid income.) We consider below alternative estimates of the labor share but since the range of possibilities is not too wide, it is instructive at this point to further draw out the inferences which would follow if the average wage rate were indeed the appropriate measure of labor returns for agricultural labor as a whole.

2. Although there is uncertainty with respect to the income received by operators of small farms in their role as producers and sometimes owners, it is very probable that for the five bottom deciles such income ranges from 15 to 30 percent of the total income of the decile. It rises rapidly to a level of possibly 90 percent for the upper three deciles.

3. White-collar workers and administrators are found in the top two deciles.

4. The pure labor share varies dramatically by decile from probably less than 10 percent in the upper decile to about 80–100 percent in the lower ones. It is impossible to be more precise since no definition of the pure labor share (including that cited above) is fully convincing for the lower deciles.[14]

5. The capital share is very high on the largest farms, possibly about 85 percent but almost certainly above 75 percent. Note that the upper decile corresponds essentially to operators of farms of 20 or more hectares.

Evidence on Changes in Income Distribution over Time

More limited evidence than the above can be brought to bear on the question of how distribution has changed over time and to consider possible causes of the apparent changes. Pertinent information is much scantier for the years before 1960, and it is also difficult to quantify subsequent developments because, though there have been sample surveys in agriculture following up the 1960 census, they have not been sufficiently parallel in concept to permit satisfactory comparisons.

The nature of the 1960 distribution does suggest that knowledge of the time path of the labor share would give some feel for changes in overall skewness and particularly for changes in the proportion of income received by the poorest sector of the population. Using wage rate data collected on a municipal level for over 30 years (albeit with

---

14. An argument can be made that the producer income on small plots is almost exclusively capital income since the opportunity cost of the labor is zero or close to it. The key point here is that regardless of how the imputation between labor and capital income is made for small producers, the pure labor share of low-decile income is much greater than that of high-decile income.

weaknesses and biases), one can compare estimates of the wage bill and value added to produce an estimated labor share. The evidence is startling. Real daily wage rates appear to have been about the same in the latter part of the 1960s as they were in the mid-1930s. They underwent a decline in the late depression years and the early 1940s, then rebounded and continued to increase until the early 1960s, and have since leveled off (see table 3.6).[15] During the same period (since 1935) average income per person engaged in agriculture appears to have risen at an average rate of 2–3 percent per year. If it is legitimate to assume that daily wages are a reasonable indicator of pure labor income[16] (on this see n. 20), the pure labor share must have fallen substantially; a best-guess time series is presented in

15. It may seem dangerous to base our conclusions about trends in the distribution of agricultural income so strongly on wage statistics, whose quality is believed to be relatively low. Despite their undisputed weaknesses, these data are in our judgment sufficiently within the ball park to convince us that the wage share has fallen significantly. For a detailed discussion see A. Berry, *The Development of the Agricultural Sector in Colombia,* forthcoming, chap. 5 and statistical appendix. Suffice it to point out here the following.

(1) When the series encompasses more than 30 years, the percentage change in error of observation over time must be quite large to account for an error of, say, 1 percent in the estimate of annual growth of real wages. We doubt that the wage estimates are likely to have been in error by more than 30–40 percent at any time and would expect any trend in this error to have been less than this (i.e., if downward biased at the start, it is very probable that they would also be downward biased at the end).

(2) The use of alternative deflators such as the blue-collar cost-of-living index of the nearest city or the national GNP deflator rather than the one actually used (food prices in the capital of the department) does not appreciably alter the results. Given improvements in transport, we might expect rural prices to have risen, if anything, faster than urban ones over this period.

(3) Since the wage figures are collected on a municipality basis, it is possible to test for gross inconsistencies (e.g., 100 percent) by comparing the reported wages of neighboring municipios. Such differentials do not appear to occur.

16. Perhaps the greatest weakness in the linking of these two variables (wages and income distribution) is the possibility that average number of paid work days per year may change over time. There is some evidence of such a phenomenon for Colombia (also for Japan). However, for the wage share to have remained constant, assuming that the figures on daily wages are accurate, the number of days worked per year would have to have increased by almost 70 percent during this 35-year period. This appears implausible, so with some caution it seems safe to conclude that a decrease in the wage share along with a decrease in the price of labor relative to those of land and capital together has occurred. This event would suggest that the personal and family distribution of income has been worsening over time.

Table 3.6
Index of Real Agricultural Wages, by Department and
Climate and for Colombia as a Whole, 1935/37–64/67
(1963 = 100)

	1935–37	1938–39	1940–41	1942–44
Antioquia				
Hot	78.3	59.1	67.7	50.7
Cold		80.1	84.7	47.4
Atlantico				
Hot	81.0	69.6	63.2	80.0
Bolivar[a]				
Hot	80.6	91.3	81.0	67.5
Boyaca				
Hot	73.9	72.1	78.0	64.6
Cold		80.6	87.2	68.2
Caldas				
Hot	127.0	99.6	122.4	84.4
Cold		105.4	122.2	79.4
Cauca				
Hot	102.8	71.9	70.4	70.3
Cold		87.6	99.3	69.1
Cundinamarca				
Hot	73.0	72.3	86.2	64.8
Cold		79.2	108.4	66.8
Huila				
Hot	74.7	66.6	81.2	61.5
Cold		66.2	79.9	60.5
Magdalena				
Hot	86.0	87.7	75.1	63.4
Cold		82.8	85.3	51.8
Nariño				
Hot	95.9	83.8	85.0	62.9
Cold		79.2	81.1	75.2
Norte de Santander				
Hot	91.3	62.7	80.7	70.8
Cold		82.6	99.4	72.8
Santander				
Hot	80.9	84.0	87.8	77.8
Cold		71.9	83.9	54.3
Tolima				
Hot	71.5	84.9	75.7	63.5
Cold		77.4	76.6	57.6
Valle del Cauca				
Hot	116.2	112.2	117.7	92.1
Cold		132.4	111.4	98.2
National				
Hot	99.8	84.3	77.2[b]	
Cold		91.4	82.0[b]	

Table 3.6 (continued)

	1945–49	1950–54	1955–59	1960–63	1964–67
Antioquia					
Hot	60.1	69.9	83.2	92.7	88.9
Cold	72.3	81.0	85.3	92.7	90.8
Atlantico					
Hot	72.9	71.8	66.3	91.0	94.5
Bolivar					
Hot	81.7	80.2	73.2	95.2	87.2
Boyaca					
Hot	76.5	78.2	79.9	99.5	102.1
Cold	72.3	78.9	79.2	97.7	105.8
Caldas					
Hot	102.1	99.7	103.4	97.8	102.6
Cold	86.8	87.3	91.6	93.0	99.8
Cauca					
Hot	90.4	92.6	85.2	96.2	100.4
Cold	85.6	90.9	87.8	97.0	98.4
Cundinamarca					
Hot	81.7	86.0	92.4	95.9	112.4
Cold	85.6	80.2	85.3	94.2	113.0
Huila					
Hot	78.5	80.0	84.6	108.3	92.9
Cold	75.0	77.6	80.3	101.8	91.2
Magdalena					
Hot	85.2	86.9	78.5	96.2	102.0
Cold	82.0	72.1	86.0	100.5	105.1
Nariño					
Hot	89.0	84.6	76.4	98.6	89.8
Cold	80.0	83.0	77.8	93.9	85.4
Norte de Santander					
Hot	75.7	87.5	84.2	96.6	93.8
Cold	79.6	93.5	85.8	102.4	100.0
Santander					
Hot	84.6	89.7	88.7	97.8	95.6
Cold	71.8	70.7	75.8	94.2	80.7
Tolima					
Hot	59.4	91.7	94.3	102.3	93.6
Cold	66.8	88.3	92.7	98.4	89.9
Valle del Cauca					
Hot	96.7	97.0	96.9	102.5	99.8
Cold	98.1	86.1	102.1	106.9	100.3
National					
Hot	78.5	83.5	81.9	94.7	96.2
Cold	73.6	84.3	87.7	98.3	97.6

[a] Includes Cordoba.
[b] 1940–1944.

Source: A. Berry, *Development of Agricultural Sector*, chap. 5 and table A-135.

Table 3.7
Pure Labor Share as a Percentage of Agricultural Value Added,
Selected Groups of Years

1935–39	66–84[a]
1940–44	56–79[a]
1945–49	46–47
1950–54	40–47
1955–59	34–42
1960–64	35–43

Note: The labor share figure used here has been calculated by multiplying the average male agricultural wage (figures from DANE) by the estimated labor force in agriculture. It would tend to overestimate the labor share since there are some, but not many, women and children (with lower average wages) in the labor force, and it would perhaps tend to underestimate the labor share, though this is uncertain, in that it assumes that the average quality of labor inputs is that of the paid worker. To the extent that the quality of the labor force has probably risen a little over time the figure would not quite refer to the income of the same type of labor over time.

[a]It must be remembered that figures on agricultural output and wages probably become worse and worse the further back the period to which they refer. The much higher labor share that emerges from our calculations for early years almost certainly reflects errors in these figures. But for labor's share not to have fallen at all the errors would have to be greater than suggested by consistency checks.

table 3.7. Changes in land and capital inputs are hard to estimate accurately and direct information on their prices is scarce; the data we have does suggest that the rental price of one or both has risen over this period.[17] In any case, whether because of greater relative amounts of these factors or increases in their price, the share of income generated in agriculture going to capital and land together has almost definitely risen substantially.

It is not possible to make a neat delineation between agricultural laborers and farm operators in Colombia, since many farmers have

17. If we assume, to take round figures, that between 1935 and 1965 the labor share fell from 60 percent to 40 percent, then, given that the real wage rate did not change, the ratio of each to labor would have had to increase by 125 percent for the real rental of land and capital to have also remained unchanged. In fact the evidence suggests that the ratios rose about 50 percent over this period (capital/man a little more and land/man a little less). This would suggest that the average of their two prices must have increased by about one-third. Direct evidence, although scanty, would not contradict such a development. Land prices appear to have risen considerably (though this does not necessarily mean that land rent has).

The Distribution of Income in Agriculture

a little land but not enough to provide a full-time job or a subsistence income without working on someone else's land.[18] Frequently a small plot of land is made available to the worker by the owner of the farm, partly to tie down the desired labor supply. Since all combinations of operator–laborer exist (in terms of the income share from each), it is not clear for how many people the absence of a positive trend in the real wage rate over this period implies a failure of total income to rise.[19] As of 1960 about 80 percent of the labor force earned the majority of its income from labor (paid or imputed), and probably from one-half to two-thirds earned more than 75 percent of their income from labor on other peoples' land. Thus a nonincreasing wage rate probably indicates a nonincreasing or very slowly increasing real income for a majority of the labor force.[20]

18. This is not to say that landless workers are employed year round. We have assumed an average of 250 days worked per year in calculating the annual agricultural real wage. We have no information as to whether persons earning most income from their own land or persons working mainly on others' land put in more days of work per year.

19. It is possible that real annual incomes have grown despite the failure of the daily wage to do so, as noted above. The text should be read with this qualification in mind.

20. We have neither tried to present a single formal model within which to evaluate the distributional implications of the wage and other data presented, nor tried to go beyond probability statements (albeit strong ones) with respect to how distribution has evolved. This is partly because we are uncertain of the degree to which the Colombian agricultural sector during this period approximated a neoclassical system and the degree to which it approximated a labor-surplus system. And it is partly because we feel that the evidence points toward a worsening distribution regardless which of these two models one accepts as the most relevant.

Consider, for example, a labor-surplus model in which the real wage does not change over time (not quite equivalent to the Colombian experience, in which it fell and later rose again) and the modern (capitalistic) sector expands. Now the income share of modern sector capitalists would only drop if the capital share in modern agriculture were falling faster than a certain rate. But there is no evidence of this—rather the contrary. There seems to have been considerable substitution of capital for labor in this modern subsector during the last four decades. Although we have no direct information, it is to be presumed that the capital share climbed. Even if the income share of modern capitalists were constant or rising slowly, some overall improvement in distribution (as measured, for example, by the Gini coefficient) could occur if the modern sector wage were above the average traditional sector earnings and if the latter earnings were rising on a per capita basis as people moved to the modern sector. Although evidence is scanty on the former question, it seems unlikely at this point that the modern sector wage is above the per capita income of most small-scale operators. The annual

For a fuller picture of distribution changes over time, it would be necessary to know how the distribution of land has changed, but there is almost no information on this subject. Increasing and decreasing concentration seem about equally likely. Continuing breakup of minifundia has been a frequent phenomenon in some parts of the country but breakup of large farms has occurred elsewhere, and the colonization of new lands tends to provide a partial safety valve against concentration. All in all, no easy balance can be drawn.

Some Tentative Explanations of Changes in Distribution over Time

To evaluate the likelihood that the apparent worsening of the income distribution in agriculture will continue into the 1970s (barring changes in exogenous determinants or in policy), it is worthwhile to review some possible explanations for such change. Since a major factor in the worsening has been the sluggish behavior of the real wage and the decline in the wage share, it is useful first to explore possible causes of this phenomenon. The first hypothesis that should

---

wage is approximately equivalent to the income generated on a farm of 1–2 hectares. (The issue is confused by the fact that so many families earn income from both sources.) On the second question, it must be remembered that the total labor force in the traditional sector has probably been roughly constant during most of the period under consideration—although emigration to modern agriculture and to nonagriculture (mostly the latter) has been continuous, natural population growth has at least offset this factor. Total traditional sector output has indeed been rising, though slowly, over time and there has probably been a gradual increase in output and income per capita in this sector. But it is too slow, especially in view of the apparently small modern-wage/traditional-sector earnings differential, to satisfy the conditions enunciated above for an improvement in distribution even with a rising modern capitalist share. If one accepts the neoclassical framework as more relevant, the stagnant wage rate implies even more directly a worsening income distribution (see chap. 1).

Perhaps the weakest link in the chain of evidence and logic whereby we have concluded that distribution has worsened in agriculture is the implicit assumption of no more than a small change in the number of days worked per year over the period. Our wage data are provided exclusively on a daily basis; we have assumed 250 days worked per year throughout—a figure based on evidence from the 1950s and 1960s but not earlier. If number of days worked per year has risen substantially, our basic conclusion would be weakened or nullified. A more detailed consideration of this possibility is presented elsewhere (Berry, *Development of Agricultural Sector*, chap. 5), where it is argued that for plausible increases in days worked per year over this period, our basic conclusion would not be negated.

be tested is that the agricultural sector is connected to the rest of the economy via sufficient factor mobility so that wage rates and rates of return to capital are determined at the economy-wide rather than the sectoral level. The wage for a given type of labor would, for example, be the same in agriculture and in nonagriculture. The hypothesis that factor remunerations in a sector depend on structural change within it (capital accumulation, technological change, and so on) makes sense only when intersectoral factor mobility is limited, or when the sector in question looms large in the total economy so that in a sense it pulls the rest of the economy along with it. Agriculture was undoubtedly the dominant sector of the Colombian economy until the post-1950 period, suggesting that its factor prices and shares were at that time determined primarily or substantially by events within the sector; this would be less true now.

The still somewhat limited evidence available indicates a consistency of the agricultural wage pattern with that of blue-collar workers in manufacturing and construction (see tables 4.1 and 4.2 for the comparison; table 3.6 presents agricultural wage series by department). This evidence suggests that labor has been sufficiently mobile to prevent large divergences in real wage movements across sectors. The decline of the agricultural real wage (1935–43) was, it appears, accompanied during the period 1933–39 (roughly) by a parallel drop in urban wages.[21] And from the early 1940s there has been a considerable parallel in the movement of agricultural and certain nonagricultural wage series. Both agricultural and manufacturing wages rose rapidly from 1942 or 1943 to 1947 or 1948, then fluctuated with less or no apparent advance until about 1953 or 1954. Manufacturing wages then started a long upward drift that continued without pause until the early 1960s. Agricultural wages also rose over the period 1953–63 (though with sharp drops in 1956 and 1957). Construction wages are not available over 1942–50 but from the mid-1930s to the present their trends have been similar to those of agricultural wages. Taking the period after 1935 as a whole, then,

21. At least this is the evidence from a series for female factory workers in Medellin and for construction workers in Bogota. See A. Berry, "Real Wage Trends in Colombian Manufacturing and Construction During the Twentieth Century," University of Western Ontario, Department of Economics, Research Report no. 7403, 1974.

it is evident that agricultural wages have shown trends markedly similar to those in nonagriculture. Accordingly, in explaining trends in wages and the labor share economy-wide phenomena should be the reference point. But since agriculture was so important during most of the period under consideration, specific events in that sector would be expected to play a significant role in determining economy-wide trends. A combined focus is therefore warranted in the analysis of distribution within agriculture.

Although the factor markets of agriculture and nonagriculture appear to have been closely linked, the decreasing labor share observed in agriculture has not characterized the economy as a whole, at least not since 1950.[22] During 1950–60, while the paid labor share was rising by 10 percentage points in nonagriculture, it was falling by 5 percentage points in agriculture; and while the pure labor share was about constant in nonagriculture it was falling 10 percentage points in agriculture. Why this different behavior? It is related in part to the fact that labor has remained fairly homogeneous in agriculture with relatively little addition to human capital over time while nonagriculture has seen substantial improvement in the labor force. This contrast should explain some of the quite different trends in the paid labor share of the two sectors. But the dissimilar evolution of the pure labor shares cannot be explained this way; it must be associated, in effect, with different types of aggregate production functions or different types of technological change. Along with other evidence, it would suggest that in some aggregate sense technological change has been pure labor saving in agriculture and roughly neutral in nonagriculture.[23] Such a general description of the process of change in agriculture is not very enlightening, however. A useful way to classify determinants of changing functional distribution follows.

22. See A. Berry, "Changing Income Distribution under Development: Colombia," *Review of Income and Wealth*, Income and Wealth Series 20, no. 3 (Sept. 1974): 289–316.

23. Assuming that the production function in each sector has unit elasticity of substitution. If this is not the case the statement must be modified accordingly. Factor demands in nonagriculture may of course be greatly affected by changing sectoral composition of demand, so the idea of an aggregate production function is a less satisfactory one in this context.

Changes in Factor Proportions and/or Factor Price Ratios

Changes in factor proportions and, more specifically, the extent to which increases in output have been due, respectively, to increases in land under cultivation and to increases in reproducible capital may affect the path of income distribution. In general one may expect increases in land to be complementary with labor, that is, to shift the demand curve for labor to the right, other things being equal. Capital might be either a complement or a substitute for labor, but it is more likely to be competitive than is land. Given the fairly low price elasticity of demand for agricultural products, an increase in capital could lower the equilibrium wage.

With fairly smoothly working markets, changes in factor proportions make themselves felt in factor price ratios. These ratios can of course be affected also by policy, as noted below in connection with the ratio of machinery prices to wages.

The Nature of Technological Change

If technological change is labor saving it will tend to worsen the distribution of income (under almost all interesting assumptions). A bias toward capital saving will have the opposite effect.

Changes in the Relative Importance of Different Types and Sizes of Farms

If factor proportions did not depend on size or tenure of farms or other institutional conditions subject to change over time, one could evaluate without further complications the effects of capital formation, land expansion, and technological change on the demand for labor. But we have already seen that different farm sizes are anything but homogeneous. Hence the labor/land ratio, for example, could change substantially as a result of a variation in the relative importance of different farm sizes (e.g., through a redistribution of land), all else remaining equal. This heterogeneity also implies that the effect of a given technological change on labor demand depends on its relative adaptation by the different farm sizes. A particular technological change could raise the demand for labor on one group of farms and lower it on another group.

Changes in Product Composition of Demand

Changes in product composition of demand tend to alter the relative demand for the different factors since different crops use different factor proportions. It is of special interest to assess the implications of the increase and subsequent decrease in the importance of coffee. Since coffee appears at first glance to be a labor-intensive crop, its recent decline might be hypothesized to have contributed to the falling labor share. The other major transformation in output composition has been associated with the commercialization of agriculture beginning in the late 1940s and early 1950s with the expansion of such crops as cotton, rice, and sesame. The general impression is that these are capital intensive. Thus commercialization probably also tends to diminish the labor share.

Changes in composition of crop output (as opposed to composition of demand) are in part a response to the nature of the new technologies becoming available and to capital formation. To that extent they do not constitute a separate determinant of labor demand. But the changing importance of coffee, for example, is primarily a world demand phenomenon and should thus be treated as an exogenous factor.

Using the above theoretical framework, it is instructive to consider jointly the implications of the combination of land increase, capital increase, and technological change for income distribution and, in particular, for the behavior of real agricultural wages.[24] In another study it has been hypothesized that the growth of agricultural output until about 1950 was largely explained by the growth of the traditional inputs, while increasing total factor productivity was not very significant. It appears that from the late 1930s until

24. A labor force increase should be taken into account as well. Reasonably firm data are only available for censal years, but it seems that the agricultural labor force has been increasing rather systemically at 1 percent per year for some decades. With this growth rate relatively constant, variations in the rate of wage change cannot be related to it. Changes in the percentage of the labor force who are employed could be a factor, as mentioned in the text.

about 1950 only 10–25 percent of output growth was due to increased factor productivity. Since 1950 it seems that technological change has become more important, accounting for 30–50 percent of output growth.[25]

If in fact (1) there was little technological change before 1945 or 1950 and (2) land and labor tend to be complementary in use, then, unless other factors were affecting the wage rate, the behavior of wages over the pre-1950 period as a whole (see table 4.2) might suggest that capital was competitive with labor. During this period the agricultural real price index was climbing; in the absence of any technological change the increase in land per worker[26] would have been expected to exert upward pressure on the wage rate. Yet, in the period of the mid-1930s to the late 1940s, wages did not rise, but rather fell. But if technological change was not important, the decrease in wages is presumably not due to labor-saving technological change—impressionistic evidence on the use of new techniques is consistent with relatively little change during the period.[27] The main forms of capital formation were cattle, plantations, construction, and soil improvement, none of which would on the surface appear as likely to be competitive with labor as would machinery, for example.

It has often been argued that the land law of 1936 (which required landlords to pay tenants for investments they made while renting land) led the former group to dispossess the later. This action would have increased the supply of labor and helped decrease the wage rate in the late 1930s and early 1940s. The depression may also have had something to do with the decline. The subsequent wage increase (1943–50) would have been a result of the general expansion of the

25. Berry, *Development of Agricultural Sector*, chap. 2.
26. Notice that although much of the newly exploited land was devoted to cattle grazing, the figure here refers to cropped land per man; it too rose.
27. A caveat must be added here. Although technological change may not have been important as a contributor to growth, it could still have had a negative impact on the demand for labor. In a system with imperfect factor markets such that different producers face different relative factor prices, technological change can occur for one subset of producers and (1) raise their factor productivity measured at the factor prices *they* face, (2) lower the demand for a factor, (e.g., labor) but (3) not show up as an aggregate residual, in the calculation of which different factor prices are used from those facing the adopting producers. This phenomenon could have occurred during the period in question.

agricultural sector in the absence of major labor-saving technological change. Such an interpretation would suggest that capital was not sufficiently competitive with labor to have precipitated a decreasing wage rate in the face of output growth, had other things been equal.[28]

To review, declining real wages could be largely explained by the following phenomena: (1) the declining importance of some labor-intensive crops such as coffee compensated by faster growth in less labor-intensive production of commercial crops and cattle; (2) the increase of the rural proletariat by some ejection of tenants from their traditional land plots; and (3) aftereffects of the depression, during which real wages for those who could get work rose as prices fell faster than nominal wages; when prices began to rise again (late 1930s and 1940s) real wages could be expected to fall again.[29]

The explanation of changes in factor prices over the post-1950 period has more current interest, but again no clear picture emerges from the information available. The rapid burst of mechanization from the late 1940s to about 1956 did not bring (at that time) a lowering of the average wage rate, though its association with the advance of such low-labor-share crops as rice, barley, sesame, and sugar for refining (and corn and wheat when produced with machinery) suggest that it might have been expected to do so. Table 3.8 presents data on tractors, tractors/hectare of temporary crops, the tractor price/wage ratio, and the real wage. The relative price of a horsepower definitely dropped at the end of the 1940s and beginning of the 1950s, and despite some subsequent fluctuations never returned to its level before that decrease. During most of the 1960s the relative price was almost as low as in the first half of the 1950s. This decrease in the relative price of machines compared to labor could have decreased the demand for labor in agriculture from the mid-1950s. However, this factor was not sufficient to offset other pressures that led to an increase in real agricultural wages from the mid-1950s to

28. Changes in land distribution could also have been important in determining the demand for labor, but apart from possible movements between the categories tenants and landless workers, there is little evidence of large-scale changes in distribution. Certainly many people lost their lands during the *violencia*, but most large farms remained large.

29. For a more detailed treatment of this question, see Berry, *Development of Agricultural Sector,* chap. 6.

the mid-1960s, by which time real agricultural wages had reached a level slightly higher than that current in the late 1930s (see col. 8 of table 4.2).

Much more detailed analysis is necessary to test the overall effect of mechanization and technical modernization. One hypothesis is that with mechanization, better but fewer workers are required, and those hired receive relatively higher wages. Such a sequence could lead to a higher observed wage (especially if DANE data gathering reflects more the wages on relatively large farms) even though the average wage did not rise and/or the demand for labor decreased. The failure of the wage rate to rise since about 1963 could be a reaction to the continued growth of commercial agriculture. Alternatively the main determinant of wage changes may have been the ability to get a job outside agriculture; such opportunities were relatively good in the late 1940s and early 1950s. This last hypothesis may explain the decrease in real agricultural wages starting in 1962–63, when it appears the level of urban unemployment started to increase perceptibly and wage increases to decelerate.

Output Composition, Changing Factor Shares, and Changing Comparative Advantage of Small and Large Farms

It was observed earlier that an independent determinant of changes in factor shares over time would be changes in composition of demand among crops which (1) use different factor proportions and/or (2) have different adaptability to small versus large farms.[30] In this section empirical evidence on factor proportions and factor shares[31] corresponding to various agricultural commodities is presented, along with data on the relationship between farm size and product composition of output. It is essential to note carefully that factor proportions used to produce the same crop may vary tremendously among different types of farms, so the only fully satisfactory specification of the relationship among factor proportions,

30. Changes in output composition which simply reflect changing factor proportions and factor prices would of course not be an independent determinant.
31. Shares of the value added gross of depreciation (value of product minus value of purchased inputs). Theoretically, of course, it would be better to use net income, but depreciation estimates are not available. For this reason our figures overestimate the capital share.

Table 3.8
Tractorization over Time

Year	Tractor Inventory at Year End (1)	Stock of Horsepower at Year End (Thousands) (2)	Hectares under Annual Crops plus Bananas and Cocoa (Thousands) (3)	Horsepower per Hectare in Annuals plus Bananas and Cocoa (4)	Tractors per Thousand Hectares in Cited Crops (5)	Cost of Horsepower/Wage (Index) (6)	Cost of Horsepower (Index) (7)	Daily Wage (8)
1947	3,781	124.8	1,779.8	.0818	2.477			1.62
1948	4,409	145.5	1,875.7	.0914	2.771			2.02
1949	5,197	171.5	1,753.6	.1230	3.728			2.03
1950	6,537	215.7	1,970.2	.1321	4.006	89.25	224.9	2.52
1951	7,892	260.4	2,103.5	.1401	4.123	77.92	221.3	2.84
1952	8,798	294.7	1,951.7	.1726	5.153	80.96	227.5	2.81
1953	10,057	336.9	2,050.7	.2046	5.931	61.03	178.2	2.92
1954	12,163	419.6	2,194.1	.2290	6.326	55.75	182.3	3.27
1955	13,880	502.4	2,187.7	.2661	7.041	66.41	229.1	3.45
1956	15,403	582.2	1,997.0	.2995	7.679	76.21	269.8	3.54
1957	15,335	598.1	2,068.3	.3226	7.867	82.21	319.8	3.89
1958	16,272	667.2	2,170.6	.3355	7.988	125.80	572.4	4.55
1959	17,338	723.2	2,197.3	.3543	8.386	106.64	533.2	5.00
1960	18,426	778.6	2,179.0	.3909	8.824	85.15	469.2	5.51
1961	19,227	851.8	2,290.5	.3919	8.788	76.04	478.3	6.29
1962	20,128	897.7	2,241.4	.4140	9.200	79.57	536.8	6.92
1963	20,622	928.0	2,416.6	.3991	8.639	73.16	657.7	8.99
1964	20,876	964.5	2,604.5	.3832	7.983	60.52	623.4	10.30
1965	20,792	998.0	2,622.7	.3654	8.199	59.13	670.5	11.34
1966	21,294	958.3	2,489.5	.4631	9.262	61.65	727.5	11.80
1967	23,058	1,152.9	2,491.6	.5250	10.078	79.02	1,059.6	13.41
1968	25,110	1,308.2					1,274.5	

Sources and Methodology: Column (1) is an estimate made by Wayne Thirsk, "The Economics of Farm Mechanization in Colombia" (Ph. D. diss., Yale University, 1972).

Column (2), for the years 1950–68, is taken from Victor M. Espinosa, "Medicion del Cambio Tecnologico en la Agricultura Comercial Para Colombia 1950–70," paper written in the graduate course in agricultural economics, University of the Andes, 1971, table 3. The data from previous years were estimated by the author.

Column (3) is based on data from USDA Foreign Agricultural Report no. 52, *Changes in Agricultural Productivity and Technology in Colombia*, Washington, D.C., June 1969.

Column (7) is from Thirsk, ibid., p. 319, and col. (8) is data collected by the author based on information published in DANE's *Boletin Mensual de Estadistica* and *Anuario General de Estadistica*. The other columns are derived from those cited.

farm size, and crop would refer to the factor proportions for "crop i grown on type of farm j"; unfortunately, this level of detail is not available.

Despite the spotty and at times impressionistic nature of the information on factor shares for various crops and animal products, estimated shares differ so much among products that there is little danger in categorizing certain crops as labor intensive relative to certain others. Table 3.9 summarizes estimates of labor share and labor income per hectare, along with other available estimates, for the major crops and for cattle. It seems clear that the labor-intensive category (as defined by the high labor share of income generated)

Table 3.9
Labor Income and Labor Share by Products

	Value Added per Hectare		Labor Income per Hectare		Labor Share			
Perennials	1958 (1)	1966 (2)	1958 (3)	1966 (4)	1958 (5)	1966 (6)	Future (7)	Other Estimates (8)
Coffee	1950	3340	475	1,380	24	41		
Cacao	—	—	270	790	—	—		
Bananas (export)	3,700–5,500	7,300–10,900	290	840	≤8.0	≤11.5		
Platanos	—	—	250	730	—	—		
Sugar (for refining)	3,100	10,000	500	1,100	16.1	11.0		
Sugar (panela)	1,100	2,650	530–810	1,540	48–74	58		
Annuals: Relatively Commercialized								
Barley	870	1,900	80	240	9	12		
Cotton	1,340	2,300	380	1,100	28	48	15–30	
Rice	960	2,425	215	625	22	26	12	
Sesame	550	1,980	150	440	27	22	15–18	
Annuals: Less Commercialized								
Beans	600	1,700	380	1,100	63	65	12	
Corn	425	1,030	200	580	47	50	13	
Potatoes	3,200	7,325	630	1,830	20	25		45;54
Tobacco	2,890	7,630	1,960	5,700	63	74		
Wheat	510	1,350	135	390	26	29		33;44
Yucca	950	3,670	385	1,120	40	30		
Animal Products								
Cattle						25 (1960 estimate)		

Sources and Methodology: Figures on value added per hectare were based on value of output per hectare data from USDA Foreign Agricultural Report no. 52, *Changes in Agricultural Production and Technology in Colombia*, Washington, D.C., June output 1969, and on a variety of sources from which estimates of the share of output value corresponding to purchased inputs could be drawn.

Major sources of information on labor inputs for various crops were (a) the estimates by Lauchlin Currie in his *Accelerating Development: the Necessity and the Means* (New York: McGraw–Hill, 1966), pp. 174–78; (b) Caja Agraria, *Manual de Costos* (Bogota: Caja Agraria, 1967); (c) INCORA, *Informacion sobre Costos de Produccion*, Aug. 1968; and (d) ILMA (Instituto Latinoamericano de Mercadeo Agricola), *Supply Problems of Basic Agricultural Products in Colombia* (Bogota: ILMA, 1964). A variety of other sources was used for specific crops.

None of the above sources could be accepted as definitive, because most of them present figures referring directly to commercial production. Currie's estimates are the most meaningful for our purposes, but some were adjusted on the basis of more detailed studies than he had available at time of writing.

The data of col. (7) are based on figures presented in INCORA, ibid., and correspond to what the study refers to as future technologies and cost structures.

The estimates offered in col. (8) come from crop studies and are of interest due to their differences with my estimates for these products, which suggest that, whether because 1958 and 1966 were atypical or for some other reason, mine may be downward biased.

The estimate for cattle is based on the author's estimate of the number of people engaged in cattle raising (about 380,000 in 1960) and Central Bank-based estimates of value added. It is perhaps more likely to be biased up than down because the Central Bank estimate of milk production appears low. On the other hand Currie estimated a greater number of people engaged in the cattle industry (440,000).

Notes: Labor income of various products is calculated as man days times a daily wage rate, i.e., there is no attempt in this context to use a different labor cost for hired and family labor. Some attempt was made to take account of apparent differences among crops in the wages paid to hired labor. Differences are based on differences in the type of work, the region in which the crops are grown, and so on.

Labor share is likely to be unstable, at least for commercial operations and crops whose yields and/or prices fluctuate considerably. (It is equally likely to be unstable if calculated for noncommercial operations on the assumption of a fixed payment per unit of labor with returns to capital calculated as a residual.) The most appropriate measure is a long-run average labor share. Although here we did not take the desirable step of estimating the shares for a number of years, the use of both 1958 and 1966 is a step in this direction. The shares differ between the two years primarily because of changes in the relative price of labor and the products.

consists of tobacco, cane for brown sugar (panela),[32] corn, beans, and yucca. Evidence on potatoes is conflicting but they also probably belong in this group of products with labor shares in the 40–70 percent range. In contrast are the relatively commercialized annual crops (cotton, rice, barley, sesame, and so on), all of which typically have labor shares below 30 percent.[33] The tree crops, including coffee during the period of high prices, generally have labor shares below 30 or 35 percent. When prices correspond to the long-run average, coffee's labor share may well be above 35 percent[34] (our estimate for 1966 was 40 percent). The crops with high labor shares are also the ones with high labor income per hectare; coffee joins the ranks of the highest labor income crops, and potatoes surpasses some of those with higher labor shares. (These two are of course among the highest "value added per hectare" crops.)

For cattle (taking beef and dairy together) the labor share appears to be about one-fourth, making it lower than for all crops taken together (for which the figure is probably about 35–40 percent.) The smaller livestock (pigs and poultry) probably have a higher labor

---

32. It is worth remarking also in the case of panela that its processing is usually done in rural areas or small towns and as such offers substantial employment. The "trapiches" (presses), of which there were almost 60,000 in 1960–61, are scattered through much of the country. Many are small operations on small farms using family and other low-cost labor. Consideration of this stage as well as the production of cane implies a very high labor income per hectare for panela (see Izquierdo B. Victaliano, *Caña, Trapiches y Panela en Cauca, Valle, Caldas,* Asociacion Nacional de Cultivadores de Cana de Azucar, 1964).

The case of coffee is another for which inclusion of labor for on-farm processing implies that the figures presented in table 3.9 understate somewhat the farm-labor income associated with 1 hectare of the product. But the share of all coffee-related labor associated with processing seems to be small. ECLA–FAO estimated 15.2 man-hours per 100 kilograms of unthreshed coffee (coffee is normally threshed in industrial mills). This is only about 2 percent of the field hours. Almost 90 percent of the coffee farms in the ECLA–FAO sample had their own processing (depulping) plants and 88 percent of them were small and hand operated.

33. The figure of 48 percent for cotton in 1966 does not seem to be typical.

34. Theory would suggest that the labor share falls, in the short run at least, when coffee prices rise in a context where labor is not in short supply. As prices rise, land rents increase more rapidly than wages when labor supply is elastic. The much lower labor share for 1958 (the last year for which internal coffee prices were maintained at a high real level) than for 1966 is consistent with this principle. (The ECLA–FAO study estimated a labor share of value of product of about 24 percent for 1955–56, consistent with our 1958 estimate).

share, so the share for all livestock would be a little higher, though not much, since cattle is by far the most important subsector.

The average labor share for any given crop depends on the proportion produced on large commercial farms. The commercial technologies for barley and wheat generate about the same shares and so do the traditional technologies, but the average share is lower for barley because it is a more commercialized crop. For many crops (e.g., wheat, barley, rice, corn, potatoes, sugar) the labor share is likely to vary by four or five times between the commercial and the traditional technologies. The former is likely to produce a higher yield per hectare and often a higher value added per hectare, while using much less (though sometimes higher cost) labor. Table 3.10 contrasts crops according to whether they are typically produced on small farms, large farms, or both. The small-farm crops are essentially the traditional technology annuals, especially tobacco, potatoes, and wheat;[35] beans and corn also rank high in share of area cultivated in small units. The crops most characterized by being produced on large farms are cotton and rice.

It is clear from the data of table 3.9 that, at least as far as crops are concerned, changing composition of output has been related to the decreasing labor share over time. Most of the high labor share crops have had slow output growth over the last two decades or more. While the average annual output growth of panela, beans, tobacco, corn, and yucca during 1950–67 was about 2.4 percent, that of all crops was about 3.6 percent for the same period. Commercial crops (cotton, rice, barley, sorghum, sugar for refining, sesame, soybeans) had output growth of about 7.5 percent and raised their share of total crop output from about 10 percent in 1950 to about 25 percent in 1967. This change in output composition must have contributed substantially to the lower average labor share.[36] And

35. Note that because these figures refer to 1960, they may now be significantly different for some crops. The commercial share of total crop output has continued to grow over time. The shares of the farms of less than 5 hectares fell in most of the crops between 1960 and 1966, but the typical decrease was not so rapid as to suggest that overall the figures presented here would be seriously different from 1970 reality.

36. If the labor share of each crop had remained constant during this period at the value observed in 1958, the labor share for the set of traditional and commer-

Table 3.10
Tendency of Crops to be Grown on Small and Large Farms, 1960 and 1966

	Percentage of Harvested Area on Farms of ≤ 5 Hectares: 1960	Percentage of Harvested Area on Farms of ≤ 5 Hectares: 1st Semester, 1966	Percentage of Harvested Area on Farms of ≥ 50 Hectares: 1960	Percentage of Harvested Area on Farms of ≥ 50 Hectares: 1st Semester, 1966	Percentage of Harvested Area in Plots of ≤ 5 hectares: 1960	Percentage of Harvested Area in Plots of ≥ 50 hectares: 1960
Perennials						
Coffee	21.6	18.7	20.8	22.0	48.4	8.0
Cacao	16.5	15.0	29.4	29.8	63.5	3.8
Bananas (export)	13.6	13.8	43.8	40.6	52.8	25.6
Platanos	21.8	19.9	24.2	28.5	78.2	1.6
Sugar	18.4	15.7	40.0	40.7	51.9	25.8
Annuals: relatively modern technology						
Barley	21.2	31.3	39.1	41.8	44.6	23.6
Cotton	8.3	2.2	50.7	85.3	29.1	32.3
Rice	7.1	6.7	66.7	68.0	29.1	32.3
Sesame	22.2	22.5	36.3	44.0	35.1	16.6
Annuals: traditional technology						
Beans	24.2	25.5	29.3	31.7	64.8	9.5
Corn	26.6	24.6	31.2	36.9	61.7	7.6
Potatoes	31.8	39.9	19.9	20.1	67.4	4.2
Tobacco	41.0	37.8	10.2	21.8	84.8	1.6
Wheat	30.6	33.7	16.9	24.7	64.9	5.7
Yucca	24.7	19.8	24.2	35.2	87.7	.8

Sources: For all crops except cotton the 1960 figures are from DANE, *Censo Agropecuario: Resumen General, Segunda Parte.* For cotton, they are from Instituto de Fomento Algodonero, Colombia, *Su Desarrollo Agricola: Algodon y Oleaginosas, 1961–1962* (Bogota, 1963). For 1966 all figures are based on USDA Foreign Agricultural Economic Report no. 66, *Agricultural Productivity in Colombia* (Washington, D.C.: U.S. Government Printing Office, 1970), pp. 24–26. The cotton information refers only to the interior of the country; large farms are probably somewhat more important on the coast. Because of the different base, the 1960 and 1966 figures cannot be compared.

because the faster growing crops tend to be large farm crops, it has also presumably lowered the small producer's share of capital income. Although there are no reliable over time data on factor proportions for given crops, it is plausible to assume that for many the labor share has declined (holding size of farm on which it is grown constant). This might or might not explain a substantial part of the secular decline.[37]

The case of livestock is less clear-cut. Poultry has shown rapid increase and presumably has a higher labor share than cattle, but no usable information on this is available.

In short, the growing significance of crops with low labor shares has implied little increase in the overall demand for labor; this affects principally the rural proletariat and thus tends to worsen the income distribution. The greater dispersion of incomes may also be due to a decrease over time in the labor share generated on each size of farm.

Summary

Inequality of distribution of income generated in agriculture as of 1960 (to which the figures presented in this chapter refer) was extreme; the top decile of income earners appeared to receive 50–55 percent of all income generated in the sector. The pure labor share was about one-third. Distribution appeared to have been worsening

---

cial products mentioned here (including all the major crops) would have fallen from 41.3 in 1950 to 36.7 in 1967.

The relative stagnation of coffee output over the last 35 or 40 years (2.4 percent average growth from 1930 to 1965) has probably played some part in the secular decline of the labor share, but since its labor share appears to have been only marginally higher than that of agriculture as a whole (it has been lower when coffee prices were high) and its growth rate has been only about 1 percent slower than total output, this cannot be proposed as a major explanatory factor.

Observe that, because average wages are higher in some commercial crops (e.g., sugar) than in traditional crops, the impact of the shifting output composition on number of jobs is more negative than its impact on the labor share. Our labor share estimates by crop (table 3.9) take account of differential average wages by crop. With a few exceptions these differentials are not very wide (e.g., a 50 percent differential is a large one); wages seem to be determined (predominantly) by market forces. A good part of the differentials by crop are probably due basically to regional differentials.

37. This is only a proximate or mechanical explanation of course.

secularly over the last three or four decades and the pure labor share to have been falling. Some of the decrease is undoubtedly associated with the expansion of commercial crops (such as cotton, sugar, and rice) in the post-World War II period, crops with low labor shares produced with machinery and advanced technology. The decrease in the relative price of machinery has undoubtedly been another factor although its importance is much harder to evaluate. As discussed elsewhere, a decreasing pure labor share in the economy as a whole may have been a principal factor; in other words developments in agriculture may have been closely intertwined with those in other sectors.

4

Changing Income Distribution under Development: 1930s–1960s

As detailed in chapters 2 and 3, Colombia's income distribution in the mid-1960s was extremely unequal. Chapter 3 reveals a clear pattern of worsening within the agricultural sector. This chapter probes the broader and central issue of how the overall distribution has changed and is changing; an investigation of this subject may give clues as to how it is likely to change in the future.

Many less developed countries, Colombia included, have during the post-World War II period achieved what are in historical terms very respectable growth rates of total output and even of output (and income) per capita. But it is often argued in Colombia, as in many other developing countries, that recent growth has been characterized by worsening distribution,[1] stable or even declining incomes for lower-income members of the labor force, burgeoning urban slums filled with people expelled from agricultural sectors that are stagnant and archaic or whose pattern of modernization has been characterized by labor-saving technological change, swift population growth accentuating all the problems of labor surplus, and so on. Such fears are fueled also by the generally accepted belief that the growth process in the now developed countries involved a stage of worsening income distribution prior to a subsequent stage of improvement associated with the approach of economic maturity. Some students believe that this sequence is more or less inevitable since the high profit share linked to a skewed family or personal income distribution is a key source of the savings that promote

1. Especially during the post-World War II period with its tendencies to capital-intensive growth, rapid population growth, and so on.

growth. This pessimistic conclusion leads, further, to the fear that extra-labor-market steps taken in the guise of income redistribution will create disincentives and inefficiencies in the system and help to slow its growth down to unacceptable levels.[2]

Few countries have sufficient information from as far back as 20 or 25 years to provide bases of comparison with the more abundant data now available, so most judgments as to income distribution trends are of necessity impressionistic. This chapter attempts to trace specific features of the income distribution trends in Colombia during the last 30 or 40 years by piecing together diverse types of information. A rough attempt is made also to check the consistency of various alternative hypotheses that might explain the observed trends.

Methodology

The desirable data base for studying changes in income distribution —good quality surveys with comparable and appropriate definitions and corresponding to different points of time—will remain out of reach for some time in most Latin American countries, and Colombia is no exception. Whereas four or five attempts have been made at different points of time to estimate distribution,[3] only that presented in chapter 2 (for 1964) has adequate detail and methodology to lend it much confidence. Among the other studies methodology is either too crude, insufficiently spelled out, or incomparable with the 1964 study to permit useful over time comparisons.[4] Under the actual data conditions, over time comparisons of these surveys can at most serve as a check on other techniques.

In this study major reliance is placed on the wage series for various groups of workers. This, coupled with information on functional distribution over time and on changes in the occupational and sectoral structure over time, permits some appraisal of (1) changes in the overall personal or family income distribution and (2) with somewhat greater precision, changes in the distribution of labor income. A number of problems associated with differences between personal

2. E.g., wage legislation that induces capital intensity.
3. See Miguel Urrutia, "Reseña de los Estudios de Distribution de Ingresos en Colombia," *Revista del Banco de la Republica*, no. 508, Feb. 1970.
4. For a more detailed discussion see ibid.

and family income, inclusion or noninclusion of income not associated with the current production process, biasing effects of an increasing proportion of women in the labor force, and other matters are swept aside in order to paint the broad outlines of the picture; some of these problems have been discussed in chapters 2 and 3. Although the distribution of capital income is also of much interest, it is significantly harder to get at. Reference is made to some of the possible mechanisms determining changes in income distribution, but neither information nor analysis is at present sufficiently advanced to allow more than speculative hypotheses in this area.

The nature of the available data makes it convenient to partition the discussion into a number of aspects. Frequently it is possible to say with greater certainty what has happened within a given sector or time period than for the whole economy or the whole time period considered—from the mid-1930s to the present. In particular, separate information has already been presented for the agricultural sector, and it is useful to distinguish agriculture and nonagriculture. In general much better information is available on the distribution of labor income than overall or for capital income. Finally, reference of much of the available information to a number of benchmark years forces the use of periods delimited by those years. The basic conclusions of the analysis are (1) that income distribution in agriculture has worsened throughout the period since the mid-1930s (see chap. 3) and (2) that nonagricultural income distribution probably worsened from the mid-1930s until some time in the early 1950s, then improved till some time in the mid-1960s, and then tended to level off.[5] Conclusion (2) is based primarily on and therefore especially pertinent to the distribution of labor income; much less is known about the distribution of capital income and its relation to labor income. Because conclusion (2) relates to two or three basic subperiods, the discussion will be organized along chronological lines.

---

5. Evidence for the period since the mid-1960s is as yet very incomplete; some of it suggests a renewed worsening, some of it does not. Income of such groups as agricultural and construction workers has not increased substantially if at all (see table 4.1), but structural change (especially shifting from agriculture to nonagriculture) may have been extremely rapid. Any overall judgment would be premature at this point.

The Probable Worsening of Distribution, 1930s to Early 1950s: Evidence

A substantial body of evidence suggests that overall personal or family distribution (always very bad) worsened from say 1930 until some time in the early 1950s.[6] This period included the economic difficulties of the latter part of the world depression in the 1930s; the advance of industry, given an initial impetus by the obstacles to importation during those years and further stimulated during the war because capital goods were again difficult to import; and the rapid postwar industrial and overall growth associated with easing of the balance of payments. The price of coffee started to rise rapidly in the late 1940s and early 1950s. Rural violence, already fairly common in the 1930s, exploded into the famous *violencia* in the late 1940s and early 1950s, and undoubtedly contributed to rural–rural migration.[7] Growth in per capita income was fairly continuous over the period and particularly rapid during the latter part between 1945 and 1951–54, during which income per worker[8] rose at an average of 5.1 percent per year[9] while output per worker was climbing at 3.6 percent. During the decade 1934–36 to 1944–46, income per worker grew less quickly at 1.0 percent and output per worker at 1.4 percent. For the period as a whole, income and output per capita grew at 2.8 percent and 2.3 percent, respectively, as population grew somewhat faster than the labor force.[10]

Major evidence of worsening distribution is the slower income

---

6. A competing hypothesis of particular interest when only the urban sector is being considered would locate the turning point (from worsening to improving) in the late 1950s. Udall's evidence on several low-income occupations in Bogota, including the only data that separate out unskilled manufacturing workers, shows no definite rise until the early 1960s. Average blue-collar incomes began to rise quickly in the early 1950s, as is well known, but these increases may have gone largely to more skilled workers or workers of large firms. (Udall's data were from classified ads, and it is not clear how accurate an indicator they provide.)

7. Evidence and opinions are more mixed as to whether it was a factor in promoting rapid growth of the large cities. It clearly hastened the flow of rural people from Tolima and Huila to the llanos, and it generated immigration to small towns and cities—some of the people left again after the violence died down in the countryside.

8. More precisely, per member of the labor force, although during these early years open unemployment was quite low.

9. Based on net national income estimates.

10. The substantial differences between income and output growth over this period are due to sharp shifts in the terms of trade.

growth for unskilled labor than for other groups, especially in agriculture.[11] (In fig. 4.1 are plotted relevant series for the major occupational categories for which information is available, and in table 4.1 percentage changes over specified periods are indicated.)

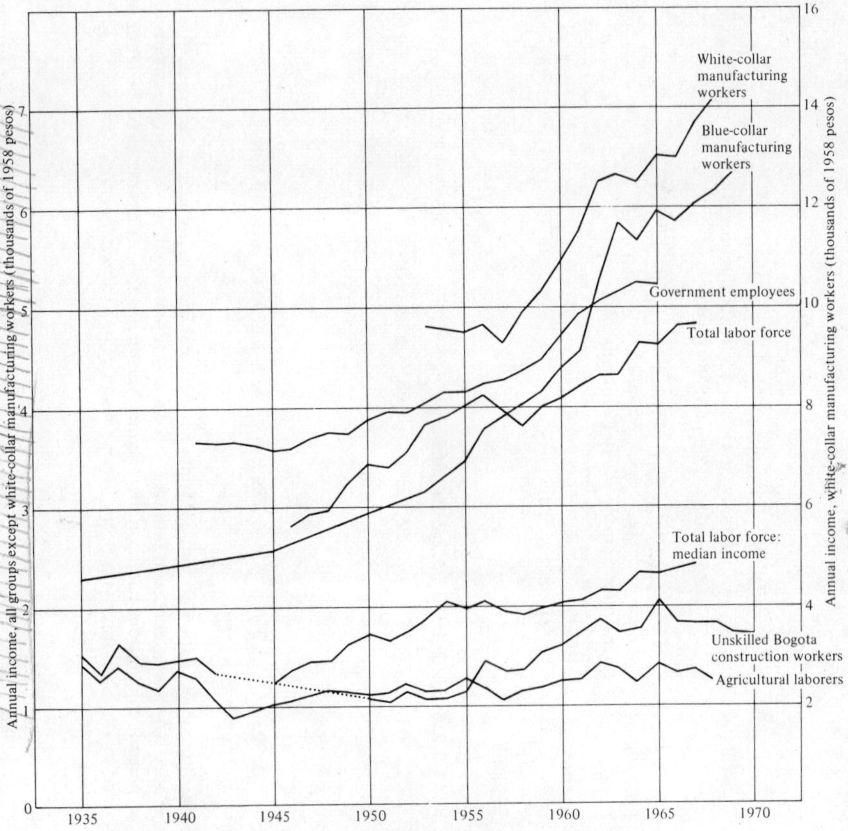

Fig. 4.1. Historical trends in the income levels of selected occupational groups from 1935.

11. For agricultural workers slow income growth characterized the whole period after 1935. Between 1935 and 1968, average income per capita in agriculture probably rose by about 150–175 percent while the daily real wage appears not to have risen at all (see, however, n. 14).

Table 4.1
Changes in Average Income by Periods and by Occupational Categories
(Annual income in 1958 pesos)

	Labor Force (1)	Agricultural Labor Force (2)	Male Agricultural Blue-Collar Workers (3)	Factory Manufacturing Blue-Collar Workers (4)	Bogotá Construction Workers (5)	Agricultural Labor Force excluding Male Blue-Collar Workers (6)	Factory Manufacturing White-Collar Workers (7)	Government Employees (8)	Nonagricultural Labor Force[n] (9)	Labor Force Median Income[o] (10)
Period I (1934-36 to 1950-54)										
Average income										
Beginning of period	2,280	1,144–1,218	1,102–1,377,[d,e]	2,280–2,365			5,650–6,400	≈3,080	4,201–4,335	
End of period	3,685[a]	2,300[b]	1,158[e]	3,193[g]	1,081[i]	3,060[k]	9,600[g]	≈3,900	5,364	≈1,840
Annual rate of increase	2.8	3.7–4.2[c]	–1.0–0.25[f]	1.8–2.0[h]	Decrease[j]		2.3–3.0[l]	1.4	1.26–1.45	
Period II (1950-54 to 1964-66)										
Average income										
End of period	4,746	2,903	1,336[e]	5,878	1,880[i]	3,948[k]	13,038	5,197[m]	6,413	≈2,354
Annual rate of increase	1.9–2.3	1.8	1.1	4.6	4.2	2.0	2.0	2.2	1.35	

Note: The deflator used for all incomes is the national accounts net national income implicit price index. Annual wage series for some of the occupations included here are presented in table A2. Except where indicated, average implies mean.

[a] Net national income per person; calculations based on the *Cuentas Nacionales* and my estimates of the labor force.
[b] Agricultural output divided by the labor force (see Berry, *Development of Agricultural Sector*, chap. 5).
[c] 1935 to 1950–54.
[d] Refers to 1936.
[e] Assuming the reported daily wage of 250 days worked per year.

^{f}A literal reading of the wage statistics indicates a decrease of 15.9 percent over the period 1935–37 to 1950–54, i.e., of about 1 percent per year. It is argued elsewhere (Berry, ibid.) that the observations in the 1930s are probably above equilibrium wages because prices were falling and money wages could have lagged behind prices in this descent. The decrease of the GDP deflator from 1927–28 to 1935–37 was a little over 20 percent, and that of the GNP deflator was probably about the same. It would seem implausible that the wage lag would cause an overestimate associated with falling prices of more than 15 percent, although there could also have been a wage lag related directly to the fact that the real wage was falling. Perhaps a total overestimate of 20 percent would provide an upper limit, thus implying a wage increase over the period of about 0.25 percent per year.

^{g}Refers to 1953.

^{h}1936 to 1953; these annual rates correspond to total real wage increases of 35 and 40 percent, respectively.

^{i}Assumes 275 days worked per year.

^{j}There is some question of whether the figures for the 1930s and the 1950s refer to the same groups, but it seems unlikely they are very different.

^{k}Assuming crudely that 40 percent of the agricultural labor force were workers (col. 4); there is some imprecision in this assumption but it probably does not lead to a large bias in the estimate made. As explained elsewhere, there is no simple delineation of laborers and others.

^{l}Assuming a total increase over the period of 50–70 percent. During 1944–45 to 1953 we have estimated an increase of 48.3 percent. Prior to 1945 the evidence is more problematic. For 1936–42, data on a set of firms of varying composition suggested a decline of about 18 percent, although the series was erratic. Possibly there was some increase over 1942–45. Overall the increase would seem likely to fall in the range 50–70 percent as assumed here.

^{m}Refers to 1963–67.

^{n}All figures in this column are calculated on the basis of cols. (1) and (2) and of data on the share of the labor force in agriculture. The method of calculation underlying cols. (1) and (2) is somewhat different, with col. (1) probably having some upward bias relative to col. (2). However, it seems unlikely that these problems generate a significant bias in the growth rates calculated in col. (9).

^{o}Assuming the same median/mean ratio as found by Urrutia–Sandoval in 1964, i.e., 4175/8410, or. 496 (see Miguel Urrutia and Clara Elsa de Sandoval, "La Distribucion de Ingresos Urbana para Colombia en 1964," *Revista del Banco de la Republica* 42, no. 503 (Sept. 1969): 1227–89).

In 1938 landless or nearly landless workers accounted for 47.5 percent of the total agricultural labor force; by 1951 this figure had risen to 55–57 percent.[12] Whereas income per capita in agriculture increased rather systematically over the whole post-1935 period, real wages were lower in 1950 than in 1935 (having bottomed out in the early 1940s); the 1950–54 average was about 20 percent lower than in 1935, according to the figures.[13] It seems probable that these figures give a downward-biased measure of real wage change during the period.[14] However, even if this is the case, it appears certain that labor income in agriculture grew less rapidly than per capita income in the sector [3.7–4.2 percent over the period 1935 to 1950–54 according to the author's estimates (see table 4.1)].

In agriculture, at least during this early period, only moderate injustice is done to the facts by assuming two factors: homogeneous,

12. This figure includes family helpers in 1951; whether it does in 1938 is unclear but it seems probable. When the figures are excluded, they are of course lower. Perhaps the most relevant ratio that can be derived from the census data is paid blue-collar workers/employers + independent farmers + paid blue-collar workers. This was 50.5 in 1951 (excluding people not reporting their occupational position). The comparable figure for 1938 is not deducible from the census, because family helpers (assuming they are included at all) are not separated from paid workers. If the family-helper/paid-worker ratio had been constant between the two years, it would have been about 43 percent in 1938. Since a number of paid blue-collar workers are sons who will inherit land, these ratios overestimate the percentage that might be thought of as a permanently landless class. Moreover, most of them have some land, so the line separating "landless" and "landed" is a rather arbitrary one. The percentages referred to for 1951 appear not to have changed significantly in subsequent years.

13. See Berry, *The Development of the Agricultural Sector in Colombia*, forthcoming, chap. 5.

14. Evidence from several countries, including Japan, suggests that wage rates may have been above their equilibrium levels (or merely overreported) during the early years of the depression, when prices were still falling or constant. In other words the suggestion is that wages lagged behind prices in their descent during the depression. [For a discussion of the Japanese case see Ryoshin Minami, "The Turning Point in the Japanese Economy," *The Quarterly Journal of Economics* 82 (Aug. 1968): 380–402.] Unfortunately, wage statistics are not available prior to 1935 in Colombia to verify this hypothesis, but the similarity of the pattern with Japan in particular does suggest it as the most likely interpretation for the wage rate decrease at the time. (This issue is discussed in greater detail in the author's *Development of Agricultural Sector,* chap. 2.) Whether the decrease in the observed real wage corresponds to a decrease in welfare of people at that time is unclear. It may be that the wages reported during the previous years were accompanied by such employment difficulties that they do not constitute a good indicator of real income.

relatively unskilled labor- and land-capital. (This is not to deny that many farmers earned income from owning quantities of both factors, but in this sector, unlike manufacturing, labor did not have an important human capital component related to education or particular learned skills. Education was concentrated among the large landowners.) Thus a wage rate climbing more slowly than average income was essentially equivalent to a worsening of the distribution between labor and capital, or between laborers and capitalists.[15]

Wage statistics for the nonagricultural sector are scarce before the 1950s. It does appear, at least during the late 1940s and early 1950s, that the distribution of labor income in manufacturing was worsening: a comparison of the 1945 and 1953 industrial censuses suggests that between those two years average blue-collar wages rose by about 25 percent while average white-collar wages were increasing by about 50 percent.[16] The fast growth of manufacturing during these years and the special focus on import substitution would be expected to contribute to such a trend. The white-collar blue-collar comparison cannot be made for the universe of manufacturing firms before 1945. Data from the firms reporting to DANE during the period 1936–42 (between 400 and 1,000 according to the year) suggest approximately a 5 percent increase in real wages for blue-collar workers and a 10 percent decrease for white-collar workers, which is consistent with the pattern of a quickly widening white-collar–blue-collar differential beginning after World War II. This widening was reversed beginning some time in the early or mid-1950s.

As indicated in table 4.1 and figure 4.1, white-collar wages in

---

15. Given the context of little difference between the wage and traditional sector earnings and little tendency for the latter to rise over time, partly because of the continued pressure of rising population (see chap. 3, n. 15 for a lengthier discussion).

16. See Albert Berry, "Trends in Real Wages in Colombian Manufacturing and Construction," University of Western Ontario, Department of Economics Research Report no. 7403, 1974. Note that this figure does not mean that white-collar earnings rose by 50 percent for a given occupation. There was undoubtedly an upgrading of average education and training of the white-collar workers in this period. (The number of engineers and certain other professionals probably rose markedly.) Still the increase for the representative occupation must have been substantial.

manufacturing were far above the mean or median incomes of the economy at each point in time, so the rapid increase for this period as a whole, and particularly the postwar part, constitutes per se a factor tending to worsen the overall distribution. Blue-collar workers in the factories included in the DANE surveys from which the above estimates were made also are above the median income, though a little below the mean. Their 35–40 percent increase for the entire period was somewhat below the overall average; depending on which aspects of the income distribution are of particular concern, this could constitute either a positive or a negative factor. However, the trend does suggest a worsening of the urban distribution.

No good estimates of the purchasing power of manufacturing output[17] for this time are available. Physical output per person seems to have risen at about 4.7 percent, and if one judges by the cost-of-living indices that include manufacturing items in the miscellaneous category, the relative price may have drifted up somewhat.[18] The fact that the increase in average wages (blue and white collar together) was somewhat less than the increase indicated by the figures for average labor productivity[19] would suggest that the gross capital share rose and that income of industrial capitalists probably increased somewhat faster than wages,[20] and certainly faster than average income of the total labor force, therefore contributing to a worsening of distribution.

Earnings of artisan workers are not available for this period; it

17. And hence of total income (labor plus capital) generated in manufacturing.
18. David S. C. Chu ("The Great Depression and Industrialization in Latin America" (Ph.D. diss., Yale University, 1972) estimated that the relative price of nontraditional manufactures climbed dramatically in the early 1930s and remained high relative to the 1920s at least through the mid-1940s (when his study ends). Because the relative price of imported inputs rose less rapidly, the relative price of value added in manufacturing (determined by the prices of output and inputs) can be characterized as high during the 1930s and early 1940s (ibid., p. 82).
19. As shown in table 4.1, white-collar wages rose at about the same rate as did average labor productivity, and blue-collar wages a bit more slowly. Since the relative number of white-collar workers was growing during this period, the average wages (white and blue together) rose at about 3.4 percent—faster than a simple weighted average of the increases for the two categories.
20. It is unclear how quickly depreciation charges may have been rising, but it seems unlikely that their behavior could imply that net capital income rose less rapidly than labor income. Because average firm size was growing, it seems especially improbable that average capital income per capitalist was rising more slowly than average income as a whole.

seems unlikely that they could have been rising rapidly, since there is little reason to believe that physical productivity was doing so.[21] The share of all industrial workers in certain artisan sectors was decreasing, especially in the textile and clothing sectors, where modern factory industry was driving out traditional production. This could even have implied downward pressure on artisan incomes; industrial growth was for the most part taking place far from the areas of artisan production, so most artisans would have had little chance to switch to the factory sector. Although no overall judgment can be made, it seems unlikely that income per worker was rising as fast as the 2.8 percent that characterized the labor force as a whole during this period.

The movement of average wages of government employees (a category so heterogeneous[22] that it is doubtful it can be given much interpretation) is somewhat different (see table 4.2) from that of white-collar workers in manufacturing; it seems not to have been increasing in the years preceding the end of World War II. A five-year moving average of wages for all levels of government rises moderately over the succeeding decade (1945–55) and more quickly in the following years. The movements are different for the various levels of government, in particular for the national government and the other two levels.[23] One interesting subgroup, the primary school teachers, underwent real wage declines during World War II, an approximate constancy until some time in the early 1950s, and then a rather swift increase. The wage determination of both this subset of government employees and the category as a whole probably

21. Or that the composition of output was altering significantly (as it has in the last couple of decades).

22. It includes professionals, teachers, police, street sweepers, and a host of other categories. A breakdown by blue collar/white collar would be useful but has not yet been achieved. Alan Udall did study the wage trend for Bogota street sweepers and showed that, taking 1937 and 1950–54 as end points, an increase of about 10 percent was registered. But there were violent fluctuations in this real wage during the period; it then fell in the 1950s. [See Alan Udall, "Migration and Employment in Bogota, Colombia" (Ph.D. diss., Yale University, 1972), chap. 2.]

23. The figures here probably understate the real increase through failure to take adequate account of the increase in fringe benefits (*prestaciones sociales*). Moving averages are used since nominal wages are inclined to change in steps in the government sector, with the result that real wages fluctuate rather violently and probably do not reflect short-run market phenomena.

Table 4.2
Real Wage Indices of Government Employees
(Five-year moving averages, centered on the middle year)

	National Government (1)	Departmental Government (2)	Municipal Government (3)	Weighted Average of Three Government Levels (4)
1924[a]	59.9	59.9	39.4	55.8
1939[a]	69.5	72.3	56.9	68.3
1940[a]	76.5	77.7	61.1	73.9
1941	86.13	75.94	58.00	76.43
1942	86.18	75.41	57.38	76.11
1943	88.83	73.65	56.26	76.24
1944	91.13	70.93	54.74	75.77
1945	89.69	68.85	55.50	74.52
1946	90.43	67.31	58.44	74.78
1947	93.63	67.84	61.44	76.88
1948	95.32	68.21	61.92	77.80
1949	93.54	69.04	63.60	77.75
1950	91.48	77.76	66.34	80.96
1951	89.16	80.90	68.28	81.68
1952	88.38	81.74	69.04	81.86
1953	88.82	84.04	74.26	84.00
1954	91.66	85.88	79.10	86.84
1955	95.76	80.00	80.50	86.40
1956	98.54	80.58	81.84	88.02
1957	98.94	81.64	85.10	89.25
1958	100.50	83.68	87.56	91.18
1959	101.14	87.40	89.44	93.30
1960	102.16	94.36	95.64	97.74
1961	106.38	99.10	101.36	102.46
1962	107.89	104.1	103.22	105.44
1963	108.07	108.12	106.01	107.68
1964	110.43	108.54	108.25	109.24
1965	109.93	108.08	109.39	109.08

Sources and Methodology: The source for the nominal wages on which the data of this table are based is in the majority of years the *Anuario General de Estadistica*. For years in which information could not be found in the *Anuario*, data from the publication *Estadisticas Fiscales y Administrativas* were used. The published data (in both cases) gave the total wage cost and the number of permanent employees. Various types of bias may come from assuming that the ratio of these two figures measures the wage rate, for example when in different years a different share of the wage bill goes to temporary workers. It is also true that the apparent noninclusion of fringe benefits in the labor cost data introduces a negative involves considerable nonmarket elements,[24] so their remuneration may not parallel too closely the general trends for people of comparable skill.

Persons in the employ of the three government levels increased from 2.4 to 3.1 percent of the labor force between 1938 and 1951. Assuming that a good number, apart from the teachers, required relatively little preparation and that skills were less important determinants of their employment, it is not necessarily surprising that they should not have shared in the rapid increase in white-collar wages that characterized the manufacturing sector.[25]

In the construction sector data are scarcer and more difficult to interpret. Nevertheless a comparatively clear hypothesis emerges from a comparison of the scattered information on unskilled construction worker wages with the agricultural wage figures (see table 4.3). It appears over the long run that (1) a relatively close relationship has prevailed between the two series and (2) that there has been a wage differential in favor of the urban (unskilled construction) worker. Thus in the late 1930s the typical daily wage of a peon in Bogota seems to have been 20–40 percent higher than the daily wage of peons in the agricultural regions near Bogota [compare cols. (1) and (3), table 4.3].[26] The relationship appears to have become in-

---

bias over time because fringe benefits have been an increasing share of total remuneration.

To convert the nominal figures to real ones the following indices were used. (1) 1954–56: The national white-collar cost-of-living series was used in the cases of the municipalities and departments and the corresponding Bogota series to deflate the national government salary series (given that a large part of the national government employees live in Bogota). (2) 1946–54: The Bogota white-collar cost-of-living series was used (no national series was available for this period). (3) 1937–46: A blue-collar Bogota cost-of-living series was used; not even a Bogota white-collar series was available during this period. It is clear that the methodology used to convert the nominal salaries to real ones can introduce a variety of weaknesses in the series.

[a]Values are for the year in question, not five-year averages.

24. Wage increases are probably positively correlated with budget surpluses.

25. An alternate explanation of the different behavior would simply be the heterogeneity of the group considered; probably some sets of professionals did have wage increases.

26. Udall's study of the Bogota labor market indicates that average construction worker real wages, not just those of the unskilled worker (*obrero raso*), rose about 23 percent during 1937 to 1963–64. In this period Cundinamarca agricul-

Table 4.3
Unskilled Construction Wages in Bogota Compared to Other Selected Wage Series
(All wages expressed in pesos per day)

	Current Prices				1958 Prices			
	Unskilled Construction Workers, Bogota (1)	Agricultural Laborers, Cundinamarca (2)	Agricultural Laborers, Cold Climate Cundinamarca (3)	Agricultural Laborers, Colombia (4)	Unskilled Construction Workers, Bogota (5)	Agricultural Laborers, Cundinamarca (6)	Agricultural Laborers, Cold Climate Cundinamarca (7)	Agricultural Laborers, Colombia (8)
1935	(.80)				4.44	4.90	4.85	5.60
1936	(.75)				3.85	3.77	3.74	5.15
1937	(.93)				4.91	3.89	3.85	5.77
1938	(.94)	.60	.60		4.40	4.38	4.34	5.04
1939	(.96)	.60	.60	.74	4.31	4.02	3.97	4.66
1940	(.95)	.80	.80	.78	4.40	5.74	5.68	5.38
1941	(.94)	.80	.90	.71	4.42	5.42	5.70	5.19
1942	(.92)	0.65	0.60	0.72	3.98	4.06	3.73	4.23
1943		0.60	0.60	0.73		3.38	3.34	3.52
1944		0.90	0.80	0.94		5.04	3.46	3.78
1945		1.05	1.00	1.09		4.02	3.80	4.04
1946		1.50	1.50	1.25		5.29	5.24	4.20
1947		1.75	1.50	1.62		4.86	4.17	4.42
1948		1.85	1.70	2.02		4.74	4.35	4.74
1949		2.05	2.00	2.03		5.07	4.91	4.53
1950	2.24	2.50	2.30	2.52	3.97	4.85	4.45	4.46
1951	2.34	2.90	2.60	2.84	3.81	5.08	4.55	4.55
1952	2.45	2.70	2.40	2.81	4.08	4.68	4.16	4.85
1953	2.50	2.95	2.55	2.92	3.88	4.61	3.99	4.66
1954	2.74	3.42	2.90	3.27	3.91	4.58	3.89	4.66

1955	2.93	3.67	3.25	3.46	4.14	5.16	4.44	5.16
1956	3.98	3.92	3.35	3.54	5.32	5.32	4.55	4.76
1957	4.30	4.37	3.90	3.89	4.92	4.91	4.38	4.25
1958	5.01	5.05	4.50	4.55	5.01	5.05	4.50	4.55
1959	6.00	5.25	4.75	5.00	5.60	5.02	4.52	4.78
1960	6.50	5.90	5.25	5.51	5.84	4.90	4.35	5.05
1961	7.60	6.50	5.80	6.29	6.28	5.24	4.69	5.08
1962	8.50	7.10	6.55	6.92	6.85	5.99	5.49	5.66
1963	10.20	9.15	8.40	8.99	6.23	5.73	5.25	5.52
1964	12.55	10.10	9.75	10.60	6.52	5.60	5.06	4.92
1965	15.00	11.65	11.60	11.28	7.50	6.78	6.30	5.60
1966	16.00	13.72	12.60	13.17[c]	6.70	6.15	5.63	5.33
1967	17.00[a]	15.67	14.20	14.07[c]	6.58	7.33	6.76	5.52
1968	18.00[a]	16.80	14.50	14.82	6.58			5.13
1969	19.00[a]	18.50	17.22	17.03[d]	6.31			5.15
1970	20.00[a]			18.18[d]	6.21			5.15
1971	21.57[b]				6.30			

Sources and Methodology: For the years 1950–58, col. (1) is based on unpublished data kindly supplied by Robert Merrill; for subsequent years the lower figure of the CAMACOL series and the ICT series was chosen. In certain years in which ICT was paying the minimal wage the CAMACOL (Camara Colombiana de la Construccion) figures were lower still, and the assumption is that the market wage was in fact below the minimum wage at those times. In the last years the CAMACOL figures have been above those of ICT (Instituto de Credito Territorial) and also above figures suggested by data from CEDE, DANE, and experts in the field. For this reason we have accepted the ICT figures for 1965, 1966, and 1967. (It would be possible to verify more completely the consistency with the CEDE data during 1963–66 if we knew the educational distribution among the unskilled workers, but we do not.) It should be noted that there is some difference of opinion as to whether real construction wages have risen over the last few years. The fact that the figures presented here for 1967–70 were simply interpolated obviously implies that they are open to doubt. However, the data for 1965 and 1966 seem reasonably good, with no reason to believe they

Table 4.3, *Sources and Methodology* (continued)

are overstated. The 1971 figure is probably the most solid of all. Figures for 1935–42 come from Bogota municipal government records, as reported in Miguel Urrutia and Mario Arrubla, eds., *Compendio de Estadisticas Historicas de Colombia* (Bogota: Direccion de Divulgacion Cultural, Universidad Nacional de Colombia, 1970). Columns (2) and (3) are based on DANE information published in the *Anuario General de Estadistica* and/or the *Boletin Mensual de Estadistica*. For col. (2) the cold and warm regions of Cundinamarca were weighted equally in the calculation. Columns (4) and (6)–(8) through 1965 come from Berry, *Development of Agricultural Sector*, chap. 5. (The original sources are the two just cited.) The specific sources for the subsequent years are cited in the footnotes. Column (5) is col. (1) deflated by the Bogota blue-collar cost-of-living index constructed by DANE.

[a] Interpolated by guessing.

[b] First semester. Calculated as 20.39 (the figure reported by a DANE survey and excluding fringe benefits) plus an estimated 1.5 for those benefits.

[c] Interpolated (in the absence of access to the correct figure) taking into account an estimate of the change in the real agricultural wage between 1967 and 1968.

[d] Based on equal weights for warm and cool regions.

verted in the early 1950s with the agricultural wage slightly higher, perhaps in part a result of the *violencia*. The typical long-run differential then reappeared in the late 1950s and since then it has been fluctuating between 10 and 25 percent. It seems to have narrowed in the last five years, perhaps due to a slowdown in building or perhaps to increasing efficiency of the labor market. Some uncertainty attaches to this interpretation due to the fact that the wage figures presented in column (1) for 1935–42 are public sector wages, whereas the post-1950 figures refer primarily to the private sector. In any case these public sector unskilled construction wages for Bogota bore a fairly consistent relation to the Cundinamarca agricultural wages over the 1935–42 period: the real construction wage showed no measurable change while that in agriculture fell a little.[27] No data are available for 1942–50, but if it be assumed that the recorded public sector wages for the 1932–42 period corresponded to the same skill level (or more generally to the same labor market) as those of the 1950–70 series (not exclusively or even primarily public sector), then it would be concluded that the real wage fell by about 20 percent (from an index of 75 to one of 61) over the period.[28] Thus the suggested 1935–50 wage movement clearly fits a worsening distribution pattern.

For the country as a whole, unskilled construction wage series are unavailable before 1950. A less close relationship between construc-

---

tural wages climbed by 35–50 percent and those in Boyaca by about the same amount (see Udall, "Migration," pp. 10–14).

27. The figures indicate that unskilled construction workers received a lower real wage in the late 1930s than in the early 1930s; as the decade began, sharp real wage increases accompanied the rather rapid fall in prices. But it seems probable, as noted above, that during both these periods the market was in disequilibrium. The rising real wages of the early 1930s were probably associated with the increasing employment problems, so that in a more general sense there may have been no increase in real income. Conversely, the decrease in the measured real wage probably was accompanied by improved employment possibilities and is therefore a misleading indicator when taken by itself. There are no figures for agricultural workers in the early 1930s, but the similarity of pattern from the mid-1930s on between agricultural and construction wages, and especially the parallel decline around the late 1930s, hints strongly that real agricultural wages also rose during the early 1930s as prices fell.

28. Deflating by the Bogota blue-collar cost-of-living series. Meanwhile the Cundinamarca agricultural wage grew by 28 percent, about the same in the cool climate regions around Bogota as in the hot zones.

tion and agricultural wages would be expected at the national level due to different regional weightings for the two occupations and other factors, but it is worth noting that the evidence available for the post-1950 period is consistent with a rather close tie.[29] In view of this it seems unlikely that the country-wide average unskilled construction wage differed markedly from that for Bogota over any extended period, especially because the two agricultural wage series have quite parallel movements.[30] Consequently, it seems probable that construction wages in general suffered a decline in the 1930–50 period as a whole, or at least the 1935–50 period.

For Bogota, Udall's figures on wages in commerce fit the general pattern precisely; he finds a decrease between 1936 and 1954[31] and a subsequent sharp increase until 1963–64.[32] According to Udall, maids' wages in Bogota rose rapidly during 1936–45, fluctuated near the 1945 level until about 1950 when a sharp dip appeared, and then enjoyed a recovery which, however, only brought the wage back to its 1945 level by 1958–60. Subsequently a substantial percentage increase occurred amounting to more than 25 percent during the 1958–67 period.[33]

29. As of 1971 (first semester) construction wage differences among cities were not dramatic. [See Berry, "Some Determinants," table A-2, which indicates that 7 of 10 cities sampled had average "helper" wages in the range 18.5–20.7 pesos per day and all but Cali (affected by construction for the Pan American Games) had average "official" salaries between 25 and 35 pesos per day.] It seems probable that regional differences were greater in earlier years, when geographic mobility was more limited, just as agricultural wages varied more by department in earlier years.

30. It may be observed also, in connection with stability in wage structure, that construction workers other than those in the unskilled obrero raso category appear to have received about the same extent of wage increases as that group. The wage structure in the industry therefore has not altered much, at least as far as can be judged by Bogota data.

31. The 1936–54 change is open to some question both (1) because of the small sample in both years and possible differences in the definition of *small*, and (2) because of the fact that Udall had to assume the same ratio of average wages to average incomes in the two years, the two pieces of data apparently only being available together in 1954 (see Udall, "Migration," p. 67).

32. For 1963–64 Udall used wage data from CEDE's unemployment surveys to arrive at his estimate.

33. Udall obtained an observation every 2–4 years since 1945 based on classified advertisement data. Although the methodology leaves room for some doubt, it is consistent over time. It is more doubtful that the calculated change over 1936–45 is accurate since the sources of information were different. One might speculate

To summarize, the information on wages for agriculture, blue-collar manufacturing, construction, and commerce all show comparatively small or no increases from some point in the 1930s to some point in the 1950s. All plainly advanced less than the average income per member of the labor force. Maids' wages in Bogota, the weakest series in terms of methodology, are a partial exception—according to Udall's figures—depending on the specific period chosen. White-collar workers in manufacturing and government both showed moderate or rapid increases at least over 1945–55, suggesting a widening of the overall white-collar–blue-collar gap.[34] It thus appears that during this period there was an excess supply of labor in a number of sectors with the corresponding downward impact on wages.

A glance at figure 4.1 may suggest that the dividing line between periods is arbitrary. If relatively short-run phenomena are smoothed out it could be argued that the distinction between the two periods—before the mid-1950s and after—is not a striking one. Still, if regression lines are fitted to most of the series discussed above, their slopes tend to be lower during the first period than that calculated for the average income series. This is in contrast to a subsequent period (beginning some time in the early 1950s and extending to some time in the early or mid-1960s, according to the sector) during which blue-collar wages advanced rapidly and white-collar–blue-collar gaps narrowed. This period is discussed in more detail below.

Although empirical information on capital incomes is scarce, theory and some observation would suggest that the import-substitution policy begun in the 1930s but reaching significant proportions especially after the war, raised capital income in manufacturing (and commercial agriculture to some extent) and also led to a less equal distribution of labor income. Information on the capital share is shaky, so there is no definite empirical support for this hypothesis.

---

that Alfonso Lopez's social legislation had some impact on these wages though it would be surprising if a money wage series would catch much of it.

34. Even if the ratio of white-collar wage to blue-collar wage did not rise, the fact that white-collar workers, with wages far above those of blue-collar workers, were a growing minority of the total labor force would constitute a factor tending to increase inequality (e.g., in terms of the Gini coefficient) in the distribution of labor income. The reasoning involved is that when the upper tail of the frequency distribution expands, the Gini coefficient rises.

In manufacturing the capital share appears to have been fairly stable or falling between 1944–45 and 1953. In 1953 the labor share of gross value added (at factor cost) appeared to be a little more than 30 percent;[35] a rough estimate based on data kindly made available by David Chu suggested a somewhat lower figure for 1944–45.[36] In agriculture an increase in the capital share does appear to have occurred, though it is unclear how much of it was associated with import substitution. Since import substitution was occurring during the war as well as after it (in the former period it was a result of the restrictions on world trade associated with the conflict), one might not therefore have predicted any increase in the capital share in industry during the period 1945–53 but rather over, say, 1935–50. Note also that import substitution might have raised the capital share primarily through changes in the relative size of different sectors, e.g., a decrease in relative importance of agriculture (which had at that time a comparatively high labor share) and an increase in that of industry. Therefore, although there is no clear evidence from existing information to confirm a positive correlation between capital share and the process of import substitution, the presumption is reasonably strong. It would be worthwhile to try to obtain more data and test this hypothesis thoroughly.

But changes in overall income distribution depend not only on changes in the relative incomes of occupational groups at different positions in the distribution (our focus so far) but also on changes in their relative sizes. Certainly the major structural change during this period (and in subsequent ones) was the decreasing share

---

35. Using DANE's upward-biased value added figures, 28.7 percent; but not all purchased inputs were subtracted out in DANE's calculations of value added.

36. Considering only the industries (modern ones) for which Chu estimated (net) value added in 1945, his figures imply a labor share of net value added equal to 25.4 percent in 1944–45. For the same industries the census shows a share of 34.2 percent of gross value added in 1953. At the same time this set of industries has a below-average labor share (as a group), and their increasing weight between 1944–45 and 1953 would suggest a smaller increase in the overall labor share. Only limited credence can be given to the comparison in any case because the estimated changes between 1944–45 and 1953 labor shares seem erratic on an industry-by-industry basis. Difficulty in estimating 1944–45 value added in petroleum products was particularly noteworthy. With a lower limit value added in petroleum the 1944–45 labor share (of net value added) in these industries would have been about 28 percent.

of the agricultural relative to the total labor force. At the start of the period the agricultural sector accounted for about 65 percent of total labor force (mid-1930s), so the small but increasing size of the non-agricultural sector, with its substantially higher average income, could have worked toward an overall worsening.[37] As of 1945 the average income in agriculture was probably about 35–40 percent of that in nonagriculture; in 1935 it was perhaps 30–35 percent.[38] In 1964 the inequality of the agricultural personal income distribution was about the same as that of the urban distribution when unemployed persons were included in the latter.[39] Since the agricultural income distribution appears to have worsened substantially over the period 1935 to 1964, whereas the evidence for nonagriculture is somewhat mixed and suggests a smaller deterioration, it may be speculated that the agricultural distribution was less skewed 30 or 40 years ago than that of nonagriculture. If this was the case, the gradually increasing share of people in the nonagricultural sector would be expected to worsen overall distribution both because of the difference in average incomes of the two sectors and because of the greater inequality within the nonagricultural distribution.[40] (But see the reservation of n. 37.)

37. The argument was used by Simon Kuznets in discussing the implications of the rural-to-urban labor force transfer. [See Kuznets, "Economic Growth and Income Inequality," *American Economic Review* 45, no. 1 (March 1955): 1–28.] This effect would be expected if (1) the growing high-income sector is considerably smaller than the other one, and if (2) within each of the two groups into which the labor force was divided, everyone had the same income, or if the income distribution was at least as unequal in the growing sector as in the other one. The result would follow from most but not all combinations of intragroup income distributions. In a case such as that discussed here, the observed sequence at best creates a likelihood of a worsening distribution because not enough is known about the intrasectoral distributions to say more.

38. See Berry, *Development of Agricultural Sector*, chap. 1.

39. See ibid., 2. The measure of inequality used was the Gini coefficient.

40. In 1951 about 54 percent of the labor force was found in agriculture. The differential between average income in nonagriculture and average income in agriculture was about 2:1 although it had been higher in earlier years, before the dramatic increase in coffee prices. As discussed in chap. 1, n. 25, with a 2:1 income differential and no income variance in either of the two sectors, the transition from worsening to improvement of distribution would occur when about 59 percent of the labor force was in agriculture. Since our evidence points to a greater inequality in nonagriculture at that time, it would appear that about 1951 the transfer of labor to nonagriculture was probably still contributing to increased inequality in

A crude quantification of the effect of these factors on distribution in the period 1934–36 to 1950–54 may be obtained by assuming that for agricultural wage earners, for the rest of the agricultural labor force, and for the nonagricultural labor force, income is distributed in the same way (around a different mean) at the beginning of the period and at the end.[41] If this assumption is not too far from being accurate, distribution worsened during the period (see table 4.5). The top deciles would have increased their share of the pie; the bottom deciles would have suffered a decrease.

Possible Improvements in Distribution between the Early 1950s and the Mid-1960s

Although conclusions naturally remain somewhat speculative, the weight of evidence for the urban areas suggests an improvement beginning in the 1950s and going through the mid-1960s. For the labor force as a whole this is less definite since it seems fairly certain that the distribution of income in agriculture continued to worsen during this period. For the period 1950–54 to 1964–67 average income per worker rose at 1.9 percent per year.[42]

We turn first to the nonagricultural sector. As noted above, blue-collar real wages in the factory industrial sector rose dramatically after the early 1950s: the average annual increase between 1953 and 1964–66 was 4.6 percent, well above the overall urban sector average. This factor would not contribute to an improvement in income

---

the overall distribution (with some reservations because we have not analyzed formally the case in which there is intrasectoral variation of incomes). However, since the nonagricultural/agricultural income differential was higher than 2:1 in the 1930s and 1940s (see Berry, *Development of Agricultural Sector*, chap. 1), this conclusion is not very solid. Probably the transfer was worsening distribution but perhaps not very significantly.

41. Although scattered information is available on income trends in some categories of the nonagricultural labor force, it would be difficult to piece it together in such a way as to use such information effectively. We limit ourselves here to the crude assumption of no change in distribution within the whole nonagricultural labor force.

42. Based on net national income at market prices per worker. When one uses income of families and nonprofit institutions per worker, deflated by the private consumer goods price index, the indicated increase is about 2.3 percent. The increase would be smaller the more investment goods entered the deflator since their price rose more quickly than that of consumer goods.

distribution, since average income of these workers was above the urban mean at the beginning of the period and still further above it at the end. Meanwhile, wages in smaller factories and the income of artisan workers increased less quickly, although they still appear to have risen faster than urban incomes as a whole. They tended to be less than the median urban income at the beginning of the period so their growth may be thought of as contributing to a decrease in inequality.[43] Finally, white-collar incomes in industry rose much more slowly than those of blue-collar workers, averaging an increase of about 2.2 percent over the period (1953–64/66) in question.[44]

Further evidence that urban distribution improved during this period comes principally from the lower-income sectors of construction workers, workers in small-scale commerce, and—though with considerably less confidence in the figures—wages of maids. Wages of street sweepers in Bogota also fit the pattern from the late 1950s on; their sharp ascent began later than for construction and manufacturing workers.

From 1950–54 to 1964–67 real wages of unskilled workers in construction rose by perhaps 70–75 percent in Bogota, an average annual increase of 4.2 percent, with the increase somewhat concentrated in the period 1958–65. (Udall's figures, together with those of table 4.2, suggest that the period 1936–55 as a whole witnessed no increase, a pattern more extreme than that in manufacturing, and slightly more so than that in agriculture also.)

Data from the 1954 and 1967 commerce censuses suggest that real wages paid by small establishments rose, in some cases very substantially, and perhaps overall about the same as in small manufac-

---

43. Wages in plants of fewer than 10 workers advanced by about 1.5–2.2 percent annually over 1953–66 (see table 4.3). This was more rapid than the increase in urban income per member of the urban labor force, though very probably not above the average rate of increase of income for persons in the urban labor force. The first ratio referred to is pulled down by the arrival of many low-income immigrants.)

44. The important piece of evidence, that the average white-collar wage in manufacturing did not grow rapidly in the post-1953 period, could be misleading if the composition of this group changed over the period, e.g., if an increasing share of the people were messengers or other low-wage subgroups. There was a relative increase in office workers compared to professionals, a fact of interest because it hints that the representative white-collar worker may have had a more rapid increase in real income than indicated by the average figure cited.

turing firms and among unskilled construction workers. Real wage changes in these latter two categories (over roughly the same period) were about 20–30 percent (1953–66) and 50–60 percent (1950–70), respectively,[45] while in small-scale commerce they appear to have been 20–40 percent (1954–67) (see table 4.4).

As observed earlier Udall calculated that maids' wages in Bogota took a sharp dip about 1950 followed by a fairly rapid increase through about 1967; the increase over 1958–67 was about 50 percent and from 1950–54 to 1964–67 perhaps 60–70 percent.[46] Udall's Bogota street sweepers' wages indicate an increase of 18–21 percent from 1950–53 to 1964–66.[47]

In summary, the wages in all low-income occupations for which data are available increased more rapidly than average per capita income, thus suggesting strongly that income distribution improved in the urban sector.

As was true for the previous period, little is known about the distribution of capital incomes and how it may have changed during this recent period or about the relationship between capital incomes and labor incomes. As discussed elsewhere, the share of income going to physical capital[48] appears to have decreased.[49]

The only piece of evidence possibly throwing some light on distribution of capital incomes is information from tax returns. Urrutia cites ECLA's estimate that in 1953 the 2.9 percent of taxpayers reporting the highest income had 35.7 percent of national income. Meanwhile a comparable figure calculated by Urrutia in 1965 indicated that they accounted for only 12.1–14.1 percent of national income in that year.[50] It may be assumed that almost all the indivi-

---

45. During 1954–67 the increase was greater but wages fell in absolute terms in the succeeding years.
46. Because of the small sample and a somewhat doubtful methodology, these data are not hard. But they are suggestive.
47. See Miguel Urrutia and Mario Arrubla, *Compendio de Estadisticas Historicas de Colombia* (Bogota: Direccion de Divulgacion Cultural, Universidad Nacional de Colombia, 1970), p. 80.
48. Income related to current production, i.e., excluding capital appreciation.
49. Berry, "Changing Income Distribution under Development: Colombia," *Review of Income and Wealth*, Income and Wealth Series 20, no. 3 (Sept. 1974), p. 305.
50. Miguel Urrutia, "Variacion Historica de la Distribucion del Ingreso en Colombia," *Revista del Banco de la Republica* 43, no. 509 (March 1970): 344–53.

duals in question (natural persons as opposed to juridical persons—although the very high figure of 1953 suggests that there may have been a confusion) were in the nonagricultural sector since it is well known that farmers are normally able to almost completely evade taxes. If such a sharp decrease occurred, it would demonstrate that the highest incomes represented a smaller share of national income in 1965 than in 1953. But these statistics warrant very careful scrutiny before being used. They are mentioned primarily as additional evidence to confirm the finding that income distribution improved after the early 1950s, following some deterioration in the previous decades. Using 1937 figures from the Contraloria General de la Republica, it can be concluded that the concentration was similar in 1937 and 1964. In 1937 the richest 1 percent of the population declared about 7 percent of all income; in 1964 this group controlled about the same percentage. Pending further checking of the tax figures, they are consistent with the conclusion that income distribution deteriorated in the first period considered only to improve again starting in the 1950s.

This result holds also under the assumption that within each of twelve occupational categories[51] distribution did not vary over the period.[52] The combined effect of the shifting occupational distribution of the labor force and the changes in relative mean incomes among occupations had in fact a substantially positive impact within the upper part of the distribution, as shown in table 4.5. The share of the top decile would, under these assumptions, have fallen by from 3 to 7 percent.[53] Distribution could have worsened only if there had

51. Agricultural wage earners, other members of the agricultural labor force, blue-collar manufacturing workers, white-collar manufacturing workers, government employees, commerce workers (excludes large capitalists), artisans, construction workers, maids, technical professionals, nontechnical professionals, and "other labor and capital."

52. For several occupational categories the distribution assumed within each category was based on DANE's 1970 household survey, the only source of such information on a national level to date. For other sectors CEDE's eight-city unemployment survey of 1967 was useful [Rafael Isaza and Francisco Ortega, *Encuestas Urbanas de Empleo y Desempleo: Analisis y Resultados* (Bogota: CEDE, Universidad de los Andes, Jan. 1969)].

53. A range is presented since there is uncertainty as to the changes in size of some of the categories used, and hence also in the residual category "other labor and capital." The two values are designed to provide lower and upper limits for the change over 1951–64 at a rather high confidence level. (Because the data for

Table 4.4
Selected Real Annual Wage Series
(1958 Prices)

	Construction	Manufacturing				Commerce		Maids
	Unskilled Construction Workers Bogotá	Paid Factory Workers (White-Collar and Blue-Collar)	Artisan Manufacturing	Plants of <5 Workers[a]	Plants of <10 Workers[a]	Establishments of <5 Workers	Food and Beverage Stores with Sale of <100,000/Year (1967 pesos)	(Index 1958 = 100)
	(1)	(2)	(3)	(4)	(5)	(6)	(7)	(8)
1950	1,091							
1951	1,048							
1952	1,122							
1953	1,067	3,598						
1954	1,075				2,320			
1955	1,138	4,286						
1956	1,463	4,391	2,517					
1957	1,353	4,476		2,390				
1958	1,378	4,643				2,000–2,500	1,070	100
1959	1,540	4,763						
1960	1,606	5,227						
1961	1,727	5,513						
1962	1,884	6,068						
1963	1,713	6,372	3,129					
1964	1,793	6,339						
1965	2,071	6,557						
1966	1,843	6,520		2,820–3,080	2,800–3,060			
1967	1,810	7,086				2,900	1,680	130
1968	1,810	6,821						
1969	1,735							
1970	1,708	7,176						

Sources and Methodology: Column (1) is based on the nominal wage series of table 4.3, deflated to 1958 prices and assuming 275 days paid per year. Column (2) is from A. Berry, "Trends in Real Wages in Colombian Manufacturing and Construction," University of Western Ontario, Department of Economics Research Report no. 7304 (1974), p. 12. Column (3) is from Miguel Urrutia and Clara Elsa Villalba, "El Sector Artesanal en el Desarrollo Colombiano," *Revista de Planeacion y Desarrollo* 1, no. 3 (Oct. 1969): 43–78. Columns (4) and (5) are calculations by the author making use of John Todd's correction factors for 1966 (to offset a bias introduced by DANE's methodology in the years since 1962). See John Todd, *Size of Firm and Efficiency in Colombian Manufacturing* (Ph.D. diss., Yale University, 1972). Columns (6) and (7) are based on the commerce censuses of 1954 and 1967, respectively. In col. (6) the 1954 estimated range is preliminary; data are not fully comparable between the two censuses. The estimates of col. (7) are from A. Berry, "Unemployment as a Social Problem in Colombia: Some Preliminary Hypotheses and Interpretations," mimeo, p. 98. Column (8) is from Alan Udall, "Migration and Employment in Bogota, Colombia," (Ph.D. diss., Yale University, 1972).

[a] And less than 24,000 pesos output.

Table 4.5
Income Distribution Comparisons, 1934–36, 1951, and 1964

		1934–36	1951	1964
Nonagriculture				
Gini coefficient			.599–.644	.601
Share of top	5 percent		35.21–38.80	31.71
	10 percent		47.44–51.95	44.63
	20 percent		62.67–67.01	60.36
	30 percent		73.30–77.07	70.66
	50 percent		88.05–90.55	84.66
Bottom	20 percent		1.15– 1.56	—[a]
All Sectors				
Gini coefficient		.553	.602–.633	.57
Share of top	5 percent	38.41	40.00–42.22	35.66
	10 percent	48.16	51.15–53.90	47.87
	20 percent	60.79	64.95–67.68	63.10
	30 percent	70.14	74.29–77.01	73.73
	50 percent	83.79	86.14–88.00	86.84
Bottom	20 percent	3.78	2.49–3.00	3.30

Sources and Methodology: The 1964 distributions are basically those of Miguel Urrutia and Clara Elsa de Sandoval ["La Distribucion de Ingresos entre los Perceptores de Ingresos en Colombia—1964," *Revista del Banco de la Republica* 43, no. 513 (July 1970): 978–1006], with a few minor alterations to take account of more recent information. The 1951 distributions on which these figures are based have been estimated using data on employment by occupational category in 1951 (basically from the population census of that year), estimates of increases in mean income by occupation (based on the sources cited in tables 4.1–4.3), and the assumption that intraoccupational category distribution did not change between 1951 and 1964. Alternative assumptions were made as to some of the mean income changes based on shakier data and some of the employment estimates that were also not firm. The occupational categories used were agricultural wage earners, other agricultural workers, blue-collar manufacturing workers, white-collar manufacturing workers, government workers, commerce workers, artisans, construction workers, maids, technical professionals, nontechnical professionals, other labor and capital.

The same methodology by which the 1951 distribution was estimated (i.e., use of the 1964 distribution and information on changes for 1951–64) served to generate the 1934–36 distribution (use of the 1951 distribution and information on changes for 1934–36 to 1951) except for the wider categories used (only three): agricultural paid workers, the rest of the agricultural labor force, and the nonagricultural labor force. It was assumed that no intraperiod changes in distribution occurred within any of these broad groupings. (Thus, for example, the distribution observed within the category nonagricultural labor force in 1951 was assumed also for 1934.) The 1934–36 distribution is weaker than the later ones

Table 4.5, *Sources and Methodology* (continued)
both because this assumption is less plausible for such broad categories and because the income series are less convincing. In particular, estimates of wage income in agriculture (directly from wage data) and estimates of total agricultural income (see table 4.1) are to all intents and purposes inconsistent in the mid-1930s, the implicit nonwage income being too low. It was accordingly assumed that the nonwage income was higher than is implicit in the figures of table 4.1 (specifically, 1,941 pesos per person); the lower of the two alternative wage rates shown in table 4.1 was used. This adjustment had the effect of damping the distribution worsening, which, however, still emerges from a comparison of the 1938 and 1951 figures. It is our impression that the data weaknesses are not so great as to overturn the result that distribution worsened. Very possibly, worsening occurred within the three categories that were distinguished in 1934–36. This would mean that distribution in 1934–36 was less unequal than estimated (all else assumed to be accurate).

[a] The presence of extensive open urban unemployment in 1964 and lack of information as to the income of the unemployed make it especially hazardous to estimate this value.

been substantial worsening of the intraoccupational distribution, a matter on which we have to date no empirical evidence.

In agriculture wages climbed slowly (about 1 percent on the average) over the period; this was considerably less than the increase in average earnings of the people involved in agriculture (nearly 2 percent).[54] Distribution of capital income may have been worsening; a rapid advance of commercial agriculture was especially characteristic of the late 1950s and early 1960s.[55] Still, it seems probable that overall worsening was less than in the previous period.

Trying to judge how overall distribution moved involves putting the results for the agricultural and nonagricultural sectors together and allowing for the fact that the relative importance of agriculture

---

both years suffer many weaknesses, the level of confidence with respect to the absolute figures is of course not high.)

54. For the period beginning in 1950 the national accounts data permit some estimates of changes in functional distribution. Functional distribution is a comparatively reliable indicator of personal or family distribution for certain nonagricultural sectors whose independent workers are relatively unimportant, such as the factory sector in industry. The evidence on changes in functional distribution tends to reinforce that from earnings series for the period in question (the early 1950s to the mid-1960s). In agriculture both a declining paid labor share and a wage rate rising less rapidly than average income suggest that income distribution probably worsened again during the period. Both in nonagriculture and in the economy as a whole, the paid labor share grew substantially and the capital share fell slightly (see Berry, "Changing Income Distribution," pp. 308–12).

55. See Berry, *Development of Agricultural Sector*, chap. 2.

in output and employment was diminishing. Table 4.4 indicates that, if no intraoccupation alterations of distribution occurred, some improvement occurred within the top 40 or 50 percent of the distribution. The top decile share decreased by 3–6 percent; the top 50 percent may not have suffered any decrease. And there may have been some small increase in the share of the bottom 20 percent, although this is very tentative since the data are particularly weak in the bottom deciles of the distribution. The calculated Gini coefficient fell from the range .60–.63 to .57.

For 1934–36 to 1964 as a whole, table 4.4 suggests some decrease in the share of the top decile, definite gains for the next two deciles, no change for the next two, and some decrease for the bottom 50 percent as whole and for the bottom 20 percent as well. The relative worsening of these latter two groups appears to have characterized only the first of the two subperiods. The only group whose share moved in the same way (up) in both subperiods was composed of deciles 2 and 3. The calculated Gini coefficient increased from .55 to .57. This result confirms the casual impression of a certain degree of prosperity in the so-called middle-class, whose growth in fact provided a limited but sufficient market for the import-substituting industries that developed after the war.

Though the temptation to draw too much out of the still shaky data base used here must be resisted, the consistency of much of the pattern shown here with Kuznets's "worsening, then improving" hypothesis on income distribution in the development process is noteworthy.[56] The shift from agriculture to nonagriculture has played a role in the apparent 1951–64 improvement. Assuming such an improvement really did occur, one might be tempted to assume optimistically that Colombia had turned the income distribution corner and could anticipate a continuation of the positive trend. Certainly such a conclusion is not yet warranted, but the pessimistic opposite is even less warranted.

Income from Asset Appreciation

Perhaps the major doubt with respect to the conclusions reached

---

56. Kuznets, "Economic Growth and Income Inequality."

above, and especially with respect to the judgment that distribution may have improved over the second period considered, is the failure to take account of changes in the value of capital assets.

For a full appreciation of variations in income shares, one should treat capital appreciation as a form of income. The ratio of appreciation of physical capital to other forms of income in the period concerned has probably been in the range of .10–.20 in Colombia.[57] But no studies permitting one to assign this income by classes are yet available, so any judgment as to whether its omission creates a bias or not must be impressionistic.

Certainly the logical hypothesis is that income from asset appreciation is quite concentrated, but since the overall distribution is also quite concentrated it may not be measurably worsened when the appreciation is taken into account. It does seem likely that the distribution of income from asset appreciation is similar to the distribution of wealth, possibly even more skewed since it seems likely that only large-scale capitalists are able to take advantage of situations of rapid capital appreciation. Therefore, the tentative judgment is that if we were able to take account of capital gains, distribution would be somewhat worse.

Income Changes of Lower-Income Groups and Their Relationship to the Overall Rate of Economic Growth

It has been argued on occasion that lower-income groups in developing societies are inclined to suffer absolute income and welfare decline over time (we call this hypothesis 1). It is also argued (hypothesis 2) that *rapid* growth can lead not only to a worsening of distribution—apparently consistent with the record in Colombia—but also to lower absolute income for this group. This latter hypothesis could, if one placed sufficient weight on the lower-income

57. A crude estimate by the authors suggests a ratio of tangible wealth held by individuals to national income of about 4:1 in 1956. It seems probable that the annual real appreciation of these assets falls in the range of 2–5 percent. This would imply an appreciation income equal to 8–20 percent of the regular national accounts income. The roughly half of the capital that corresponds to urban land and real estate (including houses) probably appreciates at almost the upper margin of the range set, but some other assets may not tend to appreciate at all. (Appreciation of financial assets appears quite limited.)

groups, imply that the faster growth rate could lower the welfare of the society as a whole.[58]

The first hypothesis, that major groups have suffered decreasing absolute incomes over substantial periods of time, receives little support from the Colombian statistics. The only group for which the argument could be taken seriously is the agricultural workers, whose reported real wages appeared in the mid-1960s to be only at about their mid-1930s' level. But, as mentioned earlier, it seems that the figures for the mid-1930s were probably well above those of, say, the 1920s, so that over the longer run and certainly over the course of the twentieth century, this group has seen a substantial income increase.[59] The same goes for such other unskilled groups as construction workers, artisans, and small-scale commercial workers.

The more interesting question in the Colombian context is whether

---

58. A conclusion supported by a calculation made by McGreevey [William P. McGreevey, *An Economic History of Colombia 1845–1930* (Cambridge, England: Cambridge University Press, 1971), p. 132].

59. Hypothesized causal relationships between growth and distribution are legion, only a few of which we will mention here.

1. It is commonly believed that the marginal propensity to save is an increasing function of income so that income inequality promotes high total savings and faster growth. Probably more persuasive is the hypothesis that the savings rate out of profits is much higher than that out of labor income; of course, profits usually accrue to relatively high-income people. Neither variant would in general foster the expectation that rapid growth would lead to an absolute income decline for low-income groups.

2. Fast growth is associated with labor-saving technological change, which keeps the profit rate high. When such new technology is available, fast growth is natural because profits can be made through its innovation, and labor displacement and declining labor incomes are natural given its labor-saving feature. This mechanism could underlie hypothesis 2 in the text.

3. Fast growth is likely to be associated with inflationary finance (partly because such finance will be more sought after when high-payoff investments can be made and partly because the low capital costs associated with inflationary finance make more projects attractive), and inflation itself tends to cause labor incomes to lag behind their equilibrium levels. Eventually, institutions would arise to narrow the gap between actual and equilibrium wages, but before this happened a declining labor share could be induced.

The discussion of the text is not designed to test any one of these specific mechanisms but simply to ascertain whether hypothesis 2 is consistent with the facts. Recent cross-country evidence is compiled and presented by Montek Ahluwalia in Hollis Chenery, Montek Ahluwalia, Clive Bell, John Duloy, and Richard Jolly, *Redistribution with Growth, An Approach to Policy* (Washington, D. C.: International Bank for Reconstruction and Development, 1974).

these groups benefit or are harmed by *rapid* as opposed to slow economic growth. Colombia provides a good laboratory setting in terms of fairly lengthy periods of slow and rapid income growth. If the hypothesis is alleged to be related to output (as opposed to income) growth (and this might be the more normal version of it), the laboratory is less useful because there were smaller fluctuations. However, they were in the same direction as those of per capita income so we can more or less freely take the period 1934–56 as one of especially rapid growth and 1956–66 as one of slow growth.

One might hypothesize that different low-income groups would be affected in different ways by growth since some, such as small-scale manufacturing workers, could be essentially in competition with the dynamic sectors, whereas construction workers (at least as long as construction technology is reasonably stable—as it appears to have been in Colombia) and maids might be considered complementary. Unfortunately, adequate figures on the income of several of the low-income subgroups are not available to allow an overall comparison between these periods; table 4.6 summarizes some of the relevant information. For several groups actual income decreases do appear to have occurred during the first period of relatively quick growth. Although blue-collar manufacturing workers as a group received income increases almost as fast as the economy-wide average, it is not improbable that the small-scale firms did not share so successfully in the growth. Were this the case, the only low-income group listed here with a gain close to the overall average would be maids.[60] Almost all the categories had increases equal to or above the average during the slow growth period 1956–66, and all those for which comparisons are possible did better than in the earlier, fast growth period.

We have referred earlier to the problems of using wage data to infer trends in income distribution in the agricultural sector—especially when this sector displays certain labor-surplus characteristics (see pp. 10–15). The issue is whether the movement of selected wage rates is a good indicator of income gains for low income people in general. We know that low-income people can gain under labor-surplus conditions, although no wage rate rises—as they shift from the traditional to the modern sctor. And in fact our

60. Who provide a service clearly complementary to the success of high-income people.

Table 4.6
Annual Percentage Income Change of Selected Occupational Groups
Compared among Periods of Slow and Fast
Overall Income Growth

Occupational Group	Period 1 1935±–56 (Fast growth)	Period 2 1956–66 (Slow growth)
Agricultural wage laborers	−0.70 to +0.37[a]	1.5[g]
Unskilled construction workers (Bogota)	Small decrease– small increase[b]	3.8
Blue-collar manufacturing workers		
Total	2.18–2.36[c]	4.8
Small plants (<25 workers)	—	3.3[h]
Large plants (≥25 workers)	—	3.9[h]
Commerce workers		
All		1.3[i] (1954–67)
Small establishments (<5 workers)		1.2–2.9[j] (1954–67)
Food retailing	Decrease[d]	
Maids	Substantial increase[e] (Bogota only)	3.9 (Bogota only)
Average growth of income per member of the labor force	2.76[f]	1.68[g]

[a]See table 4.1 for discussion. The higher figure shown is the more probable.

[b]It seems improbable that an increase over this period could have been greater than, say, 1 percent per year; it could well have been less.

[c]See table 4.1. End of period defined as 1955–57.

[d]Udall, "Migration." Based on Bogota data. It is interesting to note that Udall's figures (large-store clerks) indicate a considerable increase over 1945 to 1954–58, so unless there was a drop in the period from the mid-1930s to 1945, a considerable increase must have occurred over the period as a whole.

[e]Udall, ibid. There is some uncertainty here since Udall estimates the whole increase in question to have occurred before 1945, a period during which his sources of information were not internally comparable.

[f]1934–36 to 1955–57.

[g]1955–57 to 1965–67.

[h]From Berry, "The Relevance and Prospects of Small Scale Industry in Colombia," Yale Economic Growth Center Discussion Paper no. 142, 1972. pp. 3, 32.

Table 4.6 (continued)
*From Berry, "Urban Labor Surplus and the Commerce Sector: Colombia," Yale Economic Growth Center Discussion Paper no. 78, 1973.
*From table 4.4.

estimates suggest that the bottom 25 and 50 percent of the labor force gained by 14–23 and 24–29 percent, respectively, between 1934–36 and 1950–54, a period of apparently worsening distribution. But even under labor-surplus assumptions, rapid wage increases would normally signal greater absolute improvement than slow ones, so the behavior of various wage rates is relevant.

It should be obvious that these results must be interpreted with caution.[61] It would be a contradiction in terms to argue that in the long run the welfare of low-income groups can be advanced by preventing growth. But they do raise questions. If in fact rapid growth has been causally related to worsening distribution, can the nature of growth be altered so that this price need not be paid? Or can alleviatory institutions be developed to lower the costs of growth and thus provide "social lubrication" for the process? The evidence is suggestive enough to call for additional empirical work to permit more confident acceptance or rejection of the relationship which seems to have surfaced here and for theoretical work on the mechanisms that may have generated it.

Price Indices for Various Social Classes

Throughout most of the discussion of income trends for various occupations and social groups, it has been implicitly assumed that all earnings could be deflated by a common price index to arrive at trends in real incomes. It is important to verify whether this assumption is realistic since if the prices of the typical consumption baskets of different social classes increase at different rates, changes in nominal earnings differentials will not reflect accurately the changes in real differentials.[62] Fortunately for our historical analysis, it appears

---

61. Entirely apart from the fact that the observed relationship under discussion may be spurious. Other factors were no doubt important in determining some of the income changes in question. For example, the *violencia* may have helped push people into low-income urban jobs toward the end of the first period, contributing to the bad experience of some of the groups.

62. For example, if the goods with high import content usually consumed by rich individuals increased in price more rapidly than the price of food, which

that the prices of the goods and services consumed by different income classes have moved in quite parallel fashions. As table 4.7 shows, over the period 1961–70 three price indices, based on the consumption budgets of low-, medium-, and high-income families, reveal almost identical rates of growth.[63] It is relevant to note that the parallel movement of the three indices in table 4.6 is not due to similarities in consumption patterns. On the contrary, these patterns are very different, but differences in price behavior among goods tend to compensate one another.

Table 4.7
Price Indices for Three Income Classes in Bogota
(Pesos)

	Income Groups [a]		
	0–1,999	8,000–10,999	30,000 and more
1961	100	100	100
1962	107	106	106
1963	124	125	126
1964	128	131	133
1965	150	150	153
1966	170	181	183
1967	190	195	197
1968	204	206	210
1969	218	216	219
1970	238	241	240

Source: Special estimates were constructed from DANE and Banco de la Republica price data, and consumption weights were derived from a CEDE family budget survey.

[a] The income groups refer to 1967–68 data from the CEDE family budget studies.

In summary, this evidence suggests that in Colombia comparisons of income distribution through time will not be invalidated by the

---

weighs heavily in the budget of the poor, the distribution of income in real terms would improve more than indicated by an over-time comparison of nominal earnings differentials between poor and rich.

63. The indices were constructed primarily from DANE price data; prices of some goods consumed by high-income families were obtained specially for this study by Banco de la Republica. Price changes of the various goods and services were weighted according to their relative importance in total expenditures by each income class, according to the CEDE family budget study.

use of the same price deflator to estimate real earnings trends among different income classes.[64]

64. For a more complete description of the data used and tables disaggregating price changes for each income class, see Miguel Urrutia, "Indices de Precios para Diferentes Clases Sociales," *Revista del Banco de la Republica* 45, no. 533 (March 1972): 397–402.

5

Changes in Regional Income Distribution over Recent Decades

A frequently important aspect of a country's overall income distribution—at a point of time and over time—is the distribution among regions. Until about twenty years ago there was little economic integration among Colombia's four or five principal zones. There was and is considerable variation in income levels from region to region. Although the differentials do not reach the extremes that characterize countries such as Brazil or the Philippines, they are nevertheless worrisome and give rise to a policy dilemma of whether the poorer regions are best aided by "taking economic activity to them" or by encouraging their residents to emigrate to more dynamic regions.

Colombia's Regional Inequality Compared to That of Other Countries

Before turning in detail to Colombia's own regional distribution, it is helpful to get some feel for how it ranks relative to other countries (see table 5.1). Cross-country comparisons are especially dangerous and difficult to interpret in regard to this form of inequality because data for the various countries are often provided by arbitrary and noncomparable administrative or political divisions. In a country whose states or provinces tend to be quite heterogeneous internally, there may be a great deal of inequality at the level of fairly small regions but little at the level of large regions. The data of table 5.1 naturally suffer from this problem; still it is possible to conclude that regional inequality tends to diminish with the level of development. In terms of the measure used here (see notes for table 5.1), the developed countries have almost without exception an index of less than

200, whereas no developing country in this sample registers less than 200. Given its income level, the regional inequality in Colombia appears to be below average. This may be due in part to its relatively balanced urban development—several important cities as opposed to the one or two that dominate most Latin American countries.

The tendency for developed countries to have low indices warrants special attention because this phenomenon appears to be explained in great part by the increasing regional integration that characterizes the process of development—an integration involving greater interchange of both goods and factors. The traditional theory of international trade suggests that both processes may be expected to augment the income levels of residents in all regions and to diminish differences in factor productivity among regions.[1] However, neither process would necessarily reduce income differentials among regions. Migration of labor should have this effect but that of capital might not. When capital moves among regions, the effect is to equalize its marginal productivity and remuneration among regions. But the owner of capital does not always move with the factor, so that if capital owners are regionally concentrated the same will be true for income, even though capital (in terms of its use) is well spread out across the country. In the case of labor, the region of its use is almost always the region of residence of the income recipient. Given the relatively high capital share of income in Colombia,[2] there may be a considerable lack of coincidence between the region in which income is generated and the region of the recipient.

Another cause of the comparatively even regional distribution in developed countries is almost certainly the relative unimportance of the rural sector. There is almost always a substantial gap in average

1. Among the exponents of the opposite theory, to the effect that the process tends to widen differences and even to worsen the absolute situation of the poorer regions, Gunnar Myrdal is prominent [see, e.g., chap. 13 of his *An International Economy* (New York: Harper and Row, 1955)]. One part of the literature on poles of development has the same implication.

2. Probably about one-third of income generated in the current production process (see A. Berry, "Changing Income Distribution Under Development: Colombia," *Review of Income and Wealth*, forthcoming). When capital gains income is included, the capital share might be about 40–45 percent. Harberger uses an estimate of 40 percent, which is considered acceptable by Sarmiento [see Eduardo Sarmiento, *Crecimiento Economico y Asignacion de Recursos* (Bogota: Fedesarrollo, 1972)].

Table 5.1
Regional Distribution of Income in Selected Countries

Countries, Arranged in Categories Suggested by Kuznets	Year of Study	Measure of Regional Dispersion $(V_w)^a$	Area (Square miles)
Australia	1949/50–1959/60	.058	2,974,581
New Zealand	1955	.063	103,736
Canada	1950–61	.192	3,845,774
United Kingdom	1959/60	.141	94,279
United States	1950–61	.182	3,022,387
Sweden	1950, 1955, 1961	.200	173,374
Group I: Average		.139	
Finland	1950, 1954, 1958	.331	130,165
France	1954, 1955/1956, 1958	.283	212,659
East Germany	1950–1955, 1960	.205	94,723
Holland	1950, 1955, 1958	.131	12,850
Norway	1952, 1957–60	.309	125,064
Group II: Average		.252	
Ireland	1960	.268	26,601
Chile	1958	.327	286,397
Austria	1957	.225	32,369
Puerto Rico	1960	.520	3,435
Group III: Average		.335	
Brazil	1950–59	.700	3,288,050
Italy	1951, 1955, 1960	.360	117,471
Spain	1955, 1957	.415	195,504
Colombia	1964[b]	.271	439,617
Greece	1954	.302	51,246
Group IV: Average		.464	
Yugoslavia	1956, 1959, 1960	.340	95,558
Japan	1951–59	.244	142,644
Group V: Average		.292	
Philippines	1957	.556	115,600
Group VI: Average		.556	
India	1950/1951, 1955/1956	.275	1,221,880
Group VII: Average		.275	

Source: Adapted from Jeffrey Williamson, "National Economic Development and Interregional Inequality," (Department of Economics, The University of Texas, 1964).

[a] A measure of dispersion of regional income per capita, defined as $\sqrt{\sum(Y_i-\bar{Y})^2/n}/\bar{Y}$ where Y_i is average income (or output) per person in region i, $\bar{Y}_i$ is the national average, and n is the number of regions. When regions are weighted by population the formula becomes

Table 5.1 (continued)

$$V_w = \frac{\sqrt{\Sigma[(Y_i - \bar{Y})^2 w_i]}}{\bar{Y}},$$

where w_i is the weight for region i.

[b]Based on data of Francesco Marabelli, "Tentativa de Distribucion de Producto Bruto Interno de Colombia por Seciones Administrativas del Pais (1964)" (Bogota: Naciones Unidas, 1966).

income between urban and rural areas (often favoring the former by about 2:1). Also, there are usually differences in the proportion of people in rural and in urban areas; this means that some regional differences merely reflect differences in the rural and urban weights of each region. When the weight of the rural labor force becomes low in all regions, this effect is weakened.

In any case cross-country information on regional inequalities at a given point of time provides a useful input into the analysis that should underlie regional policy. It would be better to have evidence from developing countries as to how these inequalities have been changing over the years, but so few studies are available that much reliance must be placed on the cross-country type of information. There are theories, already noted, which contend that regional differences should diminish over time and others which affirm the opposite. The cross-country comparison buttresses the former argument, at least in relation to the more advanced stages of the development process; for Colombia there is some impressionistic evidence on both sides of the fence. In this chapter we attempt to summarize the empirical data relevant to this subject, working at the departmental level.

Departmental Distribution of Income and Output in the Mid-1960s

Data generated during the 1960s are sufficient to provide reasonable estimates of output by department (or larger region); making parallel estimates of regional distribution of income received is more difficult. In this study primary reliance will be placed on calculations by the authors for 1967 and 1954. Marabelli's output distribution for 1964 is also quite useful. Although the divisions used are larger (only five regions), in many ways the most complete information is that

Table 5.2

Income Differentials by Department, circa 1964

	GDP per Capita Marabelli, 1964 (National average=100)	GDP per Capita Implicit in Marabelli's Indices	Income per Family: Ministry of Health Sample, 1965	Income per Person: Ministry of Health Sample, 1965	Index (Colombia=100)
			Pesos	Pesos	
	(1)	(2)	(3)	(4)	(5)
Antioquia	101	2,949	10,424	1,645	105
Atlantico	101	2,949	11,718	1,916	123
Bolivar	88	2,569	9,192	1,515	97
Boyaca	71	2,073	6,752	1,165	75
Caldas	91	2,657	9,536	1,489	95
Cauca	61	1,781	—	—	60
Cordoba	83	2,423	5,705	933	60
Cundinamarca	101	2,949	3,681	716	46
Distrito Especial (Bogota)	159	4,643	16,840	3,124	200
Choco	32	934	4,115	714	46
Huila	79	2,307	5,508	926	59
Guajira	52	1,518	—	—	—
Magdalena	99	2,891	8,439	1,489	95
Meta	119	3,475	—	—	—
Nariño	53	1,548	2,048	381	24
Norte de Santander	90	2,628	5,717	887	57
Santander	104	3,037	7,006	1,134	73
Tolima	105	3,066	5,878	1,117	72
Valle	128	3,737	10,686	2,015	129
Colombia	100	2,919		1,562[a]	100

Sources and Methodology: Column (1) is from Marabelli, "Tentativa de Distribucion de Producto Bruto Interno de Colombia por Secciones Administrativas del Pais (1964)" Bogota: Naciones Unidas, 1966). Since the Marabelli study was not directly available, his absolute value estimates of GDP per capita in the various departments are not used. Column (2) is based on the assumption that his estimate of gross domestic product was equal to that of the national accounts in 1964 (53.760 billion pesos). For the estimate of income per capita shown here this value was divided by our estimate of the total population in 1964 (18.412 million persons).

Columns (3) and (4) come from data of the ASCOFAME-Ministry of Health 1965 survey and are taken directly from German Urrego M., *Distribucion del Ingreso Rural Colombiano Comparado con la Distribucion Urbana*, ICA (Instituto Colombiana Agropecuario) Boletin de Investigacion no. 18, Dec. 1971. This study presents average income per family by department for rural and urban areas; these two figures are weighted by the 1964 distribution of population between rural and urban areas as indicated in the population census. Column (4) relates income to number of persons based on the same sample and handled in the same way. However, it should be kept in mind that this sample produced very doubtful income distribution data. (For a discussion of the inconsistencies that arise when using this income data, see Miguel Urrutia, "Reseña de los Estudios de Distribucion de Ingresos en Colombia," *Revista del Banco de la Republica*, no. 508, Feb. 1970). The data in these columns should be used with great care.

*a*The departmental figures, weighted by 1964 population. Excludes Meta, Guajira, and the territories. No figure was available for Cauca so it was assumed (based on Marabelli) to have a per capita income 0.61 times the national average.

of DANE's 1970 household survey.[3] A Ministry of Health–ASCOFAME survey of 1965 provided interesting but less reliable information.

Benchmark Estimates of Regional Income Distribution

Before attempting over time comparisons of regional inequalities in Colombia, it is helpful to give special attention to those years for which the most complete estimates have been made; they are Marabelli's estimate of gross domestic product for 1964[4] and the authors' for 1967.[5] Marabelli estimated a distribution by departments and concluded that the gross domestic product per capita was about three times as high in the special district (Bogota) as in the lowest-income department of those with sizable population (Nariño). His departmental indices of gross domestic product per person are presented in table 5.2 along with the absolute income figures implicit in his indices and the national average. It is clear that a substantial proportion of the differences calculated by Marabelli corresponds to different ratios of rural to total populations (see table 5.3). Over recent decades average nonagricultural per capita income has usually been about double that in agriculture.

Table 5.4 presents the authors' estimates of output[6] and output per person by department in 1953 and 1967 for the major economic sectors (agriculture, manufacturing, and commerce).[7] The ranking of departments is broadly similar to that of Marabelli.[8] There is no

3. A recent and interesting estimate of distribution by department in 1970 reached us too late to be taken into account. See Felipe Samper D., "Distribucion del Producto Interno Bruto de Colombia, 1970, Por Departamentos (Undergraduate thesis, Department of Economics, University of the Andes, Bogota, 1973).
4. Francesco Marabelli, "Tentativa de Distribucion de Producto Bruto Interno de Colombia por Secciones Administrativas del Pais (1964)" (Bogota: Naciones Unidas, 1966).
5. Neither of them provide *direct* evidence on regional distribution of income.
6. Gross domestic product.
7. Data for other sectors were unavailable or too imprecise.
8. We do not know exactly what information Marabelli used, but it is undoubtedly true that many of his sources and ours are similar or identical. He did not have a recent commerce census on which to base estimates of output in that sector. Part of the differences between his estimate and our 1964 figures relates to our using only three sectors. Undoubtedly there are various other differences. Regional income and output estimates are early enough in their infancy in Colombia to imply that only marked differentials can be taken seriously.

Table 5.3
Average Income and Coefficient of Concentration by Region,
Rural/Urban Factor, and Sex, 1970

Region and Sex	Rural		Urban		Total	
	Average Income	Coefficient of Concentration	Average Income	Coefficient of Concentration	Average Income	Coefficient of Concentration
Total	586	0.424	1.356	0.529	1.061	0.535
Men	607	0.421	1.609	0.521	1.158	0.551
Women	413	0.329	857	0.442	771	0.451
Region						
Atlantic	716	0.423	1.300	0.538	1.085	0.563
Eastern	591	0.433	1.125	0.516	817	0.503
Bogota	902	0.381	1.697	0.530	1.689	0.526
Central	576	0.500	1.274	0.491	978	0.500
Pacific	470	0.391	1.178	0.544	880	0.546

Source: DANE, Boletin Mensual de Estadistica, no. 237. Apr. 1971, p. 85.

significant change in the degree of cross-regional differentials; during the period about as many departments saw their average output per worker move closer to the national average as away from it. Of the poorest three departments, Nariño, Cauca, and Boyaca, one (Boyaca) moved closer to the national average while the other two slipped back. Of the four highest departments in 1953 (Atlantico, Caldas, Cundinamarca, and Valle), two gained (Atlantico and Valle), one stayed at about the same relative level (Cundinamarca), and one lost (Caldas). Our preferred indicator of regional inequality, the weighted V_w statistic (see table 5.1), was 0.31 in 1953 and 0.29 in 1967. (The unweighted statistic fell a little faster, from 0.34 to 0.29).

All such aggregate statistics as those underlying tables 5.2 and 5.4 are subject to serious data deficiencies and to difficulties of interpretation, especially when the basic concern is with regional distribution of income instead of output.[9] Accordingly, it is useful to take account of the other available indicators of changing income and welfare by region. As well as providing cross-checks on the aggregate data and more direct evidence on income trends, they can enrich our detailed understanding of events by showing how certain subgroups have fared.

9. Table 5.4 and the Marabelli figures in table 5.2 refer to output per worker (or per person in the case of Marabelli).

Table 5.4
Output Per Capita in Agriculture, Manufacturing, and Commerce by Department, 1953 and 1967
(Absolute figures in thousands of pesos)

Department	1953			1967		
	Output per Worker	Output per Worker (Department/ Nation)	Share of Total Labor Force in Sectors Listed (1951 population census)	Output per Worker	Output per Worker (Department/ Nation)	Share of Total Labor Force in Sectors Listed (1964 population census)
Antioquia	2.6363	1.15	.7013	15.182	1.108	61.95
Atlantico	3.0298	1.32	.5653	21.369	1.560	40.46
Bolivar and Cordoba	2.2087	0.96	.7720	14.772	1.08	68.75
Boyaca	1.0441	0.45	.8151	9.281	.678	77.17
Caldas	3.1041	1.35	.7575	14.618	1.067	63.74
Cauca	1.6996	0.74	.8039	6.993	.511	79.72
Cundinamarca and Bogota	2.8032	1.22	.5154	16.513	1.21	40.74
Huila	1.7805	0.77	.7494	12.555	.917	68.83
Magdalena	2.4153	1.05	.7722	20.192	1.474	68.90
Nariño	1.2756	0.55	.8273	5.997	.438	78.43
Norte de Santander	1.7485	0.76	.7096	8.731	.637	61.93
Santander	1.3708	0.60	.7345	13.240	.967	65.64
Tolima	2.5885	1.12	.7761	12.889	.941	68.27
Valle	2.8397	1.24	.6951	20.676	1.510	52.68
Colombia	2.3017	1.00	.6929	13.696	1.000	61.37

Source: Tables A3 and A4.

Income Trends for Selected Groups by Department

Evidence is available over fairly long periods on relative income trends for some occupational groups (agricultural laborers, blue- and white-collar workers in factory manufacturing, departmental government employees). Although these data show no simple pattern, there appears to be some tendency toward narrowing of regional differences over time. But this trend varies: some low-income departments have clearly gained ground (e.g., Boyaca, from which out-migration has been very large); others appear to have lost ground (e.g., Nariño, which has had relatively less out-migration). The agricultural wage data indicate decreasing dispersion of wage rates from 1938 to 1964. The statistic V_w[10] (unweighted) fell from .258 in 1938 to .192 in 1951 to .175 in 1964. The weighted version takes on the values .254, .171, and .164 in the three years.

For wages in factory manufacturing (blue- and white-collar workers combined), unweighted V_w was .264, .235, .270, and .228 in 1944–45, 1953, 1958, and 1967, respectively; for the last three of those years the weighted version was .140, .143, and .110, respectively. From 1944–45 to 1967 the average wage increase in the four most industrialized departments was 134 percent, whereas that of the remaining departments was 188 percent.[11] For blue-collar workers alone the gains were 126 and 159 percent, respectively. The average blue-collar wage in the four most industrialized departments slipped from its initial advantage of 45 percent to one of 26 percent over this period. For departmental government employees, the picture is less clear. Unweighted V_w was .150, .230, .208, and .212 in 1939, 1953, 1958, and 1967, respectively; the weighted figure was .139, .228, .221, and .214.

These various indicators are definitely consistent with the more aggregate evidence presented in the previous section to the effect that regional dispersion diminished somewhat over 1953–67. The government employee and manufacturing wage data suggest that there may have been some worsening in a prior period. Overall, there is some suggestion that when overall distribution has improved,

10. Defined in table 5.1.
11. With the increase of each department weighted by the 1958 employment level.

the same has been true (though hardly clear-cut) for regional distribution. As argued in chapter 4, there was a general worsening of urban distribution from some time in the 1930s to some time in the 1950s, followed by an improvement. The regional dispersion pattern seems to reflect the latter improvement though it is less clear whether the prior worsening occurred. In agriculture national distribution worsened continuously, whereas, as we see here, wage dispersion seems to have narrowed continuously. It was unfortunate that no manufacturing data were available for the late 1930s and early 1940s.

Other Indicators of Regional Welfare Distribution and Change

Other valuable indicators of changes in the standard of living available on a departmental basis are certain aspects of housing conditions. Data on earthen floors and running water indicate quite general improvements—all departments have had definite gains.[12] No obvious, simple patterns of change in the extent of differentials show up,[13] but there is some degree of consistency with the trends adduced earlier on overall distribution. Table 5.5 suggests a worsening distribution of these housing amenities during 1938–51. The average percentage gain for the five most industrialized departments (the first five in the table) was 21.8; that for Tolima and Magdalena, perhaps the richest of the remaining, more agricultural departments, was 14.6.[14] The remaining departments averaged a gain of 8.9. Over 1951–64 gain was again more rapid in the industrialized departments but the difference seems to have been substantially reduced. The

12. In several departments the percentage of urban dwellings with a given positive characteristic dropped; this typically occurred where urbanization was very rapid. Since the migrants usually had better dwelling conditions in urban than in rural zones, the fact that they were worse off than other urban dwellers and brought down the urban average does not mean that the total population was not getting better off—as the statistics indicate, it was.

13. Behavior of these housing quality measures is rather well correlated with income measures. Rural housing improvement between 1951 and 1964 was correlated to agricultural wage increases. Relative average per capita income increases during 1953–67 were correlated with the relative housing improvements by department during 1951–64.

14. We exclude Caldas from these comparisons because of the evidence alluded to in table 5.5, that the figures are not accurate, especially those for 1951.

Table 5.5
Relative Improvements in Housing Conditions by Department, 1938–51 and 1951–64

Department	1938–51 Percentage Point Improvement in				Average Value in		1951–64 Percentage Point Improvement in					Average Value in 1964	
	Running Water	Electric Lights	Sanitary Facilities[b]	Average Gain	1938 (a)	1951 (b)	Earth[e] Floor	Running Water	Electric Lights	Sanitary Facilities	Average Gain[d]	All Four Characteristics (c)	Last Three Only (d)
Cundinamarca	21.6	14.7	24.3	20.2	17.5	37.7	19.3	22.0	19.7	20.2	20.3	58.3	61.2
Antioquia	25.3	13.0	27.8	22.0	17.7	39.7	13.3	12.3	6.5	12.5	11.2	50.8	56.8
Valle	18.9	11.1	36.0	22.0	22.1	44.2	10.4	4.5	8.8	0.1	6.0	48.6	57.0
Santander	14.4	8.0	20.3	14.2	9.6	23.5	18.9	16.1	11.7	15.5	15.6	37.9	40.8
Atlantico	19.3	13.6	59.9[c]	30.9[c]	31.4	62.3	6.8	−2.6	1.9	3.6	2.4	63.3	66.9
Tolima	13.8	7.5	24.1	15.1	8.4	23.5	19.1	4.3	5.9	3.0	8.1	27.9	38.3
Magdalena	9.3	5.7	27.3	14.1	6.8	20.9	15.7	9.5	8.8	7.9	10.5	29.6	33.1
Caldas[a]	24.0	10.7	34.5	23.1	22.1	45.1	3.6	−22.4	−16.2	−26.9	−15.5	23.2	40.5
Norte de Santander	17.8	6.8	20.9	15.2	11.5	26.7	17.9	19.5	11.3	17.2	16.5	42.7	46.9
Bolivar including Cordoba	10.9	5.1	20.4	12.1	3.3	15.4	9.9	8.2	12.0	11.0	10.3	25.8	25.7
Huila	13.6	6.2	23.1	5.2	12.9	18.1	21.2	8.2	9.2	1.2	10.0	24.2	33.0
Boyaca	4.8	2.3	7.5	4.9	2.6	7.5	15.8	14.8	8.6	9.9	12.3	18.6	20.7
Cauca	6.1	3.5	15.2	8.3	4.7	13.0	7.7	8.4	5.1	6.8	7.0	19.8	25.3
Nariño	6.9	3.6	12.6	7.7	2.5	10.2	12.0	14.6	11.8	16.1	13.6	24.3	31.4
Colombia	14.9	10.9	25.3	17.0			21.8	12.1	8.5	8.0	12.6		

Sources: The population and housing censuses of 1938, 1951, and 1964 [Direccion Nacional de Estadistica, *Censo General de la Poblacion, 5 de Julio de 1938* (Bogota: Imprenta Nacional, 1942); Departamento Administrativo Nacional de Estadistica, *Censo de Poblacion de Colombia, 1951, Resumen* (Bogota, 1955—); Departamento Administrativo Nacional de Estadistica, *XIII Censo de Poblacion (Julio 15 de 1964): Resumen General* (Bogota: Imprenta Nacional, 1967)].

average gain for the five industrial departments was 16.0, that for Tolima and Magdalena 9.3, and that for the other departments (still excluding Caldas) 11.6. If Cundinamarca is excluded from the first group, its average is 8.8. In other words this second period seems to have witnessed a continued relative gain for Cundinamarca (based on that of Bogota), while the other departments with larger cities no longer recorded bigger improvements than the poorer departments. Since the main determinant of provision of certain public services is the share of all houses in urban areas, those departments that have urbanized most quickly would naturally tend to have the fastest improvement in those respects (running water, electricity, and so on). Recorded improvement might therefore be more closely associated with urbanization than with income gains. The indicator "decrease in earthen floors" is not subject to this criticism, however. During 1951–64 the five industrial departments registered a gain of 13.7 (12.4 without Cundinamarca), Tolima and Magdalena 17.4, and the other departments 14.1. These data imply that the previous indicators may be somewhat biased toward showing widening differentials; they are inclined to confirm the position that regional distribution did not worsen between 1951 and 1964.

Educational facilities, with their potential for opportunity, are another aspect of welfare. Here the correct interpretation of recent events depends on how the different educational levels should be weighted. As primary education becomes more universal, regional differences in its coverage decline. This has been happening recently (e.g., 1951–64) in Colombia, as indicated in table 5.6. On the other hand, expansion of secondary and university training has been more rapid in the richer departments. It is difficult to draw a net balance.

Mechanisms Affecting Regional Income Distribution

The extent to which regional income differences contribute to overall income skewness is related both to regional differences in average incomes and to the distribution of people among poorer and richer regions.[15] Correspondingly the regional component of overall in-

15. This distinction is mechanical rather than causal; care must be taken not to assume that regional differentials have any *necessary* causal impact on overall inequality. Used with the appropriate caution, the distinction may help to describe what is happening over time.

Table 5.6
Indicators of Educational Advance by Department

Department	Percentage of Children 5–14 in School			Percentage of Children 5–9 with Some Primary Schooling			Percentage of Children 10–14 with Some Primary Schooling		
	1951	1964	Increase 1951–64	1951	1964	Increase 1951–64	1951	1964	Increase 1951–64
Antioquia	42.7	56.8	14.1	13.3	23.7	10.4	65.7	80.6	14.9
Atlantico	32.3	54.5	22.2	17.2	38.3	21.1	61.5	81.2	19.7
Bolivar and Cordoba	26.9	43.3	16.4	7.6	19.2	11.6	31.1	55.3	24.2
Boyaca	28.6	48.1	19.5	11.0	25.2	14.2	49.2	77.9	28.7
Caldas	38.9	52.4	13.5	15.7	28.8	13.1	65.2	82.9	17.7
Cauca	30.7	42.8	12.1	8.5	17.6	9.1	47.4	65.8	18.4
Cundinamarca	43.8	51.7	7.9	18.6	37.7	19.1	66.3	88.5	22.2
Huila	36.3	52.2	15.9	7.8	19.6	11.8	44.2	69.8	25.6
Magdalena	21.9	39.4	17.5	9.6	20.5	10.9	40.3	59.2	18.9
Nariño	31.0	46.3	15.3	11.3	19.9	8.6	49.6	66.8	17.2
Norte de Santander	39.3	57.0	17.7	12.3	25.9	13.6	27.2	70.4	43.2
Santander	33.3	54.7	21.4	11.2	26.2	15.0	47.9	76.2	28.3
Tolima	22.4	52.8	30.4	7.4	22.8	15.4	43.2	72.1	28.9
Valle de Cauca	35.5	55.3	19.8	15.2	28.6	13.4	64.9	82.6	17.7
Colombia	34.7	51.1	16.4	12.6	26.2	13.6	54.3	75.3	21.0

Source: Population censuses of 1951 and 1964.
^aThere is strong evidence that the figures for Caldas were misreported (upward biased) in 1951; hence gains over 1938–51 and losses over 1951–64 are presumably overstated. Since it is difficult to guess at the nature and extent of the misreporting, no attempt was made here to correct it.
^bToilet or latrine.
^cThe figure for sanitary facilities is suspicious so the total is also; however, there is no obvious inconsistency in the data.
^dA simple average of the percentage of houses with each characteristic listed.
^eImprovement corresponds to a decrease in percentage of dwellings with this characteristic; hence the figure used is 100 minus the percentage with earthen floors.

equality can be reduced either by decreases in cross-regional income differentials or by shifts of people from the poorer areas to the richer ones (we assume here that a majority of the people are initially in the richer areas[16]).

Mobility has undoubtedly been an important factor in the decrease in inequality of income related to regional differences. It has certainly decreased the relative population of the poorer regions,[17] a development that seems to have been particularly marked in the intercensal period 1938–51 (see table 5.7), and has probably also contributed to some equalization of factor incomes in the various zones. As discussed above, wage differentials in the several sectors or occupations studied seem to have diminished in the period after 1950, whereas prior to that there was no general trend. We do not have sufficient data on over time differentials in other factor incomes to deduce whether on balance they have diminished or not, but the overall effect of migration itself has probably been to reduce the impact of regional differences on the total skewness of the distribution via the first effect cited.

Some Ambiguous Developments

Changes in relative incomes and living standards by region would be expected to reflect both (1) changes in the relative sectoral and

16. Migration could increase inequality of distribution, at least by some measures of inequality, if the bulk of the people are found in low-income regions and migration expands the high-income tail of the distribution. However in Colombia the majority of the people are found in the higher-income and usually net-immigration departments—Cundinamarca, Valle, Atlantico, Antioquia. (Antioquia is an exception in usually being a region of net emigration, a characteristic related in part to a high natural population growth rate.)

17. Even though this does not show up strongly in the data, it seems a highly plausible conjecture. The poorest (major) departments, both in terms of statistics and impressions, are Nariño, Cauca, and Boyaca. Their share of the labor force fell from 20.7 percent in 1938 to 15.6 in 1951 to 14.2 in 1964. The four industrialized departments (Antioquia, Atlantico, Cundinamarca, and Valle) had an increase in share from 35.9 percent in 1938 to 42.6 in 1951 to 44.6 in 1964. Although it cannot automatically be concluded that migration has been a positive factor (given the significant intradepartmental differences in income levels), it seems very probable (especially during 1938–51) that this was the case. If the relative incomes by department (treating the federal district as a department) had remained unchanged over 1951–64 at the relative values indicated by Marabelli (see table 5.2), the population redistribution would have implied an increase

Table 5.7
Redistribution of Labor Force by Department,
1938 to 1951 to 1964

Department	Percentage of Total Labor Force			Average 1953	Rank in Output per Capita 1964	1967[b]
	1938 (1)	1951 (2)	1964 (3)	(4)	(5)	(6)
Antioquia	12.058	12.735	12.834	(5)	(5)	(5)
Atlantico	2.698	3.593	3.765	(2)	(5)	(2)
Bolivar (and Cordoba)	7.604	7.251	8.308	(8)	(12)	(6)
Boyaca	9.388	6.623	5.848	(14)	(14)	(11)
Caldas	7.999	9.234	7.967	(1)	(10)	(7)
Cauca	4.044	3.547	3.643	(11)	(15)	(14)
Cundinamarca (Bogota)	14.134	15.627 (6.370)	17.728 (11.151)	(4)	(5) (1)	(13) (1)
Choco		1.201	1.166		(17)	
Huila	2.645	2.605	2.405	(9)	(13)	(10)
Magdalena	3.607	3.671	4.212	(7)	(8)	(4)
Nariño	7.227	5.434	4.676	(13)	(16)	(15)
Norte de Santander	3.893	3.326	2.952	(10)	(11)	(12)
Santander	7.296	6.886	5.887	(12)	(4)	(8)
Tolima	6.017	5.902	4.905	(6)	(3)	(9)
Valle	7.035	10.618	10.316	(3)	(2)	(3)
Other	4.087[a]	1.747	3.388			
Total	100.00	100.00	100.00			

Source: Population censuses of 1938, 1951, and 1964 for cols. (1)–(3); tables A3 and A4, respectively, for cols. (4) and (6); table 5.2 (Marabelli) for col. (5).

[a]Includes Choco.

[b]Only in agriculture, manufacturing, and commerce sectors.

occupational structure of the various regions and (2) changes in income corresponding to given sectors and occupations. A comparison of sectoral and occupational structures in the 1951 and 1964 censuses (see table 5.8) reveals that structural change[18] has been highly concentrated. The poorest departments tended to have the smallest percentage reduction in the share of agricultural employment (the figures for Nariño and Cauca actually indicate a small increase) while rapid decreases occurred in Valle and Cundinamarca

---

of about 1.5 percent in total income over 1951–64. The comparable gain during 1938–51 cannot be calculated with contemporary income figures.

18. Or at least certain important types of structural change.

Table 5.8
Occupational Structure Change by Department, 1951–64
(All figures in percent)

Department	Share of Labor Force in Agriculture 1951	1964	Share in Manufacturing 1951	1964	Share of Manufacturing in Factory[a] 1951	1964	Share of Labor Force in Factory Manufacturing 1951	1964	Share in Commerce (Including financial services) 1951	1964	Share in Construction 1951	1964	Share in Government 1951	1964	Share in All Services 1951	1964	Share in Municipal and Departmental Government 1951	1954	Share in Professional, Technical, and Similar 1951	1964
	(1)	(2)	(3)	(4)	(5)	(6)	(7)	(8)	(9)	(10)	(11)	(12)	(13)	(14)	(15)	(16)	(17)	(18)	(19)	(20)
Antioquia	50.85	44.83	14.40	15.30	64.06	68.27	9.23	10.44	4.87	7.93	4.36	4.88	3.02	3.06		16.86	2.70	2.13		4.10
Atlantico	20.32	16.11	22.68	23.70	46.73	56.00	12.86	13.28	13.61	14.87	5.79	6.07	4.85	4.20		22.86	2.53	1.99		5.05
Bolivar	61.33	59.35	9.63	8.74	24.99	17.12	2.41	1.50	6.07	7.34	2.23	3.25	2.74	3.17		15.16	1.16	2.05		3.09[e]
Boyaca	72.23	68.26	7.12	7.14	20.71	26.53	1.48	1.89	2.20	3.87	1.95	2.49	2.32	3.21	13.41	13.30	1.68	1.99	1.39	2.55
Caldas	61.49	52.60	9.34	10.29	34.79	31.17	3.25	3.21	5.27	9.94	1.93	3.20		3.55		16.57	2.27	2.16		3.63
Cauca	70.90	72.20	6.16	5.17	18.21	15.53	1.20	.80	3.50	4.28	2.21	2.64	2.50	3.04	10.48	10.89	1.82	1.70	1.62	2.27
Cordoba	–	–	–	–	–	–	–	–	–	–	–	–	–	2.33	–	13.35	–	–	–	2.46
Bogota	–	–	–	–	–	–	–	–	–	–	–	–	–	7.70	38.26[d]	35.69	–	–	6.66[d]	8.42[f]
Cundinamarca (incl. Bogota)	36.09	25.37	14.71	16.96	49.60	56.82	7.30	9.64	6.89	11.28	5.62	6.07	5.05	3.60	25.33	27.88	1.49	2.07	3.96	6.44
Choco	54.87	64.04	3.07	3.17	–	7.53	–	.24	1.44	2.64	.70	1.88	2.92		7.41	8.51	2.04	2.61	1.47	2.46
Huila	63.47	61.04	8.34	7.61	11.70	10.34	.98	.79	3.10	5.54	3.46	3.15	2.76	4.55	16.48	16.72	1.77	1.98	1.56	2.83
Magdalena	62.92	60.78	8.55	7.67	11.46	10.01	.98	.77	7.17	8.09	2.56	3.72		2.32		12.06	2.38	1.72		3.11
Meta	–	64.51	–	5.67	–	21.48	–	1.22	–	6.31	–	3.53	–	5.82[c]		15.49	–	1.96		2.44
Nariño	57.88	59.23	21.95	15.84	5.65	8.93	1.24	1.41	2.71	3.75	1.84	2.07	2.18	2.40		11.36	1.86	1.80		1.98
Norte de Santander	57.22	51.80	8.64	9.58	29.08	18.28	2.51	1.75	5.37	9.14	4.37	4.59		4.05	17.57		3.02	2.68		3.79
Santander	58.54	52.35	11.08	11.77	41.38	34.08	4.58	4.01	3.87	7.67	3.00	4.26		4.86	8.81		1.55	2.06		2.92
Tolima	65.82	60.65	7.72	7.40	27.93	16.24	2.16	1.20	4.18	7.47	2.55	3.21		3.29	19.81		1.92	2.25		3.05
Valle	46.28	32.43	15.92	18.95	48.27	49.88	7.68	9.45	7.38	11.98	4.71	5.75		3.85	19.81		1.78	2.19		4.21
(Intend. and Comm.)	(63.14)		(5.75)		(27.25)	(4.24)	(.85)	(.23)	(3.37)		(3.12)									
Colombia	53.87	47.27	12.27	12.78	39.75	43.27	4.88	5.53	5.43	8.58	3.54	4.30	3.71[b]	3.91	15.93	18.04	1.91	2.03	2.32	3.92

Sources and Methodology: Columns (1)–(4) and (9)–(14) are based on the data of the 1951 and 1964 population censuses. Columns (5)–(8) also make uses of DANE annual (since 1955) data on the number of people in manufacturing plants with 5 or more workers and 24,000 pesos or more of output (The estimate of number of workers in this category for 1951 is an interpolation between the 1945 and 1953 industrial census figures.) Columns (15) and (16) relate the number of permanent employees of the state and municipal governments (the great majority of them being white-collar workers) to the active population; data on the employees are from DANE, *Estadísticas Fiscales y Administrativas*.

[a]Five or more workers and output of ≥ 24,000 pesos.
[b]Estimate made by ECLA, *Analyses and Projections of Economic Development: The Economic Development of Colombia* (Geneva: United Nations, 1957).
[c]Biased up by severe underreporting of people in activities such as agriculture.
[d]Cabecera only.
[e]The figure for Bolivar alone is 3.47.
[f]Distrito Especial.

(see fig. 5.1). The share of the labor force in factory manufacturing rose in each of the four most industrialized departments (in all of them it was already above 5 percent in 1951) and fell in eight of the ten other major departments—though the declines could not be great, because the 1951 share was invariably low. The share of the labor force in all manufacturing behaved in a generally similar fashion, although the tendency to fall in departments other than the four most industrialized ones was less marked.

This differential behavior was sufficiently extreme so that between

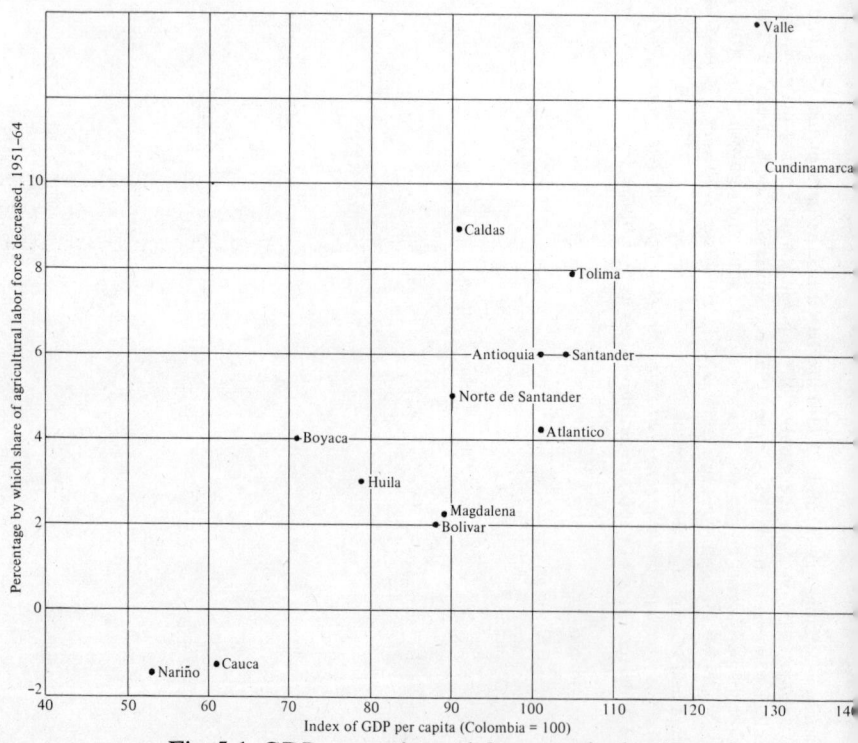

Fig. 5.1. GDP per capita and decreases in the share of labor force in agriculture by department, 1951-64.

1953 and 1964 the rest of the country had essentially no increase in factory employment, while in the four main departments an increase of 57 percent occurred. Even in terms of artisanry the increase was more rapid in the four main departments (36.8 percent) than in the others (21.6 percent).[19]

The share of the total or of the nonagricultural labor force found in industry is often taken as a measure of efficiency in the allocation of human resources. (The other side of this coin is the argument that a high share of the labor force in services is a sign of inefficiency.)[20] Observers frequently refer to the increasing concentration of factory manufacturing in Colombia as if it implies, more or less directly, a worsening regional distribution of income. But as we have already seen, this is apparently an invalid conclusion. And a glance at table A3 shows that in 1967 average labor productivity in manufacturing was not much higher (2,400 for factory and cottage shop combined) than in commerce (1,940). Cottage-shop workers, who form the bulk of the manufacturing labor force, have an average income below that of the labor force as a whole. It is therefore not obvious that an increase in the share of the labor force in manufacturing will imply rising overall incomes unless, as is so often assumed, manufacturing has greater multiplier effects than do other sectors. The inconsistency of what would have been expected on the basis of this assumption with what actually happened to the regional income distribution suggests that such facile assumptions need close scrutiny, if not

19. Possibly this tendency toward increasing skewness has diminished in the last few years. This is suggested by the relationship between the 1964 and 1967 data, which show about the same percentage increase in employment between those two years for both regions (between 3 and 4 percent in each case).

However, it is possible that the DANE sample on which the estimates of factory industry are based was better in 1967 than in 1964, especially better for the smaller-size firms that predominate in the less industrialized departments. So the growth of factory industry in the period 1953–64 may have been underestimated by these figures and overestimated in the period 1964–67. Hence no firm conclusions can be drawn from the relationship between the 1964 and the 1967 information.

20. There is a common impression that labor which generates goods is productive, whereas that which generates services is not. On a more sophisticated level than this intuition, many economists believe that industry generates linkages, multiplier effects, and the like so that its total impact on output is greater than the value of industrial product itself. A similar argument is seldom made for services.

rejection. Note further that the implications of the increasing concentration of factory industry are less clear when, as has been the case, it is accompanied by a relative decrease in factory wages in the more industrialized departments. Migration has presumably played a role in narrowing the wage gap among departments.

Somewhat similar issues are raised by the increasing concentration of population in the largest cities that has accompanied the increasing industrial concentration. It is well known that in the postwar period of rapid overall urbanization, the fastest growth has occurred in the largest cities, with the intermediate ones (many of them departmental capitals) generally growing more slowly, though with some exceptions. The period 1951–64 saw a rapid increase in the share of the total population living in Bogota, Medellin, and Cali (from about 11 to more than 18 percent); these cities had a joint annual growth rate of about 7.15 percent. Apart from the fact that these three cities grew fastest in the intercensal period, there was, over a substantial size range, little relationship between city size and growth rate. Thus the cities which in 1964 had populations of 100,000–600,000 grew at 5.3 percent while those with populations of 50,000–100,000 grew at 5.65 percent. There was substantial variation of growth rates, especially within the latter group, but no city was growing at a rate significantly below 4 percent. The rest of the urban population probably expanded at about 4 percent, so it is clear that there is a range of city sizes (relatively small ones) for which growth was slower than for the intermediate and large ones. Nevertheless, it is striking that a positive correlation between city size and population growth rates shows up in only the three largest cities and in quite small cities.

Summary

Our analysis leads to the tentative conclusion that differences in average labor productivity among departments have tended to narrow since the early 1950s. This process is suggested by the income figures and (in lesser degree) by other proxies of welfare, such as housing conditions. During the cited period redistribution of the labor force among the departments has not been great and can therefore not be credited with much of the aforementioned improvement. It is of interest to note that regional income differences appear to have decreased at a time when overall income distribution appears to have been improving (see chap. 4).

The intercensal period 1938–51 witnessed very substantial redistribution of the labor force toward the higher-income departments. Although the evidence is not consistent, it is probable that regional income differentials increased during the period.[21] Again, the trend in regional distribution appears to support the conclusion of the previous chapter that between 1938 and 1951 income concentration increased.

Of particular interest is the fact that the increasing concentration of factory manufacturing during the 1950s and 1960s seems not to have had a strong impact on regional variation in output per-capita, as reflected in the decline of this latter variance during the period.

Another interesting conclusion is that regional inequalities are less severe in Colombia than in many other developing nations, perhaps partly because they have decreased as economic and transport integration of the country proceeded in the postwar period. Also playing a role may be the dynamism transmitted to most major regions of the country by the existence of rapidly growing cities within them. The strong political regionalism in the country is not a reflection of regional inequality but rather of the continuing strength of urban centers other than the national capital.

Although a regional inequality problem of the sort present in Brazil does not exist, policy should be directed at maintaining the dynamism of the major urban areas of the country. Although balanced geographic growth seems feasible, a great effort should be made to ensure that income distribution does not deteriorate between the urban regional capitals and the extremely poor countryside of some of those regions. Probably this can be achieved only by ensuring the rapid growth of employment opportunities for rural migrants in some strategic urban centers whose sphere of influence includes these poor rural areas.

---

21. Although no overall income data are available, housing conditions improved faster in the richer departments; on the other hand agricultural wage differentials fell between 1938 and 1951. For government employees regional wage differentials increased.

PART II

THE EFFECTS OF ECONOMIC POLICY ON INCOME DISTRIBUTION

6

Sectoral Policy and Income Distribution

The previous chapters have given an idea of the degree of income concentration in Colombia. But the statistics may not convey the hardship that this level of income dispersion implies for families at the bottom of the distribution in a poor country. Given the low mean incomes in rural and urban areas, large sectors of the population—those in the lower deciles of the distribution—lead lives dominated by hunger and death. Malnutrition is such that children are permanently handicapped, both physically and mentally. Child mortality is high, the mental health situation is critical, and owing to poverty and lack of education a great number of families do not even have the hope of seeing the lot of their children improve.

Although we are not the most qualified to describe in a meaningful way the nature and severity of the poverty problem, it would be incongruous to describe the Colombian income distribution without analyzing the possible effectiveness of some policies designed to improve the welfare of the people at the bottom of that distribution.

In part II we analyze the possible impact on the distribution of income of a set of policies which are generally considered to be efficient means of channeling resources toward the poorest sectors of the population. In a sense only traditional redistribution policies are discussed. It is implicitly assumed that in the Colombian context more radical redistributive policies implying large-scale transfers of wealth and income at the expense of the upper deciles of the distribution are not presently politically feasible. And furthermore, the existing tools of economic analysis are not very well suited for evaluating the trade-offs between income redistribution and the economic stagnation and disorganization that usually accompany radical revolutionary processes.

For this reason we have chosen to analyze a set of policies which we feel may under normal circumstances help to channel a more than proportional part of the benefits of economic growth toward the poorest half of the population. However, such redistribution will seldom include a decrease in the nominal incomes of the rich, only a redistribution through time of the fruits of economic growth. Even land reform would have this effect if it is assumed that the owners are compensated for their land, albeit with amortization payments that do not reflect the real rates of return common in the economy.

The first area of policy analyzed is that of taxation and government expenditures. Because in many of the now developed countries it is believed that fiscal policy has contributed to improving the relative position of the poor, it was decided to see whether in Colombia taxation was progressive and whether government expenditure was increasing the supply of goods and services available to poor families.

We decided not to include social security expenditures in this section because in Colombia the Social Security Institute (ICSS) is self-financed and receives no government transfers. A small proportion of the labor force (about 14 percent in the late 1950s) is affiliated, and only the members have access to its medical services. These services in turn are financed partly by the employers and partly by the affiliated workers. Although there may be some income transfer to the poorer affiliated workers, the social security system as a whole probably does not redistribute income in a significant way. This conclusion could be incorrect if evidence is found to the effect that the social security fees are transferred through higher prices to the great mass of consumers who have no access to the system; in that case the redistributive effect of the system would be negative. Therefore the whole subject of the redistributive impact of social security requires further investigation.

The second area studied was that of educational policy and its capacity for affecting the distribution of income through the redistribution of human capital. In addition, it was felt that it would be useful to study the effect of changing the distribution of government expenditure among different types of education.

The other obvious instrument of redistribution in Latin America is land reform. The key issue is the potential importance of land reform as a means of improving the income of a large number of the poor in the rural sector. If little land is available, few people will benefit from land reform and the policy will not be a very useful instrument of redistribution. However, as was seen in chapter 3, land reform in Colombia could improve the welfare of a substantial sector of the rural poor. The question then is whether land reform will promote more rather than less agricultural production, and whether the rural and urban poor who could suffer if land reform led to lowered marketable surplus are more or less numerous than the rural families who would benefit directly from reform. In this area also, it seemed helpful to comment on whether land reform seems feasible given the technological constraints and beliefs common in the country and given the realities of political power.

The final area of policy that seemed most relevant when looking for ways to diminish income dispersion was that of financial policy. One school of economists, impressed by some of the successes achieved through financial reform in some Far Eastern countries, emphasizes the benefits of financial reform for growth and employment and the adjustment of relative prices to underlying supply-and-demand realities. Although at first glance it would seem surprising that a free financial system should contribute to income equalization, in the case of Colombia there was the possibility that state intervention in financial and exchange policy was actually helping to maintain a higher concentration of income than would exist in a free market environment. This was the working hypothesis used to study this area of policy intervention.

Many other types of policies that could presumably affect income dispersion have not been investigated The major ones are those of wage and incomes policy, price controls, and the behavior of government-owned industries. The reason we have not tried to cover these areas is the lack of research done to date on which to build.

Nevertheless, it may be useful at this point to make some remarks concerning the redistributive impact of wage policy since in chapter 4 the trends in real wages were analyzed in some detail. For this purpose it may be profitable to divide the discussion into two major parts: minimum wage policy and arbitration and labor union legislation.

Minimum wage policy can have quite varied effects on income distribution. An effective boosting of the minimum wage can make income distribution worse by producing unemployment among the poorest or marginal workers. Alternatively, in some fairly special cases it can raise labor income by forcing employers to pay more wages out of profits. This latter case may occur when employers are monopsonists in the labor market.

In Colombia the minimum wage has usually lagged behind market wages and therefore has seldom had any important impact in either direction. In the urban areas, where the government can police the minimum wage, very few enterprises are affected by it since it is low compared to most wages. In distant rural areas, on the other hand, where the landowners can still be monopsonists and wages are lower, it is doubtful that the government can make the minimum wage effective. In summary the government of Colombia, partly out of awareness of the presumably negative employment effects of raising the minimum wage, has seldom attempted to use this instrument for redistribution purposes. Increases in the minimum wage have probably had little if any effect on the labor share.

Legislation and government trade union policy, on the other hand, have facilitated the increase in wages of blue-collar workers, particularly between 1954–55 and 1965–66. Detailed studies[1] have shown that in this period unions probably managed to increase wages of members above the wages of nonunionized workers. Since unionized workers were concentrated in the larger modern sector establishments, government trade union policy probably caused a slight redistribution of income from the highest (employer) decile toward the seventh to ninth deciles (from the bottom), where most of these workers are to be found. This redistribution was in effect caused by the state since, given the unlimited supply of labor available to modern industry, it is very unlikely that unions could have developed without government support.[2]

To conclude, trade union policy probably helped those fortunate enough to have permanent jobs in the modern sector of the economy, but other wage policy, such as minimum wage legislation, probably had little redistributive effect.

1. Miguel Urrutia, *The Development of the Colombian Labor Movement* (New Haven: Yale University Press, 1969).
2. Ibid; chaps. 10, 13.

7

Fiscal Policy and Income Distribution

The most obvious instrument for improving income distribution is fiscal policy. Theoretically, income dispersion can be narrowed through taxation and through public expenditures and transfers. This chapter attempts to determine whether fiscal policy in Colombia has actually had this result.

Such a study is fraught with conceptual problems. For example, it may be argued that the major function of a government is to maintain a certain power structure and that taxation and government expenditure should therefore not be expected to improve the distribution of income among families. Rather, the existing income inequalities may be in part a result of the type of expenditures carried out by the state. The existing social order is maintained by a police force, an army, and judicial and education systems financed from general taxation. Viewed in this way, fiscal policy does not provide an opportunity to alter income distribution; it becomes the principal determinant and support of the existing distribution.

We do not address this broad issue but instead neglect the fact that the operations of the government do affect pretax income distribution. (In effect we assume this distribution to be determined by the relative prices of factors of production as established in free markets.) Calculation of the impact of fiscal policy on income distribution then becomes a more feasible objective. Although the substitution of private demand by government demand could bring about changes in the production structure and although the relative prices of the factors of production could therefore also change, such variations would probably be marginal. When the government budget is not a large proportion of national income, these changes in demand will affect the incomes of a limited group of individuals, and thus we may presume that the overall distribution of income is little altered.

This presumption further simplifies measurement of the impact of fiscal policies on income distribution. It is necessary to calculate the direct effects of taxation on gross income distribution and then to show how public expenditure changes the distribution of goods and services received by the various income classes. A progressive tax system, coupled with public expenditure that concentrates on providing all the population with the most basic social services, could significantly diminish the dispersion of income.

The Incidence of the Tax System

Using the most reasonable set of assumptions concerning tax incidence in Colombia, Charles McLure calculated the burden of taxation on different income classes.[1] Those estimates, along with the distribution of pretax income calculated for 1964 in chapter 2, have been used to calculate a distribution of disposable income for the same year (see table 7.1). As this table shows, the distribution of income before and after taxes is approximately the same. The percentage of income paid in taxes is similar for all the first nine deciles in the distribution and somewhat higher only for the upper decile. Although the income tax in Colombia is progressive and also an important source of revenue, indirect taxes (especially local taxes) are regressive; their impact compensates for that of the income tax.

It may be helpful at this stage to review the assumptions used to assign the tax burden. The individual income and complementary taxes were allocated on the basis of Bogota tax returns. This meant that no income tax was assigned to the lowest three deciles of the population while the highest decile paid 35.3 percent of all the income tax. The sales tax was assumed to be transferred to the consumer. Since there are various rates, family budget surveys were used to assign the revenue from the different rates to income earners according to the structure of consumption by income class.

1. Charles E. McLure, Jr., "The Incidence of Taxation in Colombia," in Richard A. Musgrave and Malcolm Gillis, *Fiscal Reform for Colombia* (Cambridge, Mass: Law School of Harvard University, 1971), pt. 2, chap. 1, pp. 239–66.

Table 7.1
Distribution of Personal Income before and after Taxes, 1966

Income Brackets[a] (1966 pesos)	Percentage of Persons (Deciles)	Personal Pretax Income[b] (Thousands of pesos)	Percentage of Personal Pretax Income	Effective Tax Rates	Total Taxes in Each Interval (Thousands of pesos)	Personal Post-tax Income (Thousands of pesos)	Percentage of Personal Postax Income
0– 1,340	10	524.7	0.9	12.6	66.1	458.6	0.92
1,340– 3,290	10	1,107.6	1.9	12.6	139.6	968.0	1.94
3,290– 3,810	20	1,574.0	2.7	10.4	163.7	1,410.3	2.83
3,810– 6,450		2,040.4	3.5	10.4	212.2	1,828.2	3.66
3,810– 6,450	10	2,623.3	4.5	13.4	351.5	2,271.8	4.55
6,450– 6,980	10	3,206.3	5.5	12.8	410.4	2,795.9	5.61
6,980– 10,060	10	4,372.2	7.5	12.8	559.6	3,812.6	7.64
10,060– 12,160	10	5,829.6	10.0	11.8	687.9	5,141.7	10.31
12,160– 20,520	10	9,035.9	15.5	13.2	1,192.7	7,843.2	15.72
20,520– 36,670	5	7,578.5	13.0	15.4	1,167.1	6,411.4	12.85
36,670– 68,675		8,141.0	14.0	15.4	1,253.7	6,887.3	13.81
68,675– 202,201		7,977.8	13.7	17.1	1,364.2	6,613.6	13.26
202,201– 562,129	5	4,019.5	6.9	19.7	791.8	3,227.7	6.47
562,129–1,073,205		265.3	0.4	19.7	52.3	213.0	0.43
Total		58,296.1	100.0		8,412.8	49,883.3	100.0

[a]It was assumed that income distribution did not change between 1964 and 1966. Therefore, income brackets were adjusted by price increases and the increase of real income per capita of the labor force to obtain brackets in incomes of 1966 from the 1964 basic information.

[b]The 1964 distribution was applied to total personal income according to the national accounts for 1966. Personal income was defined as salaries plus income of families from property and unincorporated firms plus savings of corporations, minus public debt.

The half of corporation income and complementary taxes assumed by McLure not to be shifted, one-third of the property tax, and one-third of the taxes on motor vehicles were allocated to the top three income brackets in proportion to income from capital. The total of taxes on alcohol, beer, and tobacco was allocated arbitrarily to income brackets on a somewhat less than per capita basis in the lower range and on a somewhat more than per capita basis in the upper range. The remaining two-thirds of the taxes on motor vehicles were allocated according to total consumption expenditures, on the assumption that this amount falls upon transportation and is shifted forward in the form of higher prices for all goods. The differential exchange earnings from coffee exports (essentially a tax on coffee exports) were allocated on the basis of estimated earnings by farm size.

Finally, the shifted half of the taxes on corporations, the remaining two-thirds of property taxes, all import duties, and all other indirect taxes were allocated on the basis of nonfood expenditures by income brackets. The effective rates of taxation for various taxes are given in table 7.2. This table shows which taxes have a progressive effect on income distribution and which do not, and illustrates what a shift in emphasis from some taxes to others may do to the progressivity of the system.

In a more recent study of tax incidence for Colombia[2] McLure concluded that in 1970 taxation was probably somewhat more progressive than would appear from table 7.1. However, the previous tax incidence estimate used here still appears to be generally correct. McLure notes that his latest incidence estimates "are roughly consistent with the author's previous study of incidence in Colombia."[3]

A comparison of Colombia's tax system with that of other Latin American countries shows that the nation's tax structure is relatively progressive. The income tax is an important source of revenue, and indirect taxes are less regressive than expected. But this does not mean that the system cannot be made more progressive. It is probable that an increase in the overall tax burden, with greater emphasis on property and capital gains taxes, could further improve the distribution of posttax income.

2. Charles E. McLure, Jr., *The Incidence of Colombian Taxes, 1970* (Houston, Tex.: Rice University, Program of Development Studies, paper no. 41, 1973).
3. Ibid., p. 57.

Table 7.2
Effective Rates of Taxation for Various Taxes by Income Brackets, 1966
(Rates expressed as percentage of income)

Income Bracket	Personal Income and Transfer Taxes	Corporation Income Taxes	Sales Tax	Property Taxes	Alcohol, Tobacco, and Beer Taxes	Motor Vehicle Taxes	Import Duties and Other Indirect Taxes	Exchange Earnings on Coffee	Total, All Taxes
Lowest	—	0.96	1.07	0.43	6.48	0.18	3.41	0.13	12.6
Second	—	0.89	0.77	0.41	4.61	0.17	3.13	0.46	10.4
Third	—	1.22	1.21	0.58	4.49	0.17	4.49	1.34	13.4
Fourth	0.19	1.48	1.53	0.68	2.98	0.15	5.33	0.48	12.8
Fifth	0.22	1.46	1.37	0.66	1.88	0.12	5.22	0.94	11.8
Sixth	0.96	1.52	1.41	0.70	1.34	0.13	5.48	1.68	13.2
Seventh	2.74	4.16	1.05	1.25	0.60	0.24	4.85	0.46	15.4
Eighth	5.87	4.73	0.82	1.32	0.19	0.26	3.77	0.11	17.1
Ninth	8.12	5.18	0.66	1.42	0.24	0.27	3.76	—	19.7
Average	2.13	2.68	1.22	0.92	2.26	0.20	4.63	0.62	14.8

Source: Charles McLure, "The Incidence of Colombian Taxes," 1970 (Houston, Tex.: Rice University Program of Development Studies, paper 41, 1973), table 13.

Note: Columns may not average exactly because of rounding. Rates shown here are taxes as a percentage of income, including the exchange rate differential and stockholders' shares of corporate retained earnings and taxes.

However, one of the difficulties that arise if an attempt is made to increase progressive taxation is that such taxes may discourage savings and entrepreneurial efficiency. For example, an income or property tax with very high rates tends to diminish the incentive to save, which may have an unfortunate effect on investment and the growth rate of the economy. High income tax rates also create disincentives to work for people in the upper deciles of the distribution and may incline individuals and firms to conspicuous consumption once incomes reach levels at which the income tax is more than 50 percent. They may prefer to increase costs rather than give the state a large proportion of their marginal income. But an even more serious problem with direct progressive taxation is that in a country such as Colombia, with a long tradition of capital flight and easy access to tax havens, it may lead to the export of scarce capital badly needed for development.

Some indirect taxes, on the other hand, can effectively complement the traditional income tax since they can be progressive without lowering savings or causing capital flight. Administrative reform to plug tax evasion and to get at some hard-to-tax high-income groups can also shift the tax burden toward the upper-income deciles.

Nevertheless, there is a limit to how much can be done to redistribute before tax income. The Musgrave report on fiscal reform for Colombia rightly points out that "although distributional considerations are important, it is difficult to bring about a major shift in tax burden or income distribution [though tax reform]. The primary emphasis in any such effort must lie on the expenditure side of budget policy and on the over-all strategy of development planning."[4] Therefore, it is instructive to analyze the impact of public expenditure on income distribution.

Criteria for Measuring Impact of Public Expenditure on the Distribution of Income

There are no established criteria for assigning the benefits of public expenditure to individuals within the income distribution. It is necessary therefore to describe the hypotheses that have been used in this section.

4. Musgrave and Gillis, *Fiscal Reform for Colombia*, p. 33.

The theory of fiscal incidence can be summarized as follows.[5] In a private economy each individual owns a group of assets (including the capitalized value of his labor) which produce an income that determines his economic position in relation to that of all other individuals. In such an economy the individual has no way of satisfying his "social needs," defined as those needs which can be satisfied only by goods and services consumed in similar quantities by all the population. The function of the public sector is to redistribute resources of the private sector toward the provision of goods and services that satisfy these social needs. The resulting change in the relative economic position of the individual who pays taxes and receives benefits from public services is the phenomenon that must be quantified.[6]

When studying the incidence of public expenditure a distinction must be made between two types of government expenditures: transfers and expenditures on goods and services. The incidence of transfers is easy to deal with if they are treated like negative taxes since it is known roughly who benefits from them. Public expenditure on goods and services must be treated differently.

The ideal is to add to the after-tax income distribution shown in table 7.1 the benefits produced by public expenditure. Because these benefits cannot be measured, it must be assumed that they equal the costs of providing the public services. Under this assumption the benefits received by individuals from public expenditure must be added, valued at the cost of providing such services, to disposable incomes. It is therefore necessary to determine (1) the groups that benefit from these expenditures, (2) the average cost of providing those services to each group, and (3) the location of those groups within the income distribution.

For some public services it is relatively easy to determine which groups are direct beneficiaries, for example with expenditure on edu-

---

5. See W. Irwin Gillespie, "Effects of Public Expenditures on the Distribution of Income," in *Essays in Fiscal Federalism*, ed. Richard A. Musgrave (Washington, D.C.: The Brookings Institution, 1967).

6. Assuming that the public funds are well spent, the absolute economic position of most individuals (conceivably even all individuals) will rise as a result of this reallocation of resources. As indicated in the text, quantification of benefits over costs is not normally feasible, so this overall improvement from the reallocation is not reflected in the figures.

cation, hospital care, and land reform. Although these expenditures can benefit everybody as when a higher level of literacy makes possible a freer and more democratic society or when land tenure changes make possible more rapid rates of growth, they are usually incurred for the benefit of certain identifiable groups. As a reasonable approximation these costs may be added to the incomes of said groups. In the examples given, expenditures on education benefit most directly the families of the children in schools, and in the case of land reform the families of the landed peasants who receive the expropriated land.

The incidence of expenditures on public goods such as national defense, international relations, and the judiciary is more difficult to determine. These expenditures presumably benefit all of society, and it is difficult to assign such benefits to any particular group within an income distribution. In the present quantification attempt two hypotheses are used to apportion these expenditures.

In the first hypothesis, which is pessimistic concerning the real function of public expenditure, it is assumed that the expenditures of the Colombian government on general services benefit property owners exclusively. It can be argued that expenditures on justice, the army, the police, and international relations are carried out to defend the rights of property owners. This would conform to Locke's conception of law as an instrument for protecting property. In that case the expenditures on these types of services should be distributed according to the distribution of property. Because this last distribution is not available in Colombia, it is assumed that the costs of these public services can be assigned to the upper decile of the income distribution, which presumably owns most of the property in the country. This hypothesis is used to distribute public expenditures on defense, police, judicial system, congress, public debt, and diplomatic service as well as those expenditures of the ministries of communications and mining which are not covered by user rates.[7]

The second alternative hypothesis for assigning the costs of general public services assumes that these expenditures benefit all the population by the same amount. Obviously, the distribution of the

---

7. The community action program expenditures of the Interior Ministry were assigned to the five lowest deciles of the income distribution, as was the budget for local road construction of the Defense Ministry.

Table 7.3
Public Expenditures by Major Sector or Type, 1966
(Millions of pesos)

Sector	National Government	Departmental Government	Municipal Government	Total
Education and Culture	910.6	894.3	143.8	1,948.7
Public Debt [a]	968.5	82.8	346.0	1,397.3
Public Works	721.9	309.1	—	1,031.0
Development expenditures [b]	423.4	29.2	855.9	1,308.5
Defense	916.1	—	—	916.1
National Police [c]	563.3	—	—	563.3
Public Health	281.1	88.4	82.8	452.3
Justice [d]	397.5	91.3	112.3	601.1
Labor	81.8	150.4	46.4	278.6
Agriculture	235.8	32.1	—	267.9
Government procurement agencies	24.9	42.9	91.0	158.8
Congress	104.9	7.5	—	112.4
Interior Ministry	82.7	16.5	—	99.2
Municipal administration	—	—	57.0	57.0
Foreign Relations	49.5	—	—	49.5
Communications [e]	48.4	—	—	48.4
Statistics	26.8	1.5	1.3	29.6
Fiscal control	—	—	14.2	14.2
Mining	12.2	—	—	12.2
Planning	4.6	2.6	—	7.2
Civil Service	5.3	—	—	5.3
Office of the President	4.3	—	—	4.3
	5,863.6	1,748.6	1,750.7	9,362.9

Source: The data on actual expenditures were obtained from *Informe Financiero de la Contraloria General de la Republica*, vol. 3, July 1967. Because in some cases this source did not contain a detailed discrimination by type of expenditure, the budget law was used to distribute actual expenditures into expenditures according to more detailed sectors. In Colombia actual expenditures usually differ from budgeted expenditures for two reasons: (1) Some budgeted expenditures are not carried out in the fiscal year, and (2) there are some additional budgets within the year and elimination of some budgeted expenditures in order to have funds for expenditures not budgeted. The first problem is more serious.

[a] Most of the public debt is owed to foreigners, especially IBRD, IDB (Interamerican Development Bank), and AID.

[b] Development expenditure includes expenditures in research, public housing, and subsidies to electricity generating firms and local services such as water supply and drainage. Tourism promotion is also included, as well as subsidies to bus transport.

Table 7.3 (continued)

^cIn this group we included the security forces (Departamento Administrativo de Seguridad).

^dExpenditures of the Ministry of Justice, as well as of the whole judicial branch and the Ministerio Publico, are included here.

^eCommunications and Civil Aeronautics.

benefits of general public services with this methodology produces a more equal distribution of income since it increases the revenue of individuals in different income brackets by the same absolute amount. The true distribution of these benefits probably produces a less unequal distribution than that resulting from the first hypothesis, but more unequal than that resulting from the application of the second.

Other less general types of social services such as education, health, public works, and agricultural expenditures are assigned to individuals in the various income brackets according to information on the incomes of the users of these services. The following section discusses very summarily the assumptions and the information employed to assign the benefits of this second group of public expenditures to different income classes.

Distribution of Public Expenditure among Users of Public Services

Table 7.3 shows the distribution of public expenditures by all levels of government in 1966. As can be seen, the biggest item was educational expenditure. It is therefore crucial to know who benefits from this type of expenditure.

As is shown in table 7.7, which summarizes the effect of various types of public expenditures on after-tax incomes, public support of education tends to improve the distribution of income somewhat. The improvement is not greater mainly because of the elitist nature of secondary and university education. Table 7.4 illustrates how, given the set of assumptions specified in the notes, only primary education benefits the poorer sectors of the population in a significant way. Due to the very low retention rates in the system and the lack of rural schools with more than two grades, very few poor rural children have access to secondary school and higher education.

Not surprisingly, then, the middle-income classes enjoy the greatest benefits from educational expenditures. On the other hand,

Table 7.4

Distribution of Educational Expenditures by All Levels of
Government among Deciles of the Population, 1966

Percentage Distribution of Educational Expenditures

Deciles of the Population	Primary[a]	Secondary[a]	Higher[b]	All Levels
Lowest	7.9	—	0.6	5.1
Second	7.9	—	0.6	5.1
Third	7.9	—	0.6	5.1
Fourth	10.5	—	3.0	7.1
Fifth	10.5	—	3.0	7.1
Sixth	10.5	—	3.0	7.1
Seventh	13.2	18.2	3.0	12.4
Eighth	15.8	29.4	3.0	16.3
Ninth	15.8	33.2	18.7	19.7
Second Highest 5%	—	17.8	32.3	9.1
	—	1.4	32.3	5.8
Total expenditures (pesos)	969.3	302.7	265.2	1,537.2

Sources and Methodology: For the levels of expenditure the same sources were used as those described in the notes to table 7.3.

[a]The expenditure on primary and secondary education was distributed by calculating the number of children outside the educational system and those in private schools and then assuming that those outside the system in each age group belonged in the poorest deciles and those in private schools belonged in the highest deciles. Since only the children of middle-income groups reach the last years of primary schools, it is the people in these deciles who benefit the most from both expenditures on the last years of primary and from total primary school expenditures. For example, if the number of children in the third grade were only 70 percent of children aged 9, it was assumed the first three deciles did not benefit from expenditures on third grade education. (The data on the number of children in each grade were derived from DANE, *Anuario General de Estadistica, 1966*, and the estimate of the number of children in each age group came from CEDE projections for the population for 1965–1985 by age groups.)

[b]The distribution of higher education expenditures was done by comparing the level of education of the fathers of the students in public universities with the level of education of men in the 40–59 age group according to the 1964 census. Assuming a good correlation between income and education, the education of the fathers of public university students was used to assign higher-education expenditures among deciles. Thus, if in 1964 30 percent of the men 40–59 years old had no education and only 1.6 percent of students in universities had fathers with no education, it was assumed that only 1.6 percent of the expenditures on higher education could be assigned to the first three deciles of the population. The source of the data was German W. Rama, "Origen Social de la Poblacion Universitaria," *Revista de la Direccion de Divulgacion Cultural*, Universidad Nacional de Colombia, no. 3, Apr./Aug. 1969, pp. 1–33.

more expenditure on primary education would improve the services available to the poorer families and would contribute greatly to the democratization of education. If the benefits from education are greater than the costs—and there is strong evidence of this for the primary level[8]—such change in public expenditure would contribute more toward a better distribution of income than these figures suggest. The pretax distribution could improve substantially.

In table 7.7 we also distribute expenditures on cultural services such as museums and libraries. Some expenditures, for instance those on sports, radio, and administration, were distributed on an equal per capita basis, whereas for others, such as social security of teachers and food subsidies to schoolchildren, the same distribution was applied as in the case of primary school expenditures. As can be seen in table 7.7, even though a not insignificant part of educational expenditure benefits the rich, education would appear to be one of the types of expenditure that most effectively redistributes net income.

Although less important quantitatively, public health expenditures benefit the poor even more on a per peso basis than do educational expenditures. This is shown in table 7.7, column 5, and is explained by the fact that most high-income groups use private medical services and clinics, which means that most public health expenditure benefits comparatively low-income families. For the purposes of assigning public health expenditures to different income groups it was assumed that the benefits were distributed among deciles in the same proportion as the deciles were represented among the users of one of the major Bogota public hospitals. Although this assumption seems reasonable, it could be argued that expenditures on vaccination and preventive medicine benefit all the population by similar amounts. In that case such expenditures should be allocated on a per capita basis. Although such a calculation would still imply an improved distribution of net incomes, it would change disposable incomes less than the method adopted here.

Nevertheless, whatever system is used for assigning the benefits

8. See, especially, Marcelo Selowsky, "El Efecto del Desempleo y el Crecimiento sobre la Rentabilidad de la Inversion Educacional," *Revista de Planeacion y Desarrollo* 1, no. 2 (July 1969): 5–68; and T. Paul Schultz, *Returns to Education in Bogota, Colombia* (Rand Corporation, RM 5645-RC/AID, 1968).

of public health programs, it is clear that such expenditures improve the standard of living of the poor more than proportionally and are therefore an efficient redistributing mechanism.

In contrast, expenditure in the agricultural sector does not necessarily improve the distribution of net income. Land reform expenditures definitely benefit some of the poorer sectors of the population, particularly if the land is made available to the peasants at less than commercial prices. Since the basic objective of land reform is to transfer underutilized land to the peasants at less than market prices, such a program should modify the distribution of income and wealth in a more equitable direction. Unfortunately no detailed analysis of benefit incidence has as yet been done. For this study it was assumed that government expenditure on INCORA (Instituto Colombiano de Reforma Agraria), the land reform institute, benefits the lower 50 percent of the agricultural income distribution.

In Colombia, however, other expenditures in the agricultural sector have tended to benefit high-income groups. For example, the lack of an adequate extension service has meant that only well-to-do and educated farmers have received an adequate flow of information about the new seeds and methods of cultivation developed by publicly financed research activities. The same can be said of the general expenditures on agriculture since agricultural policy is usually geared to benefit interest groups that customarily represent the wealthier elements of rural society. For these reasons the expenditures of the agricultural ministry on programs other than land reform were distributed among the upper five deciles of the agricultural income distribution.

Although currently government expenditures in the agricultural sector do not improve the after-tax distribution of income dramatically, as is shown in table 7.7, column 8, this does not mean that a carefully thought-out program of agricultural investment could not increase significantly the income of the poorest sectors of the population, which are in fact located in the rural areas. An expanded land reform program could produce large income shifts to the lower deciles of the distribution, and a massive effort to communicate technical innovations in farm management to the peasants could also have a significant effect. Unfortunately, at present small landowners do not have access to fertilizers, improved seeds, and the technical advances that have been made on government experimental farms, and the land reform program has limited resources, most of which are allocated to high-cost projects that benefit few farmers.

Budget expenditures in labor affairs do not seem to improve the distribution of net income either, since the benefits are probably received by organized workers, and there are no effective labor organizations in the rural sector or among the poorest deciles of the urban population.[9] No attempt was made to distribute the burden and benefits of social security. The assumptions used to distribute the benefits of investment in public works are more controversial. Because most public works in Colombia are related to road construction, the incidence of this type of expenditure will depend heavily on the assumptions made concerning who benefits from these roads. Such investment benefits both road users and other sectors of the population. Among the first, two categories can be distinguished: owners of passenger cars and trucks. Investment on roads benefits these groups by reducing directly the cost of transport per kilometer. In the case of trucks both the owner and the consumer of transported products gain, and in the case of taxis and buses, purchasers of the service also benefit.

Part of the cost of road building also benefits the owners of land that becomes more accessible due to a new or improved road. A property gains in value as soon as it is connected more economically with the market for labor or for goods.

Although no direct study has been made in Colombia concerning the incidence of investment in roads, in the state of Louisiana (U.S.) a study of this type suggested that landowners appropriated about 25 percent of the benefits of road construction.[10] It has been assumed here that in Colombia the benefits to landowners are similar. Because there were no data available on the relationship between property ownership and income, this part of road expenditure was distributed according to the general distribution of income since

9. Labor ministry expenditures were distributed on a per capita basis according to the income distribution of members of the Social Security Institute, who make up the bulk of organized workers, and according to the number of members in each income class.

10. William D. Ross, "Financing Highway Improvements in Louisiana," quoted in Gillespie, "Effects of Public Expenditures," p. 145.

it appeared reasonable to assume that there was a strong correlation between the distribution of property and the size distribution of income by income classes.

The rest of the benefits are assigned to the direct beneficiaries of roads, that is, to the owners of automobiles, buses, and trucks and to consumers who face lower prices because of better roads. It seemed appropriate to assign to car owners a proportion of the remaining expenditure corresponding to the percentage of gasoline they consumed, since gasoline consumption presumably reflects degree of road use.[11] This expenditure would in turn be assigned to each income class according to the number of car owners represented in each income interval. The portion of road costs assigned to trucks could be assigned to the consumer on the assumption that lower transport prices are passed on to the consumer through lower transport costs.

Because of lack of data on the actual consumption of gasoline by car owners, it was assumed that because automobile ownership is highly correlated to income, expenditures that benefit car owners could be assigned according to the general pretax distribution of income. The share of road costs assigned to trucks was apportioned among consumers according to the general pretax distribution of income on the assumption that lower transport prices are passed on through lower transport costs. This method is plausible since benefits depend on the value of goods consumed, and the distribution of consumption is in turn highly correlated with the distribution of income.

In table 7.7 a further refinement is introduced by using the rural distribution to assign the costs of local roads and the urban distribution to assign the costs of public parks and street construction in the cities. In each case the proportion of total public works expenditures assigned an income class is set at the income share of that income class.

In summary, all public works expenditures were assigned to each

---

11. Gillespie, ibid., pp. 140–45, suggests one methodology, but it is not feasible here. The methodology used here for assigning the benefits of public work expenditures is probably the least satisfactory technique used for assigning different types of public expenditures in this chapter. This is an area for which future research could have a very high payoff.

income class according to its participation in total income. The justification for this was that land and vehicles are distributed in a way similar to income and that consumers, who are the other beneficiaries of road investment, also gain from such expenditure in proportion to their income. Use of the above assumptions leads to the conclusion that public works investments do not contribute to lessening of income dispersion.

So-called development expenditures (*gastos de fomento*) are quite varied in Colombia, and different assumptions were used to assign each specific type of expenditure. For example, research subsidies seem to benefit primarily property owners, although if such research increases the demand for labor this would not be true. It was decided to assign these expenditures to the top five deciles of the population. Expenditures on the development of tourism were assumed to benefit the top two deciles, who are the only ones who can afford to spend on tourism,[12] and housing subsidies were assigned according to the declared income of the people who applied for government housing. The subsidies to bus transport were distributed on a per capita basis among the poorest 90 percent of the urban population.

The largest item included in development expenditures is subsidies to local aqueducts and power companies. Since there is some correlation between the consumption of these services and income these subsidies were assumed to be proportional to the size distribution of income for the urban areas. This method of distributing the subsidies was based on the observation that some of the poor do not have connections to the aqueduct or to electricity and that the rich have more appliances which consume water and electricity. However, it could also be argued that aqueduct and sewerage systems benefit the whole population by improving health standards. In that case distributing the costs according to the distribution of urban income underestimates the redistributive potential of this type of subsidy.

In Colombia the situation is further complicated because public utilities use price discrimination to lower the consumption costs of

12. In 1964 there was a negligible amount of international tourism in Colombia, and most expenditure went to subsidizing facilities that ten years later were still being used by Colombians. If future investment attracts foreign tourism and the tourist industry is labor intensive, the impact of this type of expenditure may be more redistributive. However, there is growing evidence that the external diseconomies of tourism are large and may affect the poor more than proportionally.

the poor. Thus, as is shown in table 7.5, a unit of electricity or water is sold to the poor at a lower price than to the rich. This arrangement gives public utilities investment a greater potential role in redistribut-

Table 7.5
Public Utility Rates for Bogota Homes, 1971
(Pesos)

Cadastral Value	Aqueduct and Sewerage		Monthly Cost of Garbage Collection	Electricity[b]	
	Cost of First 15 Cubic Meters	Cost of Each Additional Cubic Meter		Consumption	Cost per Kilowatt Hour
1– 15,000	5.00	0.75	0– 5.25	0–200 kwh	$0.13
15,001– 50,000	10.00	1.00	5.25– 17.50	201–500 kwh	$0.18
50,001– 125,000	25.00	1.50	17.50– 43.75	501–700 kwh	$0.20
125,001– 200,000	40.00	1.60	43.75– 70.00	>701 kwh	$0.23
200,001– 500,000	80.00	1.70	70.00–175.00		
500,001–1,000,000	100.00	1.80	175.00–350.00		
>1,000,001	120.00	2.00	>350.00[a]		

[a]The cost is 0.35 pesos for each 1,000 pesos of additional cadastral value.
[b]Since richer families consume more electricity, this rate is also progressive.

ing net income than in other countries and also means that the assumption used here for assigning the benefits of public utility subsidies allocates too much to the high-income groups. In reality such subsidies in Colombia may improve income more than is shown in table 7.7.

The Redistributive Effect of All Public Expenditure

Table 7.7 summarizes the impact of public expenditures on the size distribution of income. As can be seen from columns 2 and 3, taxes do not appreciably affect the distribution.[13] A comparison of the distribution of pretax income (col. 2) and of net income after taxes and the receipt of public services (col. 16 and 17) does show, on the other hand, that public expenditures improve distribution and increase the proportion of goods and services consumed by the poorest two deciles of the population. This is true even under the strong

13. As mentioned previously, however, a more recent study of tax incidence suggests that under some plausible assumptions, the Colombian tax system is more progressive than appears in this table (see n. 2).

assumption that all government expenditures on general services benefit only the richest two deciles of the population (hypothesis 1).

An analysis of table 7.7 also leads to the interesting conclusion that it is precisely local expenditures, particularly on health and education, that benefit the lower-income groups. This more than compensates for the regressive nature of local tax revenues, which are largely dependent on excise taxes. Increased emphasis on social expenditures for health and education could improve still more the net distribution. Since this type of expenditure is desirable for many other reasons as well, it would seem that a greater effort in this direction is warranted even if it has to be financed from not very progressive taxes.

Such a policy would have the added advantage of increasing the importance of local governments and advancing the process of political decentralization because education and health expenditures are logically the responsibility of local governments. Table 7.6 shows that at present these levels of government are quite poor. It appears then that a tax reform priority is the strengthenng of local government finance to make the municipalities and departments capable of radically improving educational and health services.[14]

But the major conclusion from this study of the incidence of fiscal policy on net incomes in Colombia is that the structure of government expenditure would have to change radically if it were desired to diminish income dispersion substantially via that route. Even with the optimistic hypothesis 2, in which general public expenditures are assumed to benefit each person by the same absolute amount, it appears that the fiscal system only moderately increases the goods and services received by the poor. According to table 7.7 the Gini coefficient of concentration decreases only from .58 to .57 when we pass from pretax to posttax income, and to .51 after government transfers according to whether we adopt the pessimistic or optimistic hypothesis about distribution of benefits from government expenditures. Although such a decrease in concentration is not insignificant, much more can be done. It would appear that a radical shift toward social expenditures would improve the distribution both directly and indirectly: directly by providing free services to needy

14. For recommendations of this type, consult Musgrave and Gillis, *Fiscal Reform for Colombia,* pt. 1, chap. 10.

Table 7.6
Current Expenditures of All Levels of Government, 1966
(Millions of pesos)

I. General expenditures assigned according to hypotheses I and II		4,070.9
a. National expenditures	3,204.0	
b. Departmental expenditures	621.8	
c. Municipal expenditures	245.1	
II. Expenditures assigned to users of public services, all levels of government		5,292.0
III. Total expenditures		9,362.9

Sources and Methodology:
National Government

These figures are for expenditures undertaken as found in Contraloria General de la Republica, *Informe Financiero*, vol. 3, July 1967. These expenditures were distributed according to the more detailed classifications of the budget law and the additional budgets passed during the year, although budgeted expenditures do not usually match effective total or sectoral expenditures in any year. However, there was no detailed breakdown of effective expenditures. We did not include the debt subscribed with Banco de la Republica to cover the losses of the special exchange account ($970.6 million), since this is an accounting operation that did not produce any actual disbursements.

Departmental and Municipal Expenditures
They were derived from the data published by DANE.

Comparison with National Accounts
If the data in this table are compared with that in the national accounts, the unexplained differences are small.

1966	National Accounts	Our Estimates
Tax revenue	8,561.0[a]	8,412.8
Government expenditure	9,235.0[b]	9,362.9

[a]Total income less transfers.
[b]Total government expenditures less expenditures on social security.

families and indirectly by improving the chance of the children in those families to become productive members of the labor force. There is already a voluminous literature on the long-lasting and disastrous effects of child malnutrition on the physical and intellectual performance of adults. For that reason alone, vast efforts in the area of health and nutrition are needed to avoid perpetuating pov-

Table 7.7 (Part 1)
Distribution of Income after Taxes and All Transfers
(1966 pesos)

Deciles of the Population	Pretax Income (Millions) (1)	Percentage of Total Personal Income		Public Expenditures Assigned to Users (Millions of pesos)					
		Before Taxes (2)	After Taxes (3)	Education and Culture (4)	Public Health (5)	Development Expenditures (6)	Public Works (7)	Agriculture (8)	Labor Expenditures (9)
Lowest	524.7	0.9	0.9	105.5	85.8	88.5	5.1	10.1	0.7
Second	1,107.6	1.9	1.9	105.5	85.7	47.6	42.3	27.3	1.3
Third	1,574.0	2.7	2.8	105.5	89.4	5.4	38.0	36.2	7.1
Fourth	2,040.4	3.5	3.7	141.5	89.2	6.3	43.5	26.4	6.4
Fifth	2,623.3	4.5	4.6	141.5	41.8	27.2	62.2	78.2	7.6
Sixth	3,206.3	5.5	5.6	170.9	12.7	70.0	52.1	20.0	32.5
Seventh	4,372.2	7.5	7.6	259.6	5.9	144.0	79.0	12.8	36.1
Eighth	5,829.6	10.0	10.3	297.2	—	106.3	84.2	19.6	40.9
Ninth	9,035.9	15.5	15.7	357.3	—	205.4	136.4	19.6	44.2
Second highest 5%	7,578.5	13.0	12.9	166.8	—	205.4	141.8	9.2	50.5
Highest 5%	20,403.6	35.0	34.0	111.5	—	401.7	338.3	7.8	50.7
Total[a]	58,296.1			1,962.8	452.3	1,307.8	1,023.9	267.2	278.0

Table 7.7 (Part 2)

	Expenditures on General Public Service[b]		Percentage of Total Expenditures		Income after Taxes plus Expenditures		Percentage of Personal Income after Taxes plus Expenditures	
	I (10)	II (11)	I (12)	II (13)	I (14)	II (15)	I (16)	II (17)
	6.9	409.3	3.23	7.53	761.2	1,163.6	1.28	1.96
	11.4	413.8	3.48	7.73	1,289.1	1,691.5	2.18	2.86
	13.6	416.0	3.15	7.45	1,705.5	2,107.9	2.88	3.56
	11.1	413.5	3.45	7.75	2,151.6	2,554.0	3.63	4.31
	4.1	406.5	3.87	8.16	2,634.4	3,036.8	4.45	5.13
	—	402.4	4.14	8.43	3,183.2	3,585.6	5.37	6.05
	—	402.4	5.81	10.11	4,356.8	4,759.2	7.35	8.03
	—	402.3	5.92	10.21	5,695.8	6,098.1	9.61	10.29
	2,012.0	402.3	29.66	12.47	10,620.1	9,010.4	17.93	15.21
	1,005.9	201.2	16.88	8.28	7,991.0	7,186.3	13.49	12.13
	1,005.9	201.2	20.46	11.88	18,857.5	18,052.8	31.83	30.47
Total	4,070.9	4,070.9			59,246.2	59,246.2		

Sources and Methodology: The sources and methodology used are summarized in the text and are presented in some detail in Miguel Urrutia and Clara Elsa de Sandoval, "Politica Fiscal y Distribucion del Ingreso en Colombia," *Revista del Banco de la Republica* 44, no. 525 (July 1971): 1,072–86.

Note:

I : It is assumed that with a few specific exceptions these costs are distributed between the richest two deciles of the population.

II: General public expenditures are assumed to benefit everyone in a similar way and are therefore distributed on an equal per capita basis.

[a]Owing to rounding, some of the totals are not the same as in table 7.3.

[b]General public services includes expenditures of the Interior Ministry, Foreign Affairs, Justice, Defense, Police, Congress, Tax Collection, the Presidency, Planning, Statistics, the Civil Service, Government Procurement, Communications, and other services.

erty. As will be shown in the next chapter, it also appears that in the case of education universal access may improve both future income distribution and the growth potential of the economy.

But it remains true that, although some improvement in income distribution can be achieved through fiscal policy, a significant modification of income dispersion cannot be expected from this avenue alone. It will also require ambitious structural changes to alter fundamentally the supply and demand of the factors of production. We now turn to a consideration of some policies that may have this effect.

8

Income Distribution and the Distribution of Education

As discussed in the previous chapter, if the benefits of education are assumed to be equal to costs, public expenditure on education in Colombia tends to improve the size distribution of income by providing free services to less well-off families. (The cost figures furnish the basis for the estimates of benefits to various income groups discussed in chap. 7.) Although the redistributive effect calculated in this way is not negligible, it may still understate the true decrease in income dispersion that results from giving easier access to education to all children and thus fundamentally changing the supply of skills in the economy. This would be the case if the average benefits in terms of additional future earnings plus the consumption component of education exceed the costs of investment.[1] The object of this chapter is to show to what extent the total benefits derived by poor families from certain types of education exceed the costs of providing such services.

If knowledge or, in more technical terms, human capital, is thought of as a factor of production, it is easy to see how changes in its supply will alter the distribution of income. The free supply of education implies an important transfer of capital toward families

---

1. Assuming that benefits of public education equal costs may be interpreted as implying that joint consumption and investment benefits equal costs. In fact, as will be shown here, several rate-of-return studies have indicated that returns to primary education in the form of greater earnings alone imply a very high rate of return. Adding any consumption benefits makes the case still stronger. And even in cases where marginal benefits and costs are equal, it would be expected that total benefits exceed total costs since benefit per peso spent would presumably be a declining function of total expenditures.

with low incomes. The classical economists discussed the problem of distribution in terms of capital, labor, and land, and partly owing to lack of detailed statistics, they were forced to assume that landowners and capitalists were rich and employees were poor. Given these assumptions, the problem of distribution was discussed in terms of the distribution of total production among salaries, rents, and profits. But the statistics available reveal that in Colombia the wide disparity in salaries is a primary cause of the high concentration of income. Furthermore, as in most developing nations, the proportion of salaried workers in the labor force is growing and there is evidence that labor income has increased as a proportion of national income. It thus becomes very important to study the determinants of the differentials in labor income.

This chapter analyzes the distribution of labor income and attempts to determine the extent to which the level of formal education, used as a proxy for learned skills, explains the differences in labor income.

The Distribution of Labor Income

Evidence on the dispersion of labor income can be obtained from social security statistics.[2] In Colombia all employees of medium- and large-scale firms are members of the Social Security Institute, but few farm laborers or employees of small and craft industries belong. The social security statistics do not therefore reflect the full range of labor income, since they exclude a large group of low-wage laborers; but even with this proviso in mind, the degree of income concentration shown by the data is impressive. In figure 8.1 we compare the income distribution among persons affiliated with social security in England and in Colombia.[3] As will be readily seen, the distribution of income in Colombia is much less equitable than that in England.

The more unequal distribution of property in Colombia may explain some of the greater concentration of labor incomes, but only to the extent that members of wealthy families obtain high salaries by

2. ICSS, *Informe Estadístico del año de 1969*, data for Dec. 31, 1969, p. 25.
3. The English data refer to a survey of all persons affiliated with social security, published in "Result of a New Survey of Earnings in September 1968: Part I. Distribution of Earnings by Occupation, Age and Region," *Employment and Productivity Gazette* 77, no. 5 (May 1969): 400–15.

Income Distribution and the Distribution of Education

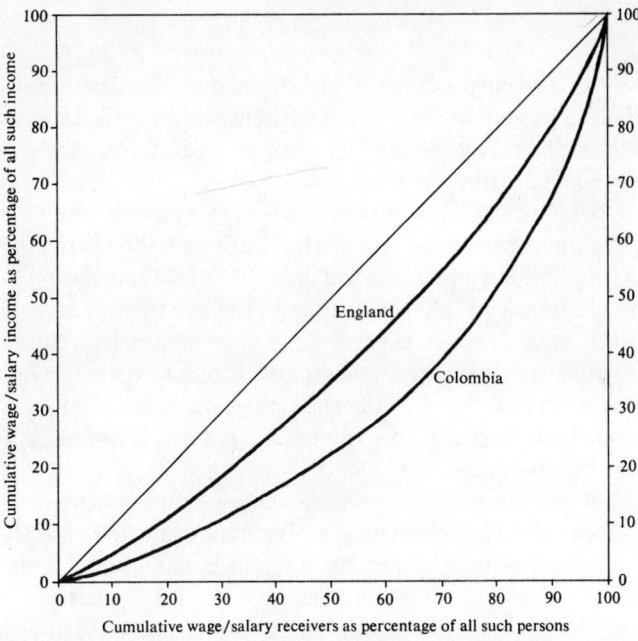

Fig. 8.1. Lorenz curves for wage/salary income in Colombia and England.

working in their own or family business or in highly paid jobs acquired through family connections. Undoubtedly, some high-prestige and high-salaried jobs do go to people with the "right" family background and connections, and firms often find highly paid jobs with not very useful functions for family members. However, it would appear that average wage differentials among occupations depend primarily on other factors.

Although some observers of the Colombian scene might not agree, the society we are analyzing does have some social mobility, and job recruitment is based to a considerable extent on ability and skills. One could argue that the most highly valued abilities and skills are not the most functional for development, but it is still very telling that in many private firms and in the public sector recruitment is often made on the basis of objective tests and that in the private sector jobs tend to have fairly strict educational requirements.

Distribution of Abilities

One of the principal determinants of income distribution is the distribution of abilities in a society. There are people with a greater ability for generating income than others, and this leads inevitably to an unequal distribution of income.

The economic ability of a person has various components. In the first place an individual when born has intrinsic abilities. In addition to the child's "intelligence" (and there is much controversy as to how intelligence can be measured and even whether it can be compared among individuals), his health, his emotional stability, and even his aggressiveness are all determinants of his eventual economic success. If any of these characteristics, some entirely biologically determined, are unequally distributed in a society, it can be expected that income distribution will also be unequal.

Psychologists have come to the conclusion that intelligence can to some extent be inherited. Although the nature–nurture controversy goes on, there is little doubt that inherited intelligence is an important determinant of economic and academic performance.[4] Although there is no agreement on the usefulness of the various measures of intelligence, it has been found that performance on IQ tests reflects a series of characteristics that are positively related to economic success in industrial societies. If intelligence as measured by IQ tests may to some degree be inherited, at least one major determinant of income distribution is biologically determined.

This theory might lead to the somewhat frightening conclusion that through biological inheritance the same families might remain in the top income brackets for generations even if the sole determinant of income were ability. However, the phenomenon of sibling regression toward the mean population IQ guarantees that no intelligence caste can be created. On the contrary, the observed differences in IQ among socioeconomic classes in developed countries

4. Arthur R. Jensen states that "the heritability of individual differences in intelligence within the white population is so well established by a number of independent studies—to the effect that genetic factors are about twice as important as environmental factors as a cause of individual differences in IQ—that this conclusion is now generally accepted by scientists who are familiar with the evidence" [*Educability and Group Differences* (London: Methuen, and New York: Harper & Row, 1973), p. 125].

are largely dependent on social mobility, which makes possible the concentration of high-IQ people in the high-income, high-status occupations.

Jensen describes this phenomenon as follows:

> Social classes are breeding populations differing in gene frequencies, especially for genetic factors related to ability and very likely for the genetic component of those personality traits which favor the development, educability, and practical mobilization of the individual's intellectual potential. But there is considerable mobility between social classes which works against their becoming castes. In fact, if social classes rigidified into castes at some period in history, genetic intelligence differences between them would most likely be reduced, since all of the IQ variability arising within classes in each generation would remain as within-class variance. A high degree of social mobility correlated with ability, on the other hand, in each generation "converts" a substantial proportion of the within-class variance to between-class variance. Thus, classes separated by more than two or three steps in the socioeconomic status (SES) hierarchy can in time undergo wide separation in the distribution of genetic factors related to ability. This trend increases the closer we approach to equality of educational and occupational opportunity and the more that SES mobility reflects ability factors rather than inequalities in opportunity.[5]

This genetic model would suggest a greater concentration of high IQs in the upper socioeconomic status occupations in developed countries than in underdeveloped countries, where clearly there is less social mobility and less educational opportunity. Since these high-SES occupations have the highest incomes, one should expect labor-income dispersion to be smaller in underdeveloped countries if IQ were the major determinant of that income. Because the opposite is true, and in Latin American countries it appears that high income and power are to some extent inherited from generation to generation, the ability factor alone must not be dominating the determination of labor-income dispersion.

5. Ibid., p. 152.

An environmental explanation of economic ability may play a role in the greater dispersion of labor income in these developing societies. The environment in which a child is brought up is definitely a determinant of economic ability (although apparently not more important than inheritance). As Burt has put it, in addition to what a child might learn, the permanent contact with an intellectual environment can stimulate his latent abilities and create a more effective motivation, a greater interest in intellectual activity, and habits of speed, care, and diligence in work.[6] It is clear that the personality of a child who grows up in a home where education and language proficiency are highly valued and where certain types of achievement are rewarded will be such as to make successful economic performance easier. The kind of environment that gives a child the opportunity to develop those personality traits useful for economic success is much more frequently found among the better-off families. The correlation between income and this type of environment produces some similarity between the distribution of useful abilities and of family income. The home environment can thus contribute to perpetrating an unequal distribution of income and can facilitate the partial inheritance of high socioeconomic status occupations even in societies with reasonable social mobility based on economic ability.

In summary the unequal distribution of economic ability, which is correlated to scholastic achievement, probably causes some degree of income dispersion in all societies with job recruitment on the basis of merit. However, since there is no evidence of a greater dispersion of IQ or abilities in developing countries such as Colombia than in developed societies,[7] the distribution of intelligence cannot explain

---

6. Quoted in Harold Lydall, *The Structure of Earnings* (Oxford: Clarendon Press, 1968), pp. 83–84.

7. The controversial studies described by Jensen do suggest that the IQs of the Negro population in the United States show less variance than those of whites. Although the racially heterogeneous Colombian population could conceivably produce greater IQ variance than that found in the developed countries, this is unlikely, and even if true would explain only an insignificant amount of the greater degree of income dispersion found in the country. For the Jensen data see the source quoted in n. 4 and A. R. Jensen, "How Much Can We Boost IQ and Scholastic Achievement?" in Stephen Wiseman, ed., *Intelligence and Ability*, 2d ed. (Baltimore, Md.: Penguin Books, 1973), p. 277.

the much higher levels of labor income concentration found in Latin American societies.

The Effect of Age and Sex on Labor Income Distribution

Another factor in labor-income dispersion is the age and sex dis-distribution of the labor force. A worker's income varies over his career because experience on the job tends to increase productivity; accordingly younger people generally have lower incomes. On the other hand, advanced age impairs the capacity for physical work, leading to relative poverty among some older groups.

In table 8.1 these tendencies can be observed in the case of Bogota workers. For all educational levels incomes increase up to the 50-year-old cohort. From this age on, incomes decrease, especially for uneducated workers who are usually manual workers and whose productivity is by then negatively affected by reasons of health. A positive correlation between the rate of increase of income through time and educational attainment can also be observed in table 8.1. While the incomes of illiterate workers increase 56 percent between the 20–24 and the 35–39 age groups, the comparable income increase for university graduates is 92 percent. People with greater formal education (and possibly with greater ability, as reflected in good performance in the educational system) are either better able to benefit from experience or are in jobs where experience tends to pay off more.

Wage differentials among age groups are, then, one determinant of income dispersion, which will be more unequal the greater the number of young people (say below 25 years) with low incomes. Above a certain age, although income continues to be related to age, it varies less. The majority of the labor force is found in this age range, and the younger workers essentially constitute a lower tail to the labor-income distribution; the bigger this tail, the bigger the overall variance. This situation may account in part for the greater income concentration found in developing countries, which have higher rates of population growth and younger populations than the industrialized nations.

The sex composition of the labor force also affects the size distribution of income. Women have an average income substantially

Table 8.1
Bogota, Income per Hour of Salaried and Independent Male Workers, 1963–66
(1966 pesos)

Schooling in Years	10–14	15–19	20–24	25–29	30–34	Age 35–39	40–44	45–49	50–54	55–59	Total
Illiterate	1.00	1.04	1.46	1.82	1.84	2.23	2.05	2.31	2.16	2.30	1.95
	(1)	(24)	(15)	(23)	(33)	(50)	(19)	(41)	(24)		(240)
1 Primary	0.81	0.92	2.36	2.10	3.13	2.82	2.46	2.78	2.18	2.62	2.45
	(4)	(13)	(25)	(28)	(29)	(28)	(15)	(19)	(17)	(2)	(180)
2 and 3 Primary	0.42	1.48	2.64	2.87	2.83	2.86	4.20	2.71	3.89	5.25	2.78
	(42)	(154)	(213)	(218)	(171)	(162)	(153)	(110)	(82)	(35)	(1,340)
5 Primary	0.80	1.63	3.30	4.21	4.10	4.70	5.00	5.85	6.00	7.63	4.12
	(20)	(234)	(312)	(339)	(289)	(259)	(192)	(154)	(122)	(61)	(1,982)
1 and 2 Secondary		3.48	4.40	5.48	5.56	5.50	6.69	5.97	4.96	11.44	5.05
		(124)	(166)	(141)	(113)	(96)	(42)	(44)	(27)	(11)	(764)
3 and 4 Secondary		3.50	4.51	6.90	10.15	9.62	11.00	10.91	14.40	21.25	8.26
		(52)	(139)	(134)	(89)	(86)	(72)	(58)	(36)	(29)	(695)
6 Secondary		3.88	7.04	11.60	16.45	18.88	21.14	21.36	22.85	(35)	16.18
		(9)	(81)	(111)	(94)	(71)	(67)	(52)	(56)		(576)
1 and 2 University		6.1	7.83	13.12	25.41	20.00	20.00	18.57	26.20		14.46
		(2)	(37)	(31)	(17)	(13)	(1)	(7)	(1)		(109)
3 and 4 University			10.40	14.63	27.00	20.72	27.36	29.62	32.00		21.22
			(13)	(47)	(30)	(22)	(22)	(8)	(8)		(150)
5 and 6 University			16.48	21.67	22.84	31.71	29.16	25.73	32.00		25.48
			(25)	(47)	(86)	(66)	(31)	(38)	(33)		(362)
All levels	0.56	2.13	4.32	6.90	8.52	8.64	9.28	8.84	10.84	911	7.14
	(67)	(612)	(1,026)	(1,150)	(951)	(853)	(614)	(531)	(406)	(188)	(6,398)

Source: Data from CEDE unemployment surveys taken from Marcelo Selowsky, "El Efecto del Desempleo y el Crecimiento sobre la Rentabilidad de la Inversion Educacional," *Revista de Planeacion y Desarrollo* 1, no. 2 (July 1969): 5–68.
Note: The figures in parentheses represent the number of observations.

lower than that of men. (Table 8.2 shows the distribution of income in Bogota according to sex in 1967.) The reasons are varied, ranging from fewer hours worked per week to more frequent job changes and pure discrimination. In any case, given this fact, income concentration tends to be greater the higher the proportion of women in the labor force (within the relevant range). They, like the young, constitute a tail of low-income earners.

Table 8.2
Employed Persons in Bogota, by Income Group and Sex, April 1967

Monthly Income Group (Pesos)	Accumulated Percentage of Men	Accumulated Percentage of Women	Accumulated Percentage of Men and Women
0– 499	25.2	64.1	39.4
500– 999	58.4	81.9	66.9
1,000–1,999	82.0	96.5	87.2
2,000–4,999	95.0	99.2	96.4
5,000 and more	100.0	100.0	100.0

Source: CEDE, *Encuestas Urbanas de Empleo y Desempleo,* Apendice Estadistico, July 1969, table OC5C.

Changes in the sexual composition of the labor force may affect income dispersion through time. An increase in the proportion of women generally increases income dispersion by adding people to the lower-paid occupations. A major occupation for women in Colombia is (low-paid) domestic service.

Schooling as a Determinant of Labor Income Distribution

As suggested above, unequal distribution of investment in human capital is probably one of the most important causes of the dispersion of labor income. Under this label we include formal and informal schooling, on-the-job training, and adult education.

It is clear that personal performance depends to a certain degree on the individual's stock of knowledge: if knowledge is unevenly distributed, the income distribution will tend to be unequal. The relationship between income distribution and informal education (the process of keeping up to date on the technical advances of a profession or occupation through reading, refresher courses, or group discussion) is hard to analyze owing to the difficulties in quantifying this type of investment. The stock of formal schooling held by individuals in the labor force can more easily be quantified, and substantial empirical work has been done on the income–schooling relationship.

A recent formulation of the effect of education on income distribution is that of Jacob Mincer.[8] In the model he develops he assumes that individuals will increase their schooling only if they expect that the additions to their future incomes due to such schooling will compensate for the private costs incurred and the income not earned during the period of study.[9] This process implies that the lifetime earnings of educated workers will be greater than those of the uneducated. The formal model can be summarized as follows.

Suppose there are two individuals with levels of formal schooling a_1 and a_2 and with n_1 and n_2 years of working life. The income differential is the difference between the present value of the lifetime earnings of the two individuals. Using continuous discounting, the present value of earnings of two individuals with a_1 and a_2 years of schooling can be written as follows:

$$PV\ a_1 = \frac{1}{r}\ Ya_1 e^{-ra_1}\ (1 - e^{-rn_1})$$

$$PV\ a_2 = \frac{1}{r}\ Ya_2 e^{-ra_2}\ (1 - e^{-rn_2}).$$

When the present values are equated to find the income differential Ya_2/Ya_1, we obtain as a first approximation

$$D = \frac{Ya_2}{Ya_1} = \frac{e^{-ra_1}\ (1 - e^{-rn_1})}{e^{-ra_2}\ (1 - e^{-rn_2})}, \tag{1}$$

where r is the rate of discount or internal rate of return of the investment, Y is income, a is years of schooling, and n is the number of years of working life.

---

8. "The Distribution of Labor Incomes: A Survey with Special Reference to the Human Capital Approach," *Journal of Economic Literature* 8, no. 1 (March 1970): 1–26.

9. There is some evidence that educated persons tend to obtain more goods and services from any given amount of income by rationalizing their consumption expenditures. This benefit from education is never included in the rate-of-return studies, which usually consider only the benefits represented by income differentials.

To simplify formula (1)[10] it is supposed that there are no differences in the length of the working life of individuals,[11] (i.e., it is assumed that $n_2 = n_1 = n$). Moreover, it may be assumed that individual 1 has no education and that individual 2 has a years of study. Making the respective substitutions in the equation, we find that the income differential is determined by the number of years of schooling of individual 2, that is,

$$\frac{Ya}{Yo} = e^{ra}. \qquad (2)$$

Equation (2) shows in a simple manner that income differentials are determined by the number of years the individual postpones his salary in order to increase his schooling. The labor income of an individual with some schooling is equal to that of an individual with no education times a function including the multiplicand of the rate of return and the level of education attained. Equation (2) can further be transformed into

$$\log Ya = \log Yo + ra \log e. \qquad (3)$$

Unless the assumption of perfect competition is made, the rates of return need not be equal to the market rate of interest and may differ among individuals.

Although some people doubt that equation (2) describes a true cause-and-effect relationship, there are good common sense and theoretical arguments for believing that it does. (In a later section of this chapter we shall go into the doubts expressed with respect to the investment in human capital approach.) Of particular interest here is the implication of the above equations that both the skewness of the distribution and the degree of dispersion of salaries will be greater, the greater the dispersion in years of schooling per worker. Furthermore, both dispersion and skewness will be larger when the rate of return is higher.

10. The formula seems complicated because the system of continuous discounting is used. The better-known formula for obtaining present value is $Y = a/(1+r)^n$, where Y is the present value of a in n years when the interest rate is r. If the interest is capitalized continuously, $Y = ae^{-rn}$. By using lifetime earnings, Mincer does not have to include any special variable for income not earned during the years in school.

11. There is some empirical evidence suggesting that the length of working life of individuals tends to be equal, and therefore this assumption seems realistic.

Thus, if education is unequally distributed and the rate of return in the economy is high, both of which conditions are common in developing countries like Colombia, a high degree of concentration of labor income is to be expected. This is well reflected in figure 8.1.

Nominal interest rates in Colombia range from 15 to 28 percent, and even when corrected for inflation it appears that from 1967 to 1973 real rates of interest would be in the range of 5–18 percent. Arnold C. Harberger estimated an average rate of return for capital of 8–10 percent in 1967.[12] All this points to high rates of return in the economy. Also, as in most countries with low average levels of education, the distribution of education in Colombia is very skewed and the concentration of schooling in a relatively small group is much more marked than in developed countries.

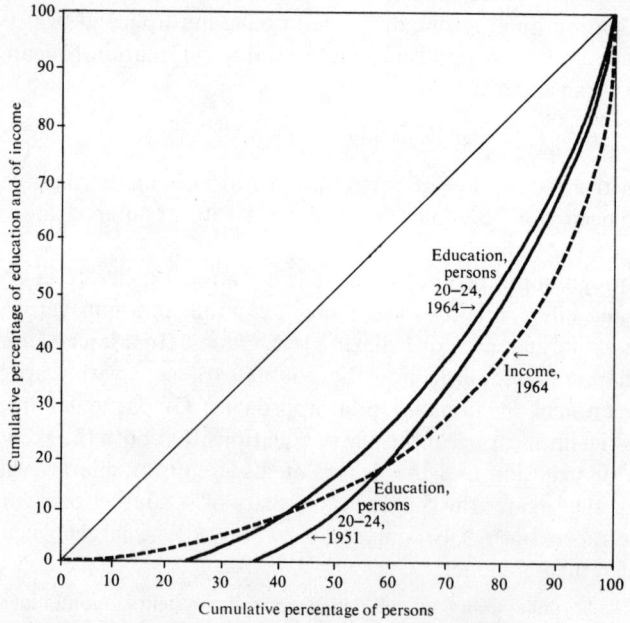

Fig. 8.2. Lorenz curves for income of the labor force and education of 20–24-year-old population.
Source: Tables A4 and A5 and chap. 2.

12. "La Tasa de Rendimiento del Capital en Colombia," *Revista de Planeacion y Desarrollo* 1, no. 3 (Oct. 1969): 13–42.

Income Distribution and the Distribution of Education

If, as suggested by the Mincer model, the distribution of schooling is a major determinant of the distribution of labor income, it is useful to try to measure the distribution of schooling in Colombia. Figures 8.2 and 8.3 show the distribution of total years of schooling of the population according to census results. Each year is given the same unit value without differentiating among primary, secondary, and university education.[13] The two graphs demonstrate a very uneven distribution of the stock of education in Colombia with no substan-

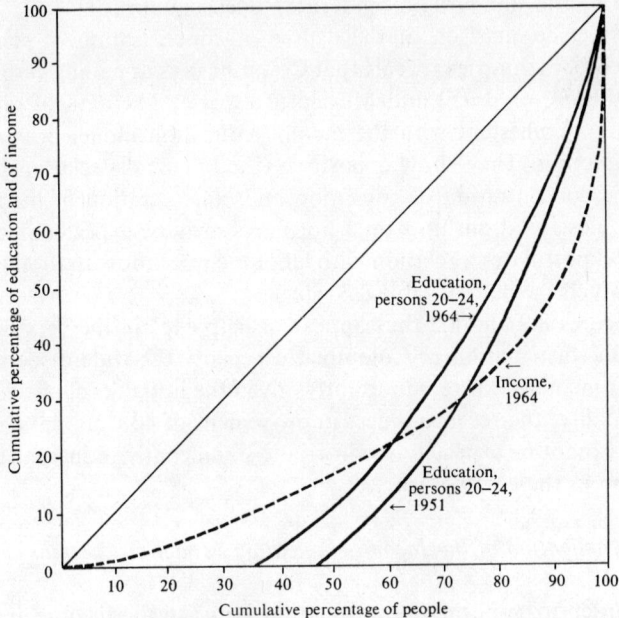

Fig. 8.3. Lorenz curves for rural income and for education of the 20–24-year-old population living in rural areas. Sources: See reference in tables A4 and A5.

13. These graphs may underestimate (or overestimate) the concentration of education because it could be argued that a more appropriate quantification would weight differently by grade in the educational ladder, either by cost or by benefits. If costs are taken as the criterion for the weights, the higher years (e.g., university) would be weighted higher than lower years (e.g., primary). If, as in Colombia, the returns on higher education are less than those at the primary level, it could be argued that university education should be given less weight.

tial improvement between 1951 and 1964. Although inequality was soemwhat less by 1964, in the rural areas it had hardly improved, especially when all age groups and not just the young 20–24-year-old group is considered. The overall improvement reflected in figure 8.2 is largely due to the greater weight of the urban areas in 1964. Figure 8.2 also compares the 1964 Lorenz curve for income distribution with the 1951 and 1964 Lorenz curves for the distribution of education in the 20–24 age group. The latter distribution is as unequal as the income distribution, which as we have seen is extreme even by the standards of underdeveloped countries.[14]

Direct comparison of the degree of concentration of schooling with other countries reveals that Colombia's is appalling (table 8.3). Only those of Brazil and Mexico are worse. The data of table 8.3 are also consistent with the income–education model discussed in this section. They show a positive (though weak) relationship between concentration of education and concentration of income. A very close relationship would not necessarily be expected, since the model postulates a relation with labor income, not with total income (to which the data of table 8.3 refer).

Figures 8.2 and 8.3 thus appear to help explain the very unequal income distribution in Colombia, especially the wide dispersion of labor incomes. More importantly, given the initial level of schooling inequality, the recent modest improvement of educational distribution cannot be expected to contribute significantly to income equalization in the coming years.[15]

Application of the Income–Education Model to Colombia

In order to confirm the correlation between the income and education distributions in Colombia and to quantify the implications

14. Since in one case we measure the concentration of years of schooling and in the other that of income. This comparison is only suggestive since the factors measured are quite different.

15. Note that one should not expect ever to have completely equal levels of education among the labor force. There are different attitudes to education, and even if there is access to schools for all, some people will prefer less education than others, among other reasons because they have different preferences concerning the distribution of income through their working lives. This in turn would lead to income differences among people of the same age reflecting the preferences of individuals rather than implying differences in welfare.

Table 8.3
Concentration of Education and Income

Country		Income Concentration Coefficients, Active Workers [a]	Coefficients of Concentration of Education, Men 25–64 [b]
United Kingdom	1951	0.40	0.18 [c]
Japan	1960		0.24 [d]
United States	1960	0.40	0.29
Canada	1961		0.30
Hungary	1960		0.33
Israel	1961		0.37
Argentina	1947	0.48	0.45 [e]
Chile	1960	0.46 (families)	0.54
Mexico	1960	0.53 (families)	0.68 [f]
Brazil	1950	0.52	0.78 [g]
Colombia	1964	0.57	0.62 [h]

Sources and Methodology

[a] See Table 3.5.

[b] Harold Lydall, *The Structure of Earnings* (Oxford: Clarendon Press, 1968), tables 7.1 and 7.2, except for the Colombian coefficient, which was calculated directly. The coefficients were calculated by generating a Lorenz curve for the distribution of schooling, but in this case each year of education was not given a unit of value. Lydall valued 1–4 years of schooling at 0.75, 5–8 years as 1 unit, 9–12 years as 1.5 units, 13–16 years as 2 units, and 17–20 years as 2.5 units per year of schooling. The principle behind this scale is that each year of schooling costs the child and his parents a certain amount of forgone income and some fees, and such costs increase as the level of education increases.

[c] Men and women in the labor force.

[d] Men of 25 years and over.

[e] Men 20 years and over.

[f] Men 30 years and over.

[g] Men 25–59.

[h] Men 15–59. If illiterate men are not included in the population, and it is not clear whether Lydall includes them in the case of the other countries, the coefficient will be 0.78.

of lack of access to education for large segments of the population, it is necessary to turn to studies that estimate the rate of return to investment in education. Fortunately, there are at least two good empirical studies along these lines. They confirm a very significant statistical relationship between income and years of schooling even when age, sex, and other socioeconomic variables are held constant. Marcelo Selowsky, for example, obtained high rates of return for education after adjusting for the effect of unemployment and participation in the labor force.[16] (Owing to the relatively low participation rates of educated women, these adjustments lower the rates of return relative to those calculated for people actually in the labor force.) Table 8.4 summarizes results obtained by Selowsky. Paul Schultz independently studied rates of return for Bogota,[17] and his results are quite comparable to those of Selowsky. Table 8.5

Table 8.4
Internal Rate of Return of Investment in Education, Men and Women, 1963–66
(Percent)

	Without Adjustment		Adjusted for Participation		Adjusted for Participation Rates and Unemployment	
	Men	Men and Women	Men	Men and Women	Men	Men and Women
3 years primary over illiterates	35	38	33	32	29	26
5 years primary over 3 years primary	30	42	28	38	28	30
5 years primary over illiterates	33	40	31	33	29	28
3 years secondary over 5 years primary	18	23	19	20	18	18
6 years secondary over 3 years secondary	29	24	31	23	31	24
6 years secondary over 5 years primary	23	24	23	21	23	21
3 years university over 6 years secondary	7	6	7	(neg.)	8	(neg.)
5 years university over 3 years university	(neg.)	13	(neg.)	9	6	10
5 years university over 6 years secondary	6	8	6	6	7	6

Source: Marcelo Selowsky, "Efecto Desempleo y Crecimiento," tables 4, 5.

16. "El Efecto del Desempleo y el Crecimiento sobre la Rentabilidad de la Inversion Educacional: Una Aplicacion a Colombia," *Revista de Planeacion y Desarrollo* 1, no. 2 (July 1969): 5–68. Given the data sources used, the Selowsky estimates really apply only to urban Colombia.

17. T. Paul Schultz, *Returns to Education in Bogota, Colombia* (Rand Corporation, RM 5645-RC/AID, 1968).

Table 8.5
International Comparison of Rates of Return to Investment in Education
(Percent)

Levels of Education	Bogota 1965 Schultz Study[a] Private Rate of Return	Bogota 1965 Schultz Study[a] Social Rate of Return	Colombia Selowsky Study[b] Urban Private Rate of Return	Mexico, 1963 Private Rate of Return[c]	Chile, 1959 Social Rate of Return[d]	Puerto Rico, 1959 Urban Private Rate of Return[e]	India 1960-61[f]	USA, 1959 Private Rate of Return for Blacks[g]
Primary in relation to illiterates	18	15	29	45	24	28	17	22
Secondary in relation to primary[h]	34	27	23	15-17	17-29	14	12-14	16
University in relation to secondary	5	3	7	40	12	15	10	10

Source: T. P. Schultz, Returns to Education in Bogota, Colombia (Rand Corporation, RM-5645-RC/AID), table 9, except the third column, which is taken from Selowsky.

[a]Men in Bogota.

[b]Men, urban areas. Internal rate of return after adjustment for participation and unemployment.

[c]Men: Martin Carnoy, "Rates of Return to Schooling in Latin America," Journal of Human Resources 2, no. 3 (Summer 1967): 359-74.

[d]Men and women: Arnold Harberger and Marcelo Selowsky, "Key Factors in Economic Growth in Chile," paper presented at Cornell University Conference on Economic Problems of Latin America, 1966.

[e]Men: H. R. Carby Samuels, "Income and Returns to Education in Puerto Rico" (University of Chicago, 1965), mimeographed.

[f]Men: A. M. Nalla Gounden, "Investment in Education in India," Journal of Human Resources 2, no. 3 (Summer 1967): 347-58.

[g]Men: Giora Hanoch, "An Economic Analysis of Earnings and Schooling," Journal of Human Resources 2, no. 3 (Summer 1967): 310-29.

[h]In some countries the calculations were made for secondary education and intermediate education with respect to primary and for secondary with respect to intermediate schooling. In those cases two rates appear.

includes the two Colombian estimates and rates of return on educational investment calculated for several other countries.

As can be seen from both tables, the internal rates of return to investment in education are very high in Colombia, except for university education. They range from 26 to 30 percent in primary school according to Selowsky and are still 15 percent in the most conservative estimate by Schultz. Such rates compare favorably with the return to most private investment (5–18 percent) and with the 8–10 percent average rate of return on physical capital in the Colombian economy, as calculated by Harberger.[18] The range of estimated rates of return for secondary education is 21–27 percent, also much higher than the average return on financial investment. Both studies, on the other hand, find relatively low rates of return for investment in university education, the range being from 3 to about 8 percent.

This empirical work confirms that disparities in the distribution of education (in years of schooling) will produce a high level of labor-income dispersion. Because education is in fact very unevenly distributed (figs. 8.2 and 8.3), it is very likely that this imbalance is a leading cause of the high concentration of labor incomes.

Criticisms of the Education–Income Model

At this point it may be useful to mention that, although considerable evidence supports the income–education model, the relationship is probably not so simple as it appears in equation (2) or in most of the models used to calculate rates of return. For example, some recent data for developed nations show no clear relation between changes in the distributions of education and income. A country such as France shows that a high degree of income concentration can coexist with a quite egalitarian distribution of education (table 8.6). However, the experience of the developed countries may not be very relevant for our study.[19] Since the concentration of education is quite

18. "Tasa de Rendimiento." Eduardo Sarmiento finds such a rate reasonable. See his "Crecimiento Economico y Asignacion de Recursos," in Hernando O. Gomez and Eduardo D. Wiesner, eds., *Lecturas sobre Desarrollo Economico Colombiano* (Bogota: Fedesarrollo, 1974), p. 198.

19. It is interesting to note that in both Colombia and the developed nations listed in table 8.6 the Gini coefficients of concentration of education are smaller

Table 8.6
Relationship between Income and Educational Inequality

Country	Coefficient of Income Concentration	Coefficient of Concentration of Education
Canada 1961	.38	.21
France 1962	.51	Women .16–Men .17
Holland 1950	.41–.45	.18
1962	.43	.17
United States 1950	.38	.22
1960	.37	.19

Source: OECD (Organization for Economic Cooperation and Development), "Conference on Policies for Educational Growth: Education and Distribution Income," background study no. 11 (Paris, 1970).

low in most of these countries, it is not particularly surprising to find that a further decrease in this concentration should not bring a parallel diminution of income concentration. Actually, in developed countries the dispersion in total income will be more a function of the distribution of assets, and the distribution of education could become a less important determinant of income inequality. In summary, education is not an all-powerful tool for redistribution policy. To some extent future earnings will still be determined by the wealth of the family and the material and environmental advantages the individual receives before entering school.

But the lack of correlation shown in empirical studies in some developed countries between changes in the two distributions can also be questioned on methodological grounds. For example, the index of concentration used for schooling does not take into account the greater costs of university education and the methods used in financing it. Many observers (e.g., Meade) have argued that in the past the increase in public elementary education in developed countries has been an important factor in the equalization of incomes. It was an investment with a high rate of return financed by general taxes and benefiting all citizens.[20] The same author goes on

---

than those of income. Although not comparable, since they measure different factors (education in one case and income in the other), one should expect this relationship between the coefficients because labor income should be less concentrated than total income.

20. Cited in OECD, Conference on Policies for Educational Growth, technical reports related to background study no. 11 (Paris: OECD, 1970), pp. 21–22.

to say that public higher education may have the opposite effect since in general it benefits a group with high incomes. In a study on this subject Hansen and Weisbrod[21] arrive at the conclusion that in the United States an increase now in public higher education might affect equity in an undesirable direction. Thus the income-distribution effect of greater equality in schooling may be very different in countries with different average levels of education per person, and it is likely that the distributional impact of educational investment will be greater in poor countries, particularly if much of the additional effort is put into primary schools.

Other criticisms have been leveled at the use of the education–income model to explain income differentials in underdeveloped nations. It has been maintained that the high positive correlation between schooling and income may be spurious, a result not of education causing higher incomes but of education being an income-elastic consumption good, so that the rich tend to be highly educated. In that case the causal relationship goes from income to education and not in the opposite direction.

It is also possible that the children of rich families obtain education partly for reasons of prestige and have high incomes from wealth or from jobs in family firms. If this is so, the correlation between education and income would be spurious. Furthermore, if access to education is limited, it may also be possible to use the level of schooling as a tool of discrimination. Education would then be a mechanism for identifying the social origins of the individual and would be used as a criterion for remunerating work. If either of the above charges were true, doubt would arise as to the appropriateness of postulating a simple causal relationship between investment in education and income.

Another possible explanation for the relationship between education and income is that in a country with unemployment, education can be used as a screening device for selecting candidates to fill the few highly paid jobs in the modern sector. In this way education

---

21. W. Lee Hansen and Burton A. Weisbrod, "The Search for Equity in the Provision and Finance of Higher Education," in OECD, ibid. Public investment in higher education may worsen income distribution if it is financed by regressive taxes and if it benefits primarily the members of well-off families. In a country such as Colombia this may also happen with secondary education.

does not increase incomes, it is merely the cost of the screening systems of employers who pay noncompetitive wages, and this cost is transferred to the state by the employers. If the state provides more education, the employers will simply raise their minimum standards for hiring, and the social benefit of increasing education becomes questionable.

This is not the place to review the arguments for and against the economic explanation of the correlation between education and earnings, since it has been done very well by others.[22] However, it may be useful to mention a few characteristics of the Colombian labor market that tend to support the impression that labor-income differentials are largely explained by the levels of formal education of different individuals. First of all, there is some evidence of general social mobility[23] and of a relatively high degree of occupational mobility.[24] These two phenomena would weaken the sociological explanation that most of the correlation between education and income is explained by the fact that the children of the rich receive more schooling than the children of the poor and that they later earn more only because they had more other advantages in life.

Although some of the observed rate of return on investment in education may be due to such a correlation between social class origins and education, the degree of mobility in Colombian society makes it unlikely that this should explain all the high rates of return observed. In other developing nations with social structures similar to that of Colombia (such as Mexico and Puerto Rico) it has been found that education does raise earnings even if we hold constant the father's occupation and the father's and mother's education.[25]

Another interesting feature of the Colombian labor market (related to high unemployment rates) is the great degree of job security found in the modern sector. Most people enter a firm and remain in it for long periods of time (turnover rates are about 50 percent of those

---

22. Mark Blaug, *Education and the Employment Problem in Developing Countries* (Geneva: International Labor Office, 1973), chap. 3.

23. See, for example, Fernando Guillen Martínez, *Raiz y Futuro de la Revolucion* (Bogota: Ediciones Tercer Mundo, 1963), and Miguel Urrutia, *The Development of the Colombian Labor Movement* (New Haven: Yale University Press, 1969).

24. See R. A. Berry, "On Occupational and Sectoral Mobility in Colombia" (mimeo, 1973) for a summary of the evidence.

25. *Education and Employment*, p. 34.

in the United States). Owing to legal and economic difficulties in laying off personnel and also to a paternalistic attitude, firms replace high-level vacancies with people lower down in the hierarchy, not with outside workers or executives. There is a lifetime commitment to the firm characterized by increased pay per number of years in the firm and a high ratio of fringe benefits to basic wages (at least 1:1 in most large firms). In these circumstances on-the-job training for specific tasks is very important, and firms hire workers with high formal education in order to be able to train them on the job in preparation for quite different tasks imposed by vertical mobility within the firm and by changes in demand for specific jobs due to technological change and product demand changes. In such a labor market it is not surprising that employers should place much value on formal education, since it facilitates further on-the-job training.

In the Colombian context the conclusion reached by Blaug concerning the value of education seems especially pertinent.

> Employers pay highly educated people more, even when their education has taught them no specific skill, because they are more achievement-motivated, are more self-reliant, act with greater initiative in problem solving situations, adapt themselves more easily to changing circumstances, assume supervisory responsibilities more quickly, and benefit more from work experience and in-plant training.[26]

Although in most countries it would appear that the economic value of education resides principally in certain social and communication skills imparted to students and only secondarily in the formation of specific skills, this would appear to be particularly true in Colombia because of the structure of the labor market. For that reason formal education is greatly valued by employers, and the correlation between years of formal education and income is quite high.

This is further confirmed by the fact that parents of all income classes consider the education of their children the only means of providing them with high incomes and a good job in the future. People generally believe that the important thing is the degree received or number of years of education, and they place less emphasis

26. Ibid., p. 38.

on the quality of schooling. This, along with the financial constraints of most families, has contributed to the proliferation of private universities and schools of dubious quality. Although the value assigned to education may be due in part to the desire for social prestige, the high cost and great importance of private education suggest that people desire schooling for more practical purposes as well. Such a great demand for private education in order to obtain prestige would be plausible only if discrimination was such that the prestige bestowed by schooling were a prerequisite for high incomes.

Viewing the issue pessimistically, one must conclude that this may indeed be the reason for the great demand for education. If educational achievement is used as a screening device for assigning the few high-income jobs in the economy, it will have a high return to the individual who manages to increase his education more than the average, but a general increase in education will not increase the income of the society as a whole. However, in Colombia, where even fairly primitive technical innovations have not been widely adopted, it is hard to believe that more education would not raise productivity. Also, because the educated self-employed earn more than those in the same occupational category who are uneducated, it is difficult to accept a theory that postulates education as only a useful screening device for modern high-wage employers.

The high correlation between years of schooling and income despite the widely varying quality of schools also suggests that a policy of expanding enrollment in primary schools would promote income redistribution even if no broad-ranging reform of curricula or school administration is carried out. In fact there is evidence from other countries to suggest that when nonschool variables are held constant, no relationship is found between academic performance and those school characteristics that have usually been considered to have significant influence on such performance. For example, the level of expenditure per student, the teacher/student relationship, the size of the class, and so on have been found to be uncorrelated with academic performance.[27] Vernon goes as far as to state that "there is rather little evidence of the effects of different kinds of schooling, or of studying different subjects in different ways, on general mental growth. But it is clear that sheer amount of schooling, even—in back-

27. OECD, *Conference on Policies for Educational Growth*, pp. 10–11.

ward countries—of low-quality education, helps to promote both school achievement and the kind of reasoning measured by nonverbal tests."[28]

The importance of the above finding, which seems to fit the Colombian case, lies in the fact that it makes the simple expansion of primary education a useful redistributive tool. This is significant because a major barrier to any effort at expansion of schooling is the argument that such a policy is useless unless the educational system is reformed and curricula and programs are redesigned to meet the specific needs of a developing economy like Colombia. Those who oppose fiscal reform to advance education have successfully used this argument though they have been unable to quantify those needs convincingly. But if it can seriously be maintained that curriculum reform is not crucial in training people for work in most jobs, it may be easier to convince policymakers of the desirability of an increasing effort to expand public school expenditure. This type of policy is relatively easy to implement in developing nations, where it is harder to improve the quality of schooling than to raise the quantity.

Democratization of Education and Income Distribution

Formal education is of course only one of the determinants of income differentials. People with the same schooling have different incomes due to different abilities and different levels of on-the-job training and informal education. The rate of return on educational investment may also vary according to the capacity for using the knowledge received and according to the degree of technical change in certain industries or occupations. But in general it can be expected that democratization of education would diminish income differentials. Other desirable but less easily quantifiable effects can also be expected. Generalized access to education will make a society more open, will facilitate social mobility, and may lead to lower rates of population growth[29]—all characteristics likely to improve the quality

28. P. E. Vernon, "Types of Social Structure of Values," in Wiseman, ed., *Intelligence and Ability*, p. 302.

29. Fertility rates vary inversely with education, and in Colombia there is some evidence that in regions where a greater proportion of children is in primary schools, the rates of population growth are lower. Greater access to education makes having children more expensive [see R. R. Nelson, T. P. Shultz, and R.

of life in developing societies. It is also probable that a more equal distribution of education will facilitate political development.

In addition it is likely that increased expenditure on primary education will increase the long-term growth prospects of the Colombian economy. As discussed, the rate of return to investment in primary and secondary education is very high, well above the average for investment in physical capital. In such circumstances a program of universal primary education will yield more growth with greater equity. Rechanneling some expenditure on university education toward primary education would have the same effects. It would improve the distribution of education and the growth rate would rise because the rate of return on primary and secondary education is greater than that on higher education.[30]

In summary, increased public expenditure on primary education will directly improve the distribution of consumption by subsidizing the consumption component of the educational expenditure of poor families, as shown in the previous chapter. And if the rate of return studies are valid, a policy of increasing and democratizing the supply of education will improve the distribution of income and consumption, and will lead to higher rates of growth, lower rates of population expansion, and possibly an acceleration of political development. It is difficult to see what other policy could have a more dramatic impact on the welfare of the population.

Slighton, *Structural Change in a Developing Economy* (Princeton, N.J.: Princeton University Press, 1971), pp. 21–22].

30. Greater access to primary and secondary education might also improve the rate of return of university education by allowing more able students to reach the universities.

9

The Financial Sector and Income Distribution

Historically there has been a popular belief in most developing countries that the financial sector is an instrument used by the rich to maintain their dominance of the economy. In the United States, for example, at the time that economic development was starting to accelerate, Andrew Jackson, a popular president, feared the concentration of power brought about by the growth of private banking. In 1833 in a letter to Polk, Jackson wrote that whoever knew him well would be aware that he had always been opposed to the United States Bank, in fact, to any bank.[1] He also claimed that although banks are useful as agencies for handling deposits and transfers, he did not think that the benefits they thus produced were sufficiently large to compensate the evils they caused, such as the creation of conditions that led to an *artificial* inequality of wealth and therefore an *artificial* inequality in the distribution of power. Jackson was convinced that if the existing system of paper money were extended and perpetuated, the great majority of the working class would have to abandon all hope of acquiring property.[2]

The leftist government of Chile under President Allende carried out the nationalization of the banking sector, and a major point of the recent common program of the socialists and communists in France for the 1973 elections was the nationalization of the part of the banking system that still remains in private hands. In France the financial sector has been in disrepute with large sections of the populace for many decades.

1. Arthur M. Schlesinger, Jr. *The Age of Jackson* (Boston: Little, Brown, 1945).
2. Ibid., pp. 78–79.

The intellectual tradition of opposition to the banking sector is also strong. Thorstein Veblen maintained that the leisure class, in which he explicitly included occupations related to financial dealings, lived off the industrial community instead of being a productive part of it.[3] Karl Marx was more radical when he wrote: "The emancipation of the proletariat is the abolition of bourgeois credit, since it means the abolition of bourgeois production and the bourgeois order."[4] In his *Class Conflict in France in 1848–1850,* Marx holds that "the closing of the bank of France would have been the deluge which would have wiped out immediately from the soil of France the financial aristocracy, the most powerful and dangerous enemy of the republic, the golden pedestal of the July monarchy."[5]

In summary a considerable segment of popular and intellectual opinion believes that the financial sector in a capitalist economy tends to concentrate both incomes and power. On the other hand neoclassical economics assigns to financial markets a vital role in the efficient distribution of resources and in economic growth and therefore considers the development of financial intermediaries indispensable for the improvement of the material welfare of a society.

Even if the conclusion of neoclassical theory that efficient capital markets could make an important contribution in nations at a stage of development equivalent to that of Colombia, financial markets are notoriously imperfect and monopoly in this sector may enable financial intermediaries to promote income concentration.

Functions of the Capital Market in a Developing Nation

The capital market and financial intermediaries may contribute to economic development in two ways. First, they may facilitate an increase in savings and therefore of funds available for investment above the level that would exist in the absence of specialized financial

---

3. Thorstein Veblen, *The Theory of the Leisure Class* (New York: Mentor Books, 1963), pp. 155–64.
4. Karl Marx and Friedrich Engels, *Obras Escogidas* [*Selected Works*] (Moscow: Editorial Progreso, 1966), p. 138 (translated from the Spanish by the author).
5. Ibid., p. 139.

institutions. For this to be true, it must be assumed that in the absence of these institutions, individuals would save only the amount of funds that they could place directly and would have less incentive to save than when specialized intermediaries offer financial instruments tailored to the particular situations and needs of different savers.

The second, and probably more valuable, contribution of the financial sector is to improve the allocation of resources among potential investors. This increases the average rate of return to capital and thus the growth rate of the economy at any given level of savings.[6] In short, the capital market contributes to development as long as it helps to channel savings to those who use resources best.

This last aspect is very important because it has been shown that countries with similar levels of savings can have considerably different rates of growth. Even though, as has been suggested in chapter 8, investment in physical capital is not the only determinant of growth, it is to be presumed that some differences in growth rates of countries with similar savings/GNP ratios are due to differences in the efficiency with which those savings are allocated.

Although under certain conditions an efficient distribution of savings is achieved when funds are assigned to the most profitable enterprises, in other cases high private rates of return do not reflect high social payoff. In those cases the state should intervene in the market to channel resources toward activities whose social rate of return is greater than the private rate.

In developing countries imperfections both in the financial sector and in industry tend to cause an inefficient distribution of investment funds that benefits highly protected monopolistic industries and producers closely connected with financial trusts. Often these activities have high private but low social rates of return.

Serious imperfections in many developing nations, especially since World War II, have been the rationing of credit, regulated interest rates and exchange rates, and diverse types of social legislation, all of which tend to push investment funds toward capital-intensive enterprises. Many economists have considered these imperfections

6. Raymond Goldsmith, *Financial Structure and Development* (New Haven: Yale University Press, 1969), pp. 394–95.

an important cause of growing unemployment in these countries, even during relatively rapid GNP growth.[7]

In the following sections the functioning of the Colombian capital market is described, and an attempt is made to determine how financial policies and foreign exchange management have affected the distribution of income.

Public Control of the Colombian Financial Market

In Colombia the monetary and exchange authorities have had substantial powers of intervention in money and exchange markets since the 1930s. Exchange control and import licensing have been a more or less permanent feature of the economy since September 1931, the controls having been eliminated or relaxed only in the short periods of high coffee prices. Monetary authorities, on the other hand, obtained wide powers of intervention in money supply only in the early 1950s. However, by 1973 the Junta Monetaria and the Central Bank had all the powers of intervention necessary to ensure control of monetary and exchange markets. In the area of exchange controls, regulation is so complete as to require the Junta Monetaria to establish monthly limits to the value of import licenses approved and to require all foreign loans to be approved by the Exchange Control Office. In addition the Central Bank in effect fixes the exchange rate because all foreign exchange must be surrendered to the bank within short periods after exports take place, and the bank is therefore the only legal seller of foreign exchange. Since only a small proportion of imports can as a rule be effected without an import license, the demand for foreign exchange is administered with some effectiveness. In contrast, the supply can only be influenced indirectly and with a lag, through changes in the exchange rate and quantum limitations on foreign credits.

In the monetary area the powers of intervention of the authorities are also extensive. Besides having broad powers to impose manda-

7. Such an interpretation is placed on this phenomenon in Colombia by the International Labor Organization. See ILO, *Toward Full Employment: A Program for Colombia* (Geneva, 1970), and Departmento Nacional de Planeacion, "El Empleo en Colombia: Diagnostico y Recomendaciones de Politica," *Revista de Planeacion y Desarrollo* 2, no. 2 (June 1970): 143–298.

tory liquidity ratios on both bank assets and liabilities, the Junta can also impose quantitative limitations on the growth of different types of credit and can limit all types of rediscount. The government also has the power to put limits on interest rates, but for political reasons they are almost always fixed at very low or negative levels in real terms. Hence monetary management is seldom attempted through interest rate policy, and the authorities must concentrate almost exclusively on direct controls designed to maintain a certain desired level of money supply.

In short, the functioning of money and foreign exchange markets is anything but free in Colombia. A proof of the importance of state intervention is that in the last two decades Colombians have almost always lived with black market exchange rates and rates of interest.

The purpose of this chapter is to compare the effects on income distribution of monetary and exchange policy as carried out by the authorities with the effects of allowing the free market to determine to a greater extent both interest rates and exchange rates.

The problem with this approach is that developing countries have very little experience with free financial and exchange markets. The comparison therefore tends to be made with respect to how free markets are supposed to function in a tidy neoclassical world. In fact, public attitudes toward financial markets are to some extent justified, and it is probable that monopoly elements in the financial market would produce results quite different from those predicted by neoclassical economics if the state decided to allow such markets to function in complete freedom. The most useful comparison is therefore with monetary and exchange policy that gives a greater but still limited role to prices as a mechanism for allocating foreign exchange and savings. Thus the analysis involves a comparison of the distributional effects of administered prices versus more or lesss freely determined interest and exchange rates.[8]

8. It would be very interesting to ascertain the effects of the financial sector on income distribution in Mexico and Brazil. In these countries financial policy in the 1960s tended to allow interest rates and foreign exchange rates to follow fairly closely demand-and-supply conditions. Although it appears that this situation has contributed to higher rates of growth in these countries through a better allocation of investment, it is also true that high rates of growth may have been accompanied by a deterioration in the distribution of income. It would be worth-

Distortions Caused by Monetary and Exchange Policy

Any system of rationing or direct controls can cause distortions in the flows of funds that lead to a greater concentration of income. In the first place, in a mixed economy they are inclined to encourage the establishment of markets parallel to those controlled. For example, if a limit is put on interest rates paid on savings by banks, some savers will lend in the extra-bank market at greater rates of interest or will take their money out of the country to invest it with international intermediaries which pay higher rates. In both cases it is the rich who have access to the parallel market so only they are able to avoid the controls. In these markets the unitary costs of transactions tend to be high and therefore can only be absorbed by those who mobilize large sums per transaction. As a result the rate of return on capital will be greater for the rich than for the poor. Moreover, parallel markets may be harmful from the point of view of growth as well as distribution. In a capital-poor country such as Colombia the flow of savings abroad is particularly harmful.

Rationing systems affect distribution in other ways. If interest rates are controlled and not allowed to go above a certain level, the large financial intermediaries, which must comply with the regulations, will ration credit directly and will inevitably place less emphasis on the profitability of the enterprises concerned and more on guarantees, friendships, and so forth. In these circumstances it has been found that credit goes to the largest enterprises (better guarantees, larger deposits, lower costs of managing their accounts), and small enterprises have difficulty in obtaining even working capital. With interest rates controlled, banks also prefer to lend to importers because they can increase the effective rate of interest with the commissions usual in foreign trade, such as those for opening letters of credit, making transfers, and conducting foreign exchange operations. Thus even if additional imports are prejudicial to the growth of the economy, interest rate policy may channel funds preferentially to that activity.

---

while to study to what extent the freeing of financial markets has contributed to both growth and income dispersion.

Foreign Exchange Management

It is likely that exchange rate management in Colombia has brought more rather than less concentration of income. The overvalued exchange rate of recent decades (certainly before 1970) probably caused some concentration of income for the following reasons.

1. The overvalued exchange rate led to a distortion in the relative prices of the factors of production. It implied a subsidy both to capital and to imported goods in general, which in turn caused the adoption of capital-intensive and import-intensive production processes and lowered the demand for labor.

2. Import controls may also have encouraged the maintenance of excess capacity in industry since, faced by uncertainty of supply conditions for capital goods, industry is inclined to import more capital and to hold larger inventories than otherwise necessary in order to assure an orderly production process in a country where labor legislation prohibits temporary layoffs of workers. The existence of excess capacity and high inventories of imported goods implies a less than optimum utilization of capital and therefore greater rates of unemployment than would be the case if exchange rates were more realistic.

3. Import controls, made imperative by overvalued exchange rates, also produce monopoly profits for those importers who manage to obtain import licenses in times of scarcity. In fact, it has traditionally been the practice at times of exchange difficulties to assign import licenses on the basis of the past record of imports. Although the system provided a rough criterion for determining the nonspeculative needs of importers, it guaranteed that the biggest and most traditional importers receive the licenses and make monopoly profits on them.[9] Since in times of foreign exchange scarcity the internal prices of imported goods will increase because of a decrease in supply but importers can buy them at a constant exchange rate, profits will be

---

9. In 1969 an investigation revealed that small importers had their licenses approved less often than larger importers. This also happens because those in charge of licensing can more easily reject licenses of small producers than of large industrialists with access to the press and political connections.

substantial. It is therefore not surprising to find that great fortunes in Colombia have been made by families connected with import businesses.

4. If exported goods are generally associated with labor-intensive production processes, an overvalued exchange rate implies a lower demand for labor and lower labor income than would have existed with more realistic rates.

Foreign trade controls have been used in Colombia primarily as an instrument for maintaining an overvalued exchange rate, and the principal beneficiaries appear to have been large-scale manufacturing and industrial enterprises and importers.[10]

Monetary Policy

Monetary policy as practiced in the last two decades has probably also contributed to the extremely unequal distribution of income. As in the case of exchange rate policy the most dangerous aspect of monetary policy from this point of view has probably been the maintenance of an unrealistic price for capital through interest rates regulated at unrealistically low prices.

As happens in many underdeveloped nations, government policy on interest rates has been dominated by the desire of politicians for a "just" interest rate. The view that interest rates are prices whose function, like that of commodity prices, is to help achieve an equilibrium between the supply and demand for money has not been widespread.

Interest rates have been controlled because politicians fear they will lose popularity if they "allow usury to flourish," but also because many policymakers, often closely identified with private business interests, are convinced that low interest rates promote investment and therefore employment creation and growth. Paradoxically,

---

10. A situation can be envisaged in which, owing to instability of coffee prices, exchange controls and import licensing would be appropriate in Colombia. Given the low internal price elasticity of some nonessential imports and the lags between import and export response to exchange rate movements, it cannot be expected that large deficits due to decreasing coffee prices be solved rapidly through devaluation. That import licensing may be a necessary tool under Colombian conditions is no reason, however, for its being used to preserve a systematically overvalued exchange rate.

this policy has probably had the opposite effects from those expected and has fostered concentration of income, underutilization of capacity, and growing unemployment as well.

The establishment by the monetary authorities of interest rate ceilings (see table 9.4) on loans made by banks and controlled financial intermediaries has, for the reasons noted above, had the effect of concentrating credit in the hands of large enterprises and large proprietors. Artisans, small industry, and small agricultural producers have had almost no access to institutionalized credit facilities. This situation is very serious from the point of view of employment creation since these sectors have the lowest capital/labor ratios and correspondingly the greatest employment potential per unit of savings. For example, the few credit programs tailored to the requirements of medium and small industry have reported ratios of investment per worker ten times lower than the average investment per additional worker in industry as a whole, which averaged 384,000 pesos of 1969 for the period 1958–1967. Thus in 1969 on the average one job was created for every 26,000 pesos in loans to small and medium-sized industry.[11]

Whereas these data show the contribution that small and medium industry could make to employment creation and to improvement in the standard of living of the poorest sectors of the population,[12] table 9.1 illustrates the extent to which credit has been concentrated in Colombia (it shows that most loans are quite large). Table 9.2 demonstrates that these loans, as might be expected, are concentrated overwhelmingly among wealthy individuals and large enterprises. According to income tax data, fewer than 30,000 persons (or less than 1 percent of the labor force) declared gross assets over 500,000 pesos (see table 9.3). Although it is likely that in tax returns assets will be undervalued while they will be inflated in credit requests, the degree of concentration shown in table 9.2 is still impressive. Comparison of the two tables also exaggerates credit concentration since table 9.2 probably includes both individuals and enter-

11. Genaro Payán López and John Eddison, "El Impacto del Credito sobre el Empleo en la Pequeña y Mediana Industria," *Revista del Banco de la Republica* 43, no. 517 (Nov. 1970): 1,623–24.
12. Small industry tends to use less-skilled workers than those found in large enterprises.

Table 9.1
Outstanding Loans of the Banking System in November 1970
(Total value by size of loan in pesos as a percentage of total bank loans)

	Total	To 5,000	5,001 to 10,000	10,001 to 15,000	15,001 to 50,000	50,001 to 100,000	100,001 to 150,000	150,001 to 300,000	300,001 to 500,000	500,001 and More
Commercial banks	100	2.8	2.9	2.5	18.3	14.5	5.8	14.7	9.3	29.2
Development banks[a]	100	5.8	4.0	5.0	17.1	14.4	6.9	11.4	7.1	28.3
Agricultural Credit Bank	100	15.7	10.5	5.7	18.9	7.9	3.4	4.3	1.5	32.1
Mortgage Bank	100	0	0	0.1	6.1	21.2	18.7	53.3	0.2	0.4
Banking system	100	5.3	4.0	3.4	16.9	14.1	7.0	15.9	6.7	26.7

Source: Unpublished study by the Superintendencia Bancaria.
[a] Includes Bancos Cafetero, Ganadero, and Popular. These banks are similar to any state commercial banks, but they were founded with the aims, respectively, of facilitating loans to the coffee sector, to cattle owners, and to relatively poor urban families. (The data for the Banco Ganadero are for June 1970.)

Table 9.2
Classification by Gross Assets of the Users of Credit, November 1970
(Percentage of credit in pesos received by individuals and firms in each asset group)

	All Asset Groups	To 10,000	10,001 to 20,000	20,001 to 50,000	50,001 to 100,000	100,001 to 300,000	300,001 to 500,000	500,001 and More
Commercial banks	100	2.3	0.9	2.2	3.0	8.2	7.9	75.5
Development banks[a]	100	0.6	2.3	3.1	2.8	7.8	7.6	75.8
Agricultural Credit Bank	100	4.2	4.0	9.7	11.2	14.7	6.1	50.1
Mortgage Bank	100	1.0	2.1	8.5	14.2	30.2	15.6	28.4
Banking system	100	2.1	1.8	4.2	5.3	11.3	8.3	67.0

Source: Superintendencia Bancaria.
[a]Banco Ganadero not included. For definition of these banks see note *a* of table 9.1.

Table 9.3
Gross Assets and Number of Taxpayers in Processed Tax Returns for 1967
(Millions of pesos)

Gross Asset Brackets	Bogota		Medellin		Other Administrations		Total	
	Number of Taxpayers	Gross Assets	Number of Taxpayers	Gross Assets	Number of Taxpayers	Gross Assets	Number of Taxpayers	Gross Assets
Up to:								
.02	110,552	429	59,623	1	222,903	42	393,076	462
.1	71,717	3,612	37,320	1,982	146,956	7,481	255,993	13,075
.5	38,416	8,060	22,493	4,731	67,481	13,863	128,390	26,654
1.0	5,239	3,606	3,365	2,345	8,259	5,672	16,863	11,623
5.0	3,325	6,163	2,338	4,439	4,794	8,743	10,457	19,345
10.0	171	1,134	160	1,101	260	1,734	591	3,969
50.0	53	865	42	582	75	1,203	170	2,650
100.0	—	—	2	119	3	182	5	301
Total	229,473	23,869	125,343	15,300	450,731	38,910	805,547	78,079

Source: Finance Ministry tabulations.

Note: The table does not include all taxpayers but a large proportion of them. In 1967, 1.4 million tax returns were received from individuals, of which about 66 percent were taxable (895,000). Nontaxable persons presumably have assets of less than 20,000 pesos.

Table 9.4
Rates of Interest of Some Financial Assets of Families

Financial Assets	Annual Rate of Interest			Conditions
	1963	1966	1969	
Savings deposits	4.06	4.06	4.06	Payable on minimum balances
Stocks of financial institutions	15.9	3.9	33.4	Dividends plus capital gains
Profits of corporations divided by their paid-in capital.	19.4	18.5	20.8	
Investment in extra-bank market (1971)	—	—	24.0	In general deposits of less than $10,000 are not accepted. Some intermediaries have 20,000 pesos and 50,000 pesos minimum.
Mortgage Bank bonds	8.1	8.1	11	Interest is tax exempt.
Government development bonds	9.2	9.2	12	Interest is tax exempt.

	1961	1962	1963	1964	1965	1966	1967	1968	1969	1970
Growth rates of consumer prices (blue-collar workers)	5.5	6.1	35.4	8.5	14.3	12.7	7.0	6.4	8.7	6.3

Sources: Banco de la Republica, *El Mercado de Capitales en Colombia* (Bogota: Editorial Andes, 1971), various chapters, and calculations by Urrutia, based on DANE and Banco de la Republica data and on personal surveys. Also Joaquin Pombo, "Algunos Aspectos del Mercado Libre de Dinero en Colombia," *Revista del Banco de la Republica* 45, no. 539 (Sept. 1972): 1,574–98.

prises. But because the ownership of large enterprises is also highly concentrated, the low proportion of credit given to individuals and small companies with few assets still seems to be a good indicator of credit concentration.

In addition to channeling funds to large enterprises, thereby facilitating growth in those sectors with the highest capital/labor ratios, subsidized interest rates may also have induced the adoption of capital-intensive methods of production.

Taking these two effects into consideration, the net effect of interest rate subsidies on labor demand may be significant.[13] It is also possible that capital-intensive industries have higher rates of saving than small producers and that therefore in the long run growth of the former will increase the level of savings. However, it is not clear that this is the case in Colombia, whereas there is no question that concentrating resources on capital-intensive industries will mean lower incomes for the great mass of unskilled labor and greater concentration of income.[14]

However, interest rate controls have not only affected the uses of funds but also the sources of funds. The law has kept interest rates on savings artificially low, both by direct controls and by requiring savings institutions to invest most of their funds (80 percent) in low-yielding fixed-interest securities of the government.[15]

For many years before 1973 the interest rate paid on savings deposits was 4 percent on minimum balances, which gave an average return of 3 percent. This was a negative real rate of interest, given Colombian inflation. Table 9.4 shows interest rates on the most widely used saving schemes compared to the rates of price increase in the

13. This subsidy is substantial in some years. For example, in the year ending in June 1973, inflation reached rates of 21–25 percent a year, while the interest rate ceiling on most bank loans remained at 14 percent. In such cases the real interest rate is negative and the subsidy large.

14. It is interesting to note that large industrial firms, which have easy access to import licenses and receive subsidized credit, also have higher capital/labor ratios than those found in medium and small firms in the same industries.

15. Before 1973, 25 percent of deposits had to be invested in Mortgage Bank papers yielding 11 percent, 32 percent in agricultural bonds and housing bonds yielding 6 percent, 10 percent in paper yielding 11.5 percent, and another 10 percent with yields of 10.5 percent. In addition, they had to keep as liquidity 3 percent of deposits at no rate of interest with the Central Bank. The average yield of 80 percent of deposits was therefore only 9.6 percent.

1960s. As can be seen, the lowest yield was for savings deposits, which are the only saving instrument used by the poorer sectors of society. Because in the early 1970s people in the lower deciles of the income distribution had no access to institutionalized credit and had to go to the extra-bank market where rates paid averaged around 26 or 28 percent per year,[16] the 4 percent paid on their savings implied a net transfer of resources from the poor to the rich.

Table 9.4 also shows that more sophisticated investors could obtain much higher returns on their savings. If they invested in stock in the early 1960s they earned dividends plus capital gains on the order of 33 percent in some years. Investment in government bonds produced three times more than savings deposits and the yield was tax exempt, thus producing higher benefits for the rich than for the poor.[17] Furthermore, except for stocks, most of the high-yield investment of the sophisticated investors had complete liquidity guaranteed by the Central Bank, thus eliminating all the risk element from the high-yielding investments.

The net transfer of wealth from the poor to the rich due to negative rates of interest on popular savings schemes may have been substantial because these deposits are limited to people with few assets. The average deposit in 1969 was 578 pesos (see table 9.5). It should be kept in mind that in 1969 $578 was equivalent to the average salary of an unskilled agricultural laborer for 30 days.

Since during the period under consideration a realistic nominal interest rate for savers would have been at least 12 percent (rate of inflation plus 4 percent) but low income savers received only 4 per-

Table 9.5
Number and Size of Savings Deposits, 1963, 1966, 1969

	Savings Deposits (Millions of pesos)	Number of Accounts in December	Average Size of the Accounts (Pesos)
1963	1,047	3,341,849	313
1966	1,725	3,893,457	443
1969	2,670	4,621,645	578

Sources: Banco de la Republica and Asociacion Bancaria.

16. See Joaquin de Pombo, "Algunos Aspectos del Mercado Libre de Dinero en Colombia," *Revista del Banco de la Republica,* Sept. 1972, p. 1,580.

17. Given the Colombian income tax rates, an 11 percent tax-exempt bond is equivalent to a taxable bond yielding 16–22 percent per year.

cent, in this sense government policy concerning yields on saving deposits deprived them of a yield of about 8 percent each year, equivalent to a total of $213.6 million in 1969. A decrease of more than half the income of the average saver means a serious decrease in the income of an old person who, having been a low-income worker, is trying to survive partly on past savings.[18]

Low interest rates on such savings are not only a subsidy paid by families with relatively low incomes to the state and to the beneficiaries of the programs financed with the funds, but they also tend to discourage private saving and therefore affect economic growth and employment negatively.

Management of the External Debt

The large amounts of external credit obtained by Colombia in the last two decades, necessitated by a chronic current account deficit (caused largely by overvalued exchange rates), has also probably had an undesirable effect on income distribution. To facilitate this discussion it is useful to distinguish between private and government credit.

Owing to the more or less permanent current account deficit, the authorities have actively encouraged private indebtedness in foreign exchange.[19] Nevertheless, the effects of this policy have often been unexpected. In periods of exchange difficulties, when it becomes necessary to follow a restrictive monetary policy to avoid increases in the demand for imports, the large traditional importers and manufacturing industries with access to foreign credit for financing imports can get around the local credit restrictions. Thus they not only consolidate their monopolistic positions (and obtain monopoly profits on the sale of imports or import-intensive local goods when the supply of them decreases) but also frustrate balance-of-payments stabilization programs. At the same time the creation of substantial foreign liabilities for the private sector has precipitated serious

---

18. An old worker living on savings of $150,000 has his income reduced from $18,000 to $6,000 a year by this interest rate policy.

19. Starting in 1970 an effort has been made to limit this type of indebtedness, but unfortunately it has been done in order to allow greater public indebtedness at a time when growing net international reserves pose a serious threat to stable money supply growth.

exchange crises when, owing to a deteriorating trade balance, foreign financial institutions ceased to roll over credits. The typical case was the 1957 crisis, when payment of the short-term private debt had to be renegotiated with foreign lenders by government representatives. Table 9.6 shows the growth of foreign indebtedness as a source of funds in the recent past.

Table 9.6
Colombia: Net Assets by Sectors
(Percent)

	Families	International Sector	Financial Sector	Banco de la Republica	Total (Millions of pesos)
1962	76.5	22.7	0.8	—	20,269
1963	73.9	19.1	7.0	—	24,631
1964	74.1	23.7	2.2	—	29,118
1965	75.7	23.5	0.8	—	33,137
1966	74.2	24.3	1.1	0.4	39,664
1967	70.7	28.7	0.6	—	47,408
1968	64.7	31.9	3.4	—	59,042
1969	63.0	32.9	3.3	0.8	71,256

Source: Banco de la Republica, *Analisis Preliminar de las Cuentas de Flujo de Fondos Financieros de la Economia Colombiana, 1962–1969* (Bogota: Banco de la Republica, 1971).

In summary, foreign private credit has had a destabilizing effect on the economy and has facilitated the monopoly profits of importers and large enterprises in periods of foreign exchange difficulties.

Foreign credit for the public sector has also probably contributed to the concentration of income. In the first place, with the exception of some of the bilateral aid given by the United States, all foreign credit to the government has been tied to the purchase of imported goods for large infrastructure projects. They in turn have usually been carried out by foreign contractors and have been capital intensive during the construction process. The projects themselves have tended to have high capital/output and capital/labor ratios and high import content. Thus public expenditures based on foreign funds have been concentrated in projects that have not significantly increased labor demand and have caused balance-of-payments problems in the long run because of their high import content and low capacity for producing exports. But in addition to the negligible employment effects of infrastructure projects, these projects tend to benefit the poorer sectors of society less than proportionally, as was suggested in chapter 7. Their impact on labor demand is positive if we assume that without foreign credit investment would have been lower. Although this is likely, much of the foreign-financed investment could alternatively have been undertaken by the private sector with foreign credit or by the government with higher tax revenues, and in both cases the capital/labor ratio of the projects would probably have been lower.

The ease with which the government has been able to finance infrastructure projects with a high import content has also meant that the investment budget has been heavily biased toward this type of expenditure because, given a politically determined tax burden, the government prefers to spend more rather than less.[20] This partiality has meant giving low priority to expenditures on education and health, which have much more desirable impacts on the distribution of income. Owing to the heavy peso counterpart requirements for infrastructure projects with foreign financing, caused by the policy of financing only the foreign costs of the project, relatively little budget money is left over for such social expenditures.

Finally, it is likely that budget support by foreign loans has led to a reduced effort in the area of tax reform. In the absence of budget support by foreign credit the government might have been forced to carry out more thorough tax reforms and to increase the tax burden since even within the Colombian political structure a government is expected to help solve *some* of the problems of the country. (Without foreign support the government investment budget would have been more than halved.) Such local financing would presumably have a more favorable redistributive effect because the fiscal system is slightly progressive and could be made more so through revenue-generating tax reform and because social programs would have been a greater proportion of total expenditures in such a case.[21]

20. Historically, the political class has believed rather simplistically that the popularity of a government is a function of the infrastructure projects it is able to complete and inaugurate. For that reason, ministers of finance and heads of planning have considered the signing of foreign credits their major accomplishments.

21. This logic could be challenged by arguing that given the political structure of society, fiscal reform could not have been carried out in any case. In that situa-

This logic could be challenged by arguing that given the political structure of society, fiscal reform could not have been achieved anyway. In that case foreign indebtedness is useful since it permits the establishment of infrastructure that can contribute to economic growth. But it could also be argued that without the loans the present political class would have had greater difficulty remaining in power.

Tax Incentives in the Capital Market

The nature of the Colombian capital market has been much influenced by the tax exemptions given to income derived from different types of financial instruments. In fact all major forms of income from savings are tax exempt although income from stock dividends and savings accounts is exempt only up to a certain amount per taxpayer.

The best-known tax-exempt financial instrument has been the Mortgage Bank bond. This paper has absolute liquidity because it is supported by the Central Bank and can be resold to the issuer at any time within its 15- or 20-year life at the issue price. In addition it is exempt from income, wealth, and death taxes. The government's development bonds, as well as other municipal bonds, have similar characteristics. For these reasons and because they are bearer bonds and therefore ideal for tax evasion, these papers are a good investment for people in the higher-income brackets. But what is worse, until recently the "cheap" funds obtained by the issuing institutions have not been used to subsidize investment programs that benefit the poorer sectors of society. Thus, although these tax-exempt instruments diminish significantly the progressiveness of income, wealth, and death taxes, it is precisely the high-income groups benefited by the tax exemptions who tend also to receive subsidized credit from the institutions concerned. For example, in 1970 the Mortgage Bank obtained $826 million through net placements of tax-exempt bonds and approved 32,322 loans worth $4,341 billion distributed as shown in table 9.7. More than 70 percent of the housing loans approved

---

tion foreign indebtedness is useful since it permits the construction of infrastructure that can contribute to economic growth. But it could also be maintained that without the loans the present political class would have had greater difficulty remaining in power.

Table 9.7
Loan Applications Approved by the Mortgage Bank in 1970
(Number of housing units and value in thousands of pesos)

Value	Total of Loans			
	Number	Percentage	Value[a]	Percentage
Up to 30	2,140	6.6	44,033	1.1
30– 50	3,082	4.5	133,526	3.1
50– 75	4,099	12.7	271,108	6.2
75–100	4,177	12.9	381,349	8.8
100–125	3,432	10.6	402,913	9.3
125–150	4,257	13.2	610,923	14.1
150–175	2,090	6.5	345,671	8.0
175–200	2,745	8.5	515,159	11.9
200–225	1,622	5.0	347,307	8.0
225–250	1,765	5.5	429,997	9.9
250–275	803	2.5	212,990	4.9
275–300	2,093	6.5	618,294	14.2
300 and more	17	0.0	22,837	0.5
	32,322	100.0	4,341,107	100.0

Source: Banco Central Hipotecario, *Informe del Gerente* (Bogota, 1970).

[a]Loans for over 4 billion of pesos were approved, while only 800 million worth of bonds were placed. The difference produced a deficit financed by the Central Bank two years later.

were for sums larger than $75,000, which means they went to families that were able to pay a monthly installment of $1,000 or more, if it is assumed that all loans had the conditions and interest rates of the bank's ordinary credit. If it is also assumed that families spend 22 percent of their current income on housing,[22] it can be estimated that 70 percent of the Mortage Bank's credits benefited people with incomes of $4,600 or more per month; only 2.5 percent of the population had incomes greater than this in 1970.[23]

Another negative aspect of the tax exemptions that favor the major existing financial instruments, which also have complete liquidity and no risk, is that they are a serious hindrance to the mobilizing of savings by the private sector. Since the private sector does not have access to Central Bank support and cannot go to the market with

22. According to the budget surveys carried out by CEDE, in the major cities expenditures going to housing increased from 18 to 22 to 25 percent as family incomes increased.
23. Polibio Cordoba et al., "La Distribucion de Ingresos en Colombia," *Boletin Mensual de Estadistica* no. 237, Apr. 1971, table 18.

tax-exempt paper, it would have to pay extremely high nominal interest rates in order to compete with the government's highly liquid tax-exempt paper. This situation has made it very difficult to develop the capital market and has forced the government to help finance the large private sector industrial projects with rediscount at the Central Bank. This policy has certainly been one of the factors that has made the control of the money supply troublesome, but its influence on the development of the capital market has also been negative.

Because competing with high tax-free interest rates, bank credit, and Central Bank rediscount is very expensive, the private sector has not found it attractive to create a market for taxable paper to tap the small saver. This is a limited market with high administrative costs and therefore not very attractive. As a result small savers with low tax rates have had no attractive financial instruments in which to invest. Since these savings are somewhat interest-elastic, as was revealed by the large increases in savings accounts when the interest rate on savings deposits was increased in 1972, the low returns available to people in low tax brackets may marginally decrease the economy's potential for saving. It is interesting to note that in 1973 further tax exemptions were introduced to encourage the development of the capital market with the result that the system became still more inequitable.[24]

Inflation and Income Distribution

Up to this point we have attempted to show that in all likelihood monetary and financial policy in Colombia have contributed to maintaining a high degree of income concentration in the last decade. In this last section we discuss very tentatively some hypotheses concerning the probable impact of inflation on income distribution through its impact on (1) wealth distribution and (2) the real incomes of different classes. Since inflation has probably been determined mostly by the monetary, fiscal, and exchange rate policies followed by the government,[25] it is essential to study its impact on the welfare

---

24. A good analysis of the effects of these new exemptions and deductions can be found in Fedesarrollo, *Coyuntura Economica* 3, no. 2 (July 1973) 80–86.
25. For a monetarist interpretation of inflation see Alberto Musalem, *Dinamica*

of the different social classes in any complete evaluation of government financial policy.

The Effects of Inflation on the Distribution of Wealth

A first step in analyzing the income-distribution effects of inflation is to study its impact on the assets and liabilities of families. For example, price increases tend to favor debtors by diminishing the real value of their debts. For this reason, in various historical situations in countries other than Colombia populist political movements have espoused easy money and favored inflation. For instance, farmers with high debt/total-assets ratios hope to increase their real net wealth through inflation. They can do this if their debts remain constant in nominal terms as their assets increase in price with inflation. The fact that in Colombia the closest thing to a populist movement, ANAPO (Alianza Nacional Popular) has on the contrary price stability as one of its major programs suggests that the petite bourgeoisie and urban workers who support ANAPO do not have high levels of debt, a situation that would make inflation less unpopular.

The high concentration of credit shown in table 9.2 suggests, rather, that high bank-loan/gross-asset ratios are found particularly among the wealthier elements of society. These groups therefore benefit from inflation; the net effect of price rises can be substantial because of frozen and low interest rates.[26] For example, in periods of accelerating inflation such as 1972 and 1973 real interest rates on bank loans with 14 percent ceilings become negative, while profits generated by the bank loans adjust upward to take account of inflation. The poor, on the other hand, who have access only to the parallel (extra-bank) financial market, do not see their real debts decrease. Interest rates in the street market adjust rapidly for in-

---

de la Inflacion: La Experiencia de Colombia, 1950–1967 (Bogota: Banco de la Republica, 1971).

26. Ceilings on interest rates were as follows in 1969: bank loans 14 percent; loans for university education, which go to the rich, 3 percent; agricultural credit 8–9 percent; medium- and long-term industrial credit 15 1/2–18 percent; long-term agricultural credit 12 percent. These were the rates in 1972, when price increases averaged about 14 percent.

flation because such loans are short term and therefore easily adjusted.

The influence of inflation on assets probably also favors families in the upper deciles of the income distribution. As has already been mentioned, only the type of financial asset held by relatively sophisticated investors has increased in real value during the inflation of the last decade. Roberto Junguito calculated that during 1961–62/1969–70[27] stocks produced a real rate of return of 8 percent per year in dividends plus capital gains. For high-income groups tax-exempt bonds were also an attractive investment during most of the decade. On the other hand, the real value of saving deposits, current accounts, and currency holdings depreciated due to general price increases above the rate of return on these assets.

It has been asserted here that savings accounts were held largely by people of little wealth. In contrast, money and current accounts, may bear a similar proportion to income for both the rich and the poor, especially if liquidity requirements are determined by the level of transactions.[28] They are in any event a greater proportion of total assets at low levels of income. Since these are the assets devalued by inflation, it would appear that the wealth of humble families is particularly hard hit.

Although more or less realistic assumptions allow us to predict the effect of inflation on financial assets, it is much harder to determine the effects of general price increases on the value of real estate. Despite the lack of reliable data on the subject, it is commonly assumed in Colombia that the value of real estate increases at least as fast as the general price level. Consistent with this is the positive correlation of rates of price increase with both the value of real estate transactions[29] and real estate values, as reflected in official

27 "Determinantes Economicos del Comportamiento Bursatil Colombiano," in Banco de la Republica, *El Mercado de Capitales en Colombia* (Bogota: Banco de la Republica, 1971).

28. Although it is possible that as the value of transactions grows, liquidity needs per transaction may diminish. This in turn may be compensated to some extent by the fact that the security provided by liquidity has a high-income elasticity of demand. But since in Colombia there are perfectly liquid financial assets such as the Mortgage Bank bonds, one would expect currency balances to be relatively higher among the poor.

29. Junguito, "Determinantes Economicos," p. 316.

cadastral data. Although average cadastral valuations are inclined to be less than the market value of property, new surveys provide fairly accurate values for land and residential construction. We therefore compared the value of land in a group of municipalities as between two cadastral surveys. Table 9.8 shows that in all areas studied except Atlantico and Santander del Norte, the value of a hectare of land increased more rapidly than the general price level. The case of Santander del Norte is explainable by the low level of economic activity in that department in the recent past. It seems, then, that real estate does maintain or increase its real value during inflation. Since land ownership is highly concentrated, as demonstrated in the chapter on agriculture, this phenomenon also favors the highest deciles of the wealth distribution.

To conclude, the inflationary process probably contributes to the concentration of wealth and therefore to the concentration of income.

The Effects of Inflation on Different Types of Incomes

From the point of view of income distribution the main effect of inflation may be the direct one on the incomes of different social classes. To appraise this effect it is necessary to establish which social groups can readjust their earned income to offset inflation.

It appears that since about 1954, when large manufacturing enterprises started to be unionized, industrial workers have been able through collective bargaining to readjust their earnings at a faster pace than price increases. White-collar workers, usually less well organized, have had less success;[30] their salaries have increased very little in real terms and have fallen in years of high inflation such as 1963.[31] In the inflationary decade 1955–65 real wages of industrial workers increased 95 percent without counting increases in fringe benefits, while the real earnings of white-collar workers only increased 25 percent. The decrease in the wage differential may be partially caused by inflation. Perlman explains this phenomenon in

---

30. Other factors than degree of organization have also played important roles in these relative developments, as discussed in chap. 4.
31. Miguel Urrutia, "Los Salarios Reales en Bogota," in CEDE, *Empleo y Desempleo en Colombia* (Bogota: University of the Andes, 1968), p. 148.

Table 9.8
Increases in Land Price per Hectare in Various Municipalities Compared with
Cost-of-Living Increases in the Same Periods

Department and Group of Municipalities[a]	Years of Cadastral Surveys[b]	Percentage Price Increase per Hectare					Variation in the Blue-Collar Price Index	
		Up to 5	5–20	20–50	50–200	200 and more		
Atlantico	(1960–61–62) (1967) 1	107	119	95	135	128	Barranquilla	111
	(1964) (1968–69) 2	44	58	25	63	−87	Barranquilla	150
Sucre	(1962–63) (1968–69) 3	187	149	187	124	257	Barranquilla	98
Cordoba	(1960–61–62) (1965–66) 4	129	122	117	100	141	Barranquilla	84
Quindio	(1960–61) (1967–69) 5	361	300	276	222	175	Manizales	141
Norte de Santander	(1960–61) (1969) 6	65	68	48	24	200	Bucaramanga	167
Meta	(1962–63) (1968–69) 7	279	149	155	176	33	Bogota	100
Huila	(1959–60–61) (1968) 8	138	235	251	334	221	Bogota	146

[a]Municipalities included are: **Cordoba**: Lorica, Valencia, Monteria, Tierra Alta, Sahagun. **Sucre**: San Onofre, Tolu, Since, Toluviejo, Ovejas, San Pedro. **Meta**: Acacias, San Carlos de Guaroa, San Martin, Puerto Lopez. **Huila**: Villa Vieja, Rivera. **Quindio**: Circasia, Filandia, LaTebaida, Salento, Genova. **Atlantico**: Palmar de Varela, Piojo, Juan de Acosta, Polo Nuevo, Santo Tomas, Malambo, Sabanagrande, Baraoa, Usiacuri (group 1); Luruaco, Sabanalarga, Tubara (group 2); **Norte de Santander**: Herran, Labateca, Chimacota, Salaz, Ragombalia.

[b]The years in this column refer to the dates of new cadastral surveys; rates of price increases were calculated between the first and second years or groups of years indicated.

terms of the reactions of the state and private employers to price increases.[32] He postulates that both types of employers attempt to maintain the real value of the income of lower-paid workers during inflation, while there is less social and political pressure to maintain the growth of real income of workers higher on the occupational ladder. Therefore, considerations of social welfare tend to facilitate the decrease of wage differentials. Underlying supply conditions are probably the basic cause of diminishing differentials since the supply of secondary school and university graduates has grown faster than that of primary school graduates, but inflation has probably facilitated changes in differentials that were hard to reduce because of well-established traditions as to what were considered appropriate income differentials for jobs of different nature and varying prestige.

To study the validity of this hypothesis, the following relationship was tested with 1955–62 data:

$$\log \frac{Sw}{Sb} = \log A + B \log Pb + C \log \frac{Ew}{Eb} + G \log d,$$

where Sw is white-collar salaries, Sb blue-collar salaries, Pb the blue-collar cost-of-living index, Ew the employment of white-collar workers, Eb the employment of blue-collar workers, and d a dummy variable to correct for the change in the sample. The estimated equation was

$$\log \frac{Sw}{Sb} = \log 1.095 - 0.3656^* \log Pb + 0.7427\dagger \log \frac{Ew}{Eb} + 0.0961 \log d,$$

where R^2 is 0.8484 and the F value is 46.64.

The correlation is high, and it can be seen that price increases by themselves explain part of the decrease in wage differentials. The equation also indicates that when the employment of white-collar workers grows faster than that of blue-collar workers, the wage differential tends to increase. It appears that since about 1968, and particularly in the recent period of very high inflation (1972–73),

---

* Significantly different from zero at the 99 percent level.
† Significantly different from zero at the 90 percent level.
32. R. Perlman, "Forces Widening Occupational Wage Differentials," *Review of Economics and Statistics* 40, no. 2 (May 1958): 107–15.

industrial workers have been less successful. But in the period under study (until the mid-1960s), it does seem that during periods of accelerating inflation blue-collar workers in large-scale industry, by the late 1950s fairly thoroughly unionized, were able to increase their real income faster than the average laborer in the economy.

On the other hand, own-account workers, employees of small industries, and small entrepreneurs, probably have insufficient mechanisms for protecting themselves against inflation. In the first place they work in highly competitive sectors with easy entry and therefore do not have much opportunity to practice price fixing. In these circumstances there may be a lag between increases in the general price level and price increases in small industry and services, a lag that works against laborers in these sectors. For example, artisan workers experienced a relative decline in income. It is suggestive that between 1953 and 1964 productivity in the sector increased at a rate 38 percent of that in factory manufacturing, while real earnings increased at only 15 percent of the rate in manufacturing.[33] Although the relative deterioration of the earnings of these workers cannot on this evidence be assigned to inflation, there are some indications that inflation favors the more organized sector. However, the whole subject requires much more research. Data concerning these sectors are scanty.

Another group clearly harmed by inflation are older people on pensions; pension payments usually remain constant in nominal terms when prices increase rapidly or are only adjusted with a lag. Chronic budget deficits, a frequent cause of inflation, reflect heavy demands on the budget and do not augur well for increasing pensions. The low elasticity of tax revenues with respect to inflation is another constraint.

The reaction of the incomes of people in the upper deciles of the distribution is also very difficult to measure. However, it would seem that people living exclusively on investment income are not favored by inflation. Since people in these circumstances are often the old, and particularly older women, inflation is usually unpopular among such groups. Although, as has been shown, the net return on stocks is such as to preserve the real value of these assets in the long run

---

33. Miguel Urrutia and Clara Elsa de Sandoval, *El Sector Artesanal en el Desarrollo Colombiano* (Bogota: CID, 1971), pp. 14–15.

even under inflation, in table 9.4 it can be seen that real returns on stocks in 1963 and 1966, both years of high inflation, were negative. Thus returns on stocks adjust with a lag to inflation, which harms people who live on investment income in the first phases of an inflationary period. The tax-exempt interest rates on bonds are also raised with a lag as inflation proceeds, as are house rents. Such lags do not harm people who can wait to realize capital gains and who can switch easily among various types of financial assets, but they may cause serious hardship on the less sophisticated older pensioners, who although relatively wealthy, will not be found in the upper decile of the income distribution. Nevertheless, it should be kept in mind that during inflation the poorer older people see their real income from savings and pensions decrease much more quickly, and therefore the income differential increases between the relatively well-off pensioners and the working-class pensioners.

The reaction of house rents to inflation also illustrates the differential impact of inflation within the upper deciles of the income distribution. The price index for house rents increased less rapidly than the general price level between 1954–55 and July 1970. In this period rents of houses for employees increased by 283 percent, while the price index for employees increased 347 percent.[34] Since on the other hand the prices of urban real estate increased more rapidly than inflation, only the landlords who were trying to live on their house rents were harmed by inflation. Those who could realize their capital gains improved their situation in the same period. Thus inflation may temporarily harm the small rentier who has to live on his investment income, while it has a positive impact on the lifetime income of a wealthier class.

In contrast, the people in the top 5 percent of the income distribution most likely do very well during inflation. Large agricultural producers, for example, can usually defend themselves from inflation because their incomes grow parallel to increases in the prices of the products they sell and because in Colombia agricultural prices tend to climb faster than the general price level during inflation. Furthermore, in an attempt to increase the supply of food during

34. The less than proportional increase in house rents may be due to an increase in the supply of housing, owing in part to increasing demand for housing as an asset that keeps its value during inflation.

inflation the authorities often provide unlimited funds for loans to the agricultural sector at subsidized interest rates. On the other hand, small agricultural producers, whose family budget is almost wholly dedicated to food consumption, do not benefit greatly from rises in food prices during inflation. The owners of monopolistic or oligopolistic industries also gain from inflation although a minority of them, subject to price controls, may suffer a profit squeeze. Moreover, since historically import controls have tended to become more stringent as inflation accelerates, the access of these same industries and large importers to import licenses generates high monopoly profits. A final consideration is that it is precisely large-scale agriculture and industry that most successfully pressure the monetary authorities to increase inflationary Central Bank credit. Inflation appears to serve these sectors well.

In summary, inflation in Colombia, as in other nations,[35] probably favors people in the upper half of the income distribution (particularly unionized workers and some entrepreneurs) and harms people in the lower deciles. Its effects on the upper decile of the distribution are hard to determine, but they are probably not unfavorable. This impressionistic conclusion should be the object of verification through much more research in Latin America. Nevertheless, the fact that the continent has been characterized by bad income distributions and by rapid rates of price increases for many decades suggests that inflation may be an effective instrument for maintaining an unjust status quo.[36]

Political Power and Privilege in the Financial Sector

For a political scientist it would be very revealing to analyze thoroughly the processes that have determined the present structure

---

35. In the United States a similar result has been found. See Edward C. Budd and David Seiders, "The Impact of Inflation on the Distribution of Income and Wealth," *American Economic Review* 61, no. 2 (May 1971): 128–152.

36. Various Mexican economists, including I. M. de Navarrete, contend that because of the inflationary policy followed by the Mexican government, development policy was inclined to accentuate an inequitable distribution of income, which tended to deteriorate in the 25 years before 1960. See Leopoldo Solis, "Mexican Economic Policy in the Post-War Period: The Views of Mexican Economists," *American Economic Review* 61, no. 3 pt. 2 (June 1971): 2–67, esp. p. 25.

of the capital market. Such a study, by determining which sectors of society have a privileged position in the financial and capital market, could give a good idea of which groups have the best instruments of power for obtaining favorable legislation and government action in Colombian society.

A quick study of legislation and regulation in the financial sector yields the conclusion that the most favored sector is that of the large commercial farmers. The state has actually created three banks to serve them, interest rates for commercial agriculture have been heavily subsidized for at least two decades,[37] and the Central Bank has frequently exempted this sector from any limits on credit growth.

In the field of foreign trade policy it is the large industrialists who gain. They have obtained high tariff protection and preferential access to import licenses. The combination of these two advantages has promoted significant levels of monopoly profits.

Subsidized interest rates, overvalued exchange rates, and ceilings on saving rates have diminished the demand for labor and therefore worked against an increase in the participation of labor in national income. In addition the inflationary policies followed by the authorities may have seriously contributed to the maintenance of an already inequitable income distribution during the last decade.

If the above conclusions are correct, a thorough reform of foreign trade and monetary policy becomes imperative. The question is whether such reforms are viable in the present political context.

37. In a recent Central Bank investigation, it was found that credit conceded under Law 26, with heavily subsidized interest rates, went to very large agricultural producers. The average size of loan in a random sample was $1,025,318 pesos.

10

The Distributional Impact of Agricultural Policy

As we have noted at various points in this study, a systematic inclusion of income distribution as relevant to policymaking is a recent concept in Colombia. Accordingly, to evaluate past policy in terms of this goal is for the most part to measure it against a standard not considered relevant at the time. This is not entirely true, however, and aspects of both agricultural policy and Colombian politics reflect public effort directed toward the improvement of income distribution. President Alfonso Lopez's Law 200 of 1936, designed to put land increasingly in the hands of the tillers, attempted seriously to improve the distribution of income in agriculture and, in a more general sense, the distribution of welfare (including the nonincome advantages of landownership). In 1961 the passage of the agrarian reform law, which created the administrative agency INCORA, was a response to distributional problems in the agricultural sector and violence in the countryside.

In other words certain highly visible political decisions have been very much related to income distribution. But the majority of the decisions taken over the course of the years, more technical in appearance and surely much more important in their ultimate impact, have not taken into account the problem of income distribution. To the extent that the decisions are not made on "technical" grounds (as they may be understood at the time), they are usually affected by the relative political power of different groups, and in this case the impact of such influence will usually be to worsen the distribution of income because of the unequal distribution of political power.

It would probably not be surprising to many Colombian decision-makers dealing with the agricultural sector that its growth over the last decades has also produced a worsening of income distribution. The most common interpretation of how the sector functions involves the idea that the larger farm tends to be more efficient and to have more potential for growth than the smaller one and that modern Western techniques of production—especially the use of machinery—are more efficient than more traditional techniques. Policy steps designed to help the small farmer are often considered part of social policy rather than economic policy. In other words they are not expected to pay off in terms of substantial output increases, and they are interpreted as essentially income redistribution devices. However, being interpreted as such reduces considerably their selling power within any government or society (even well-meaning people may not be willing to give up much output to improve distribution a little), so the efforts that might be characterized as directed toward the poorer farmer have been distinctly limited over time. Some of them have backfired.

As we saw in chapter 3, distribution of the income generated in agriculture appears to have worsened systematically since the 1930s, when information first permits a rough calculation. The labor share has fallen substantially, and there is no evidence that the distribution of capital has become less unequal. In chapter 3 several possible determinants of changes in income distribution over time were mentioned. They include (1) the combination of capital formation and technological change that has generated the rapid growth of "commercial" crops such as cotton, sugar, rice, and sesame; and (2) possible changes in the product composition of demand away from coffee and certain staple food crops that are produced on smaller farms and toward the commercial crops produced more on larger farms. No attempt was made to relate these and other possible proximate causes of changes in distribution to policy or to distinguish the extent to which they are the result of policy measures as opposed to exogenous developments. In this chapter an attempt is made to ascertain (or in some cases, more accurately, to speculate about) the impact of specific policies on distribution. In most cases no detailed empirical study has been done, so one can proceed only by deduction from the nature of the policy and what is known about the structure of the agricultural sector.

Principal Components of Agricultural Policy in Recent Decades

Agriculture is both a heterogeneous and complex sector. Partly as a result of this, public policy toward it is made by numerous institutions set up with different goals in mind and often acting in an uncoordinated way. Accordingly, it may not be meaningful to talk about the objectives of agricultural policy, let alone its effects. Theoretically, broad objectives should be set by the Ministry of Agriculture and the National Planning Department, but in fact some of the semiautonomous institutions are substantially independent, and in any event the two institutions just mentioned have not normally been able to articulate very thorough policies or to push them strongly. Our objective here, however, is only to form some judgment as to the probable effects of the various components of agricultural policy. As we see below, the overall impact on income distribution seems to have been negative.

Among the components of government policy toward agriculture that warrant consideration in this context are credit, research and extension, taxation, social infrastructure (especially roads), policy toward mechanization, price supports and controls, and land policy (whose major element is agrarian reform). It should be added that policy with respect to the education of the rural population is an important determinant of welfare levels and of income distribution in the rural area, even though it would not normally be deemed part of agricultural policy. We now consider in turn the general characteristics of these elements of policy and their probable impact on the agricultural and rural income distributions.

Credit Policy

Ever since the 1930s, credit for the agricultural sector has come from both the commercial banks and the public credit agency, the Caja Agraria (founded in 1931). At present the Caja provides more than 50 percent of all credit recorded as going to agriculture; its relative significance has been near this level (40–60 percent) for many years.

As discussed in chapter 9 credit from the official banking system is very unequally distributed in the Colombian economy as a whole. This is definitely true for the agricultural sector. Table 9.2 indicated that in November 1970 only about 8 percent of all loans by commercial banks were in quantities of less than 10,000 pesos and that about the same percentage of loans went to individuals and firms with gross assets of less than 50,000 pesos. Fifteen percent of the value of new Caja Agraria loans was in loans of less than 5,000 pesos, and a little over 8 percent went to persons or firms with gross assets of less than 10,000 pesos. When it is borne in mind that the median farm size in 1970 was still only 2–3 hectares and that the median family income was probably about 9,000 or 10,000 pesos (assuming 1.6 working members per family), it becomes clear that unless the ratio of loan received to annual family income is unusually high, only a small share of agricultural credit could have gone to families in the bottom quarter or third of the income distribution, and not too much even to the bottom half.[1] Another rough calculation shows that Caja Agraria credit does reach some small farms (of say fewer than 3 hectares), though naturally not with very wide coverage, but that the value-of-loans/value-of-output ratio was probably only one-half to one-quarter as high for these small farms as for ones of, say, 200 hectares or more.[2] Table 10.1 shows the relationship in question for the Caja Agraria. Since we may assume that virtually all commercial bank credit goes to farms of more than 5 hectares and since this credit is approximately equal in magnitude to the Caja credit, we may further assume that it roughly doubles the value-of-loan/value-of-output ratio for these larger farms as a group and therefore implies that their total value-of-loan/value-of-output ratio is at least twice as high as for the smaller farms. It goes without saying that these figures are crude estimates, but the existence of a substantial gap in this ratio between small and large farms comes through clearly.[3]

---

1. Most of the people in the bottom half of the agricultural income distribution earn most of their income working on other farms, and production on their own small plots is a secondary source. Such individuals would often not be considered appropriate credit risks in any case.
2. See Albert Berry, "Special Problems of Policy-Making in a Technologically Heterogenous Agriculture," in *Agriculture in Development Theory*, ed. Lloyd C. Reynolds (New Haven: Yale University Press, 1975), table 4.
3. For methodology see the source just cited. Information for different years

Agricultural credit has normally been made available at the most attractive interest rates used for any sector of the economy, often at about a zero real rate of interest and sometimes even negative. (Nevertheless, it is true that the effective interest rate has *normally* been positive after required minimum balances and so on are taken into account.) It is especially striking that the public agricultural credit agency, the Caja Agraria, dispenses such a great share of its total credit to relatively large-scale farmers. As indicated in table 10.1 the share of total value of loans going to farms of less than 3 hectares (roughly the median size) was only about 11 percent of all Caja credit; of total agricultural credit it might be about 6 percent.

With this highly unequal distribution of credit it would be hard to believe that its existence does not tend to worsen the distribution of income.[4] Some of the credit going to large farmers does trickle down to the smaller ones (presumably at higher interest rates) and the existence of the extra bank credit market obviously implies that more small farmers receive credit than are listed in the official statistics. But the typical real effective interest rate paid by recipients of official credit has probably been on average in the range of 5–8 percent over the last decade, whereas credit in the extra-bank market probably has a real effective rate of 20–30 percent. In short such access as the small farmers as a group do have to credit is at much higher costs.

The distribution of agricultural credit by the wealth levels of the recipients may make it look even more unequal than by income levels because a basic criterion for giving credit is the assets of the recipient. The figures of table 9.3 have already been cited in this connection.

Credit distribution has undoubtedly always been quite unequal, but the implications of this inequality have perhaps become more

---

had to be used in making the calculations underlying table 10.1, and this undoubtedly leads to some biases and errors.

4. This is not to say that Colombia's performance in this field is bad by Latin American or developing countries' standards. Some countries do not have a public credit agency for agriculture at all, and when the whole official credit operation is in the hands of the commercial banks, distribution of credit would normally be more uneven than it is in Colombia. Nor are we arguing here that it is easy to provide credit effectively to some small farmers, especially those who do not have title to their land. The implicit problems are the subject of an extensive literature. Our objective here is simply to evaluate the income distribution effects of the credit system without evaluating its efficiency.

Table 10.1
Caja Agraria Credit/Value of Output, by Farm Size

Size (Hectares)	Value of 1960 Output (Millions of 1971 pesos) (1)	Number of Loans (2)	Farms (3)	Number of Loans/Farm (4)	Value of Loans (5)	Value of Loans/Value of Output (5)/(1) (6)
<2	2,114 ⎱ 3,119	⎱ 115,000	⎱ 606,423	⎱ .190	⎱ 376.3	⎱ 12.06
2–3	1,005 ⎰	⎰	⎰	⎰	⎰	⎰
3–4	996 ⎱ 1695	⎱ 70,000	⎱ 150,182	⎱ .466	⎱ 302.1	⎱ 17.82
4–5	699 ⎰	⎰	⎰	⎰	⎰	⎰
5–10	3,004	75,000	169,145	.443	407.26	13.56
10–20	3,224	46,000	114,231	.403	383.35	11.89
20–30	1,575	⎱ 25,000	⎱ 70,549	⎱ .354	⎱ 314.06	⎱ 11.44
30–40	1,170	⎰	⎰	⎰	⎰	⎰
40–50	866	5,000	16,240	.308	105.3	12.16
50–100	2,815	9,318	39,990	.233	277.60	9.86
100–200	2,635	6,351	22,317	.285	279.81	10.62
200–500	3,143	4,500	13,693	.329	374.26	11.91
500–1,000	1,898	1,300	4,142	.314	383.41	20.20
1,000–2,500	1,536	⎱ 401	⎱ 2,761	⎱ .145	⎱ 269.79	⎱ 18.57
≥2,500	1,453	⎰	⎰	⎰	⎰	⎰

Source: Output figures are from Berry, "Land Distribution, Income Distribution, and the Productive Efficiency of Colombian Agriculture," *Food Research Institute Studies in Agricultural Economics, Trade, and Development* 12, no. 3 (1973): 199–232. The credit figures are from Berry, *Development of Agricultural Sector*, Appendix table A-79; distribution of credit by farm size, based on the distribution by patrimony, was estimated by the author. The estimates are quite crude since the methodology was indirect.

severe in recent years, so credit policy has probably been a factor in the worsening of income distribution already described in chapter 3. According to recent calculations the ratio of loans outstanding to value of agricultural output rose from .056 in the period 1940–44 to .201 in 1965–67. This rise in the availability of credit to agriculture clearly benefited primarily the larger farmers and is thus a probable source of the increasing inequality.[5]

Mechanization

As observed earlier, public attitudes toward mechanization have been very positive in Colombia. Both commercial bank and Caja Agraria credit have been readily obtainable for buyers of agricultural machinery during most of the post-World War II period.[6] Mechanization has naturally enough been considered a source of increasing efficiency and a desirable development; its advance has been rapid (see table 3.8). In fact its implications for total output are not evident without detailed analysis,[7] but this is not our prime concern here. Mechanization characterizes essentially the large farms, and it seems almost certain that its impact on income distribution is negative (i.e., that it benefits the rich more than the poor, if the latter are benefited at all). As of 1960 fewer than 1 percent of the farms listed in the agricultural census reported owning tractors, whereas about 2 percent reported making use of their own or rented tractors. These ratios

5. There are many problems with the agricultural credit data, not the least of which is the question of how many loans formally listed as going to the agricultural sector really do. But this is not of concern here, because a low-interest loan to a large farmer that is eventually used in the urban sector has still benefited that individual. For statistics on the ratio of loans to output over time see A. Berry, *The Development of the Agricultural Sector on Colombia,* forthcoming, table 3-13.

6. Several World Bank and Interamerican Development Bank loans conceded for this purpose have contributed to this condition of ready access. One IDB loan required Caja Agraria to complement agricultural machinery loans with large working capital loans to assure the full utilization of the machinery.

7. For the first such analysis of this question in Colombia see Wayne Thirsk, "The Economics of Farm Mechanization in Colombia" (Ph.D. diss., Yale University, 1972). In many countries, especially Asian ones, mechanization has very little effect on output and is merely labor displacing. The situation in Colombia is more complicated because one usual consequence is the shifting of some land on large farms from the production of livestock to commercial cropping, which is more labor intensive.

would be somewhat higher in 1970, but the number of farms smaller than 5 or 10 hectares that would be users is almost surely still below 5 percent. Mechanization thus does not directly help the small farmer except in unusual situations. It presumably leads to labor displacement in some cases, thereby lowering the welfare of that group of people (which overlaps substantially with the small-farm operators) who earn most of their income working on other people's land. Modern commercial crops, which use the machinery, have in general much lower labor shares than do traditional crops.[8]

Research and Extension

Although Colombian agriculture has been characterized by a not insignificant technical change from the 1950s on, the total impact of research and extension appears to have been far from dramatic.[9] It is true that important new varieties have been developed for some crops, but they are the exceptions rather than the rule, and according to estimates by Berry they would perhaps account for an increase in output of 0.5 percent per year.[10] At present the use of new varieties is much more noticeable in the commercial crops (such as sugar, cotton, and sesame) than in the traditional crops. It is widely speculated that this differential depends on different behavior pat-

8. See Albert Berry, "Land Distribution, Income Distribution, and the Productive Efficiency of Colombian Agriculture," *Food Research Institute Studies* 12, no. 3 (1973): 199–232. As remarked in n. 7, one major uncertainty that leaves the net distributional impact of mechanization unclear is the fact that it has been associated with the transfer of land from the very labor-extensive production of livestock to the somewhat less extensive production of commercial crops. Therefore further research will be necessary to ascertain whether there have been important distributional effects. There seems little question that, even if the total demand for labor rises as a result of mechanization thereby pulling wages up, its impact on income distribution (as opposed to that on the absolute level of incomes of the poorer members of the agricultural population) would still be negative.

9. See Berry, *Development of Agricultural Sector*, chap. 3, forthcoming.

10. If, as implicit in one calculation, biological advance constituted about 30 percent of a total residual of perhaps 1.5 percent per year (the residual is defined as the part of output growth that cannot be explained directly by the growth of the traditional inputs, land, labor, and capital). Obviously these figures are open to question, but under no circumstances could research and extension have been credited with an output increase of more than 1 percent a year in the 1950s and 1960s.

terns of smaller and larger farmers, the latter being more interested in new technologies. But it is also true that research has been directed primarily toward the crops and the variety types that could be used by the larger farmers and that the extension service has traditionally given these commercial farmers much more attention than the small farmer. In the case of corn, for example, a number of new varieties have been developed, but they are essentially adapted to large-scale production in the Cauca Valley. Little in the way of improved varieties has been made available for the highland subsistence corn producer. There is therefore little real test of whether he would change varieties if he could. Similarly, subsistence crops such as yucca and plantains have received virtually no research attention. There appears to be some rectification of this imbalance now in that CIAT (Centro Interamericano para la Agricultura Tropical) in Cali gives some attention to tropical subsistence crops.

When the same variety that suits the large producer can also be used in the more constrained situation of the typical small farmer (less ability to use modern inputs, often poorer land, and sometimes the inability to use machines), new varieties have indeed been adopted by the latter (as in the case of potatoes) and benefits reaped. But even without detailed quantification it would appear that most of the gains attributable to biological improvements and their diffusion over the last twenty years have gone to the larger farmers.[11]

That research expenditures could worsen distribution is probably less apparent to many observers (compared for example to credit distribution), but as varietal technological change hopefully becomes an increasingly important source of output growth in Colombian agriculture, this possibility warrants serious attention.

Tax Policy

Taxes effectively levied on Colombian agriculture are small if one omits coffee export taxes. Because the usual differential between the price received by the Colombian coffee producer and the world price converted at the official exchange rate is substantial, total tax take in

11. As of 1965–67 and taking 1948–60 as base, it has been calculated that perhaps 200 million 1958 pesos of additional output per year could be attributed to the biological advance (see Berry, *Development of Agricultural Sector*, chap. 3).

agriculture could be construed as reasonably high if all of this were treated as a tax. But it is debatable whether some or even any of it should be so considered.[12] Property taxes are inclined to be low and assessments seriously outdated so that in 1965 total property tax revenues in rural areas constituted perhaps only a little over 0.5 percent of agricultural income.[13] A scattering of other taxes does generate some revenue from the agricultural sector, but their total impact is very slight.[14] Agriculture is, as in most countries, an excellent base from which to avoid income taxes. Until recently the possibilities of loss write-off in agricultural operations were such that activities in agriculture not only yielded little tax revenue but decreased the revenue from income generated in other sectors. Total income tax revenue based on the agricultural sector undoubtedly remains very small.[15]

Although lack of experience with its application any where leaves it open to some legitimate question, a possibility that deserves genuine consideration is a presumptive income tax on land.[16] This tax has been legislated recently in Colombia, although with such low tax rates and assessed land values as to lose almost all its potential

---

12. If the equilibrium price of Colombian coffee were defined as the price necessary to bring forth the supply that Colombia can place in the international markets, it would be about equal to the price usually received by the producers or even a little below it at times. The world coffee price is clearly above the equilibrium price, held there by an agreement among producers and users to give the producers a certain amount of joint monopoly power. It is debatable whether coffee producers should be assumed to receive, and then have taxed away from them, part of the above equilibrium price. Furthermore, in Colombia a large part of this tax is compensated for by transport and credit subsidies and by low-cost financing of stocks. This portion of the tax can be thought of as a fee for services rendered.

13. Total income from the land (predial) tax in 1965 was 256.6 million pesos; somewhat more than half of all the assessed value of real estate was in urban areas [see DANE, *Estadisticas Fiscales, 1963, 1964, 1965* (Bogota: Imprenta Nacional, 1969), pp. 327, 387].

14. They include the slaughter tax on livestock, most of which is in any case probably passed on to the consumer.

15. See the discussion in R. A. Musgrave and Malcolm Gillis, *Fiscal Reform for Colombia* (Cambridge, Mass.: Harvard Law School, 1971), p. 33.

16. For a discussion of some aspects of the economics of this tax, see Albert Berry, "A Presumptive Income Tax on Agricultural Land: Colombia," *National Tax Journal* 25, no. 2 (June 1972): 169–81; and Roberto Jungito, *Estudio del Impuesto de Renta Presuntiva al Sector Agropecuario* (Bogota: Fedesarrollo, 1971).

effectiveness as a policy for improving the horizontal equity of the tax system, raising government revenues, or encouraging inefficient producers to sell their lands or rent them. Although it can be cogently argued that such a policy has greater opportunity for success in the sociopolitical context of Colombia than would, for example, a land reform, it had not been used until the recent passage of the legislation, despite the idea having been voiced (periodically) for at least twenty years.[17] It is also significant that the rates adopted clearly favor the cattle ranchers over crop producers, thus giving preferential treatment to the richer sectors of rural society.

Road Building

Until the post-World War II period Colombia was noted for its underdeveloped highway and road systems, a natural result of the extremely difficult terrain. Since then much progress has been made, and Colombia is now a much more integrated economic unit than it was twenty or twenty-five years ago. No attempt has yet been made in Colombia to evaluate either the overall benefits of road building or the distribution of those gains in a detailed quantitative fashion. But two of the most frequent criticisms made of the evolution of the system have been (1) the relatively great emphasis on trunk lines and the little attention given to feeder roads,[18] and (2) the fact that the location of new roads tends more often to reflect the interests of large-scale landowners than small ones and that when roads go through previously unsettled areas, the land frequently falls into the hands of large landholders with resultant negative effects on the distribution of income.[19] Whether the nature of road building has had a significant quantitative impact on distribution is hard to

17. One of the early proposals along these lines was the first World Bank Mission Report. See International Bank for Reconstruction and Development, *The Basis of a Development Program in Colombia* (Baltimore, Md.: Johns Hopkins Press, 1950). The proposal has subsequently arisen in various guises. One might argue that its suggestion by the 1969 Musgrave Tax Commission set off the serious discussion that finally led to the law's being passed, although, as indicated in the text, at such low levels as to have little potential impact.

18. One treatment of this issue is Herman Felstehausen, *Local Government and Rural Service Barriers to Economic Development in Colombia* (Bogota: Land Tenure Center, 1968).

19. See ibid.

Price Supports and Price Controls

Experience with effective price supports or controls is limited in Colombia; the price of coffee is an important decision variable and is effectively maintained. More recently IDEMA (Instituto de Mercadeo Agropecuario; previously INA, or Instituto Nacional de Abasteciemientos) has been responsible for maintaining a minimum price in the rural areas for a set of crops (wheat, corn, rice, and several others). Once again it is noteworthy that price supports have been concentrated on the crops produced by commercial farmers.[20] The success of this policy has been uneven and far from complete because of lack of storage space (especially during the earlier years), inefficient policies, and other weaknesses. It would not be plausible to assume that price control policies have had a really significant impact on income distribution. Any such effects would more likely be negative than positive judging both from theory and from experience in other countries where analyses of the issue have been carried out.[21] Price supports obviously benefit only the farmer who markets his product; this already excludes from potential benefits many small farmers, much of whose production is for subsistence purposes, for example the small-scale corn producer. And in those cases, not infrequent in the history of price supports, where either finances or storage run out fairly early in the buying process, it would be surprising if many of the early beneficiaries were not the larger producers.[22]

---

20. For a discussion of the earlier development of these programs see T. Goering, *Colombian Agricultural Price and Trade Policies* (Palmira, Colombia: Facultad de Agronomia, 1961).

21. As in the United States. See, for example, Varden Fuller, "Political Pressures and Income Distribution in Agriculture," *Journal of Farm Economics* 47, no. 5 (Dec. 1965): 1, 245–51.

22. Much of the difficulty in price support policy is that it is correctly conceived of as a necessary element if the marginal producer is to keep on producing the product in question, but thinking is very confused as to who the marginal producer is. For many crops in Colombia the marginal producer is the modern commercial farmer who switches easily from one crop to another. The intramarginal producer is the subsistence farmer who would keep on producing his corn or

Thirsk's recent analysis confirms these pessimistic expectations.[23] His calculations for 1968 lead him to conclude (1) that the costs of the program have been borne by low-income earners as a group while most of the benefits have been obtained by higher-income groups and (2) that the program imposes an efficiency cost on the economy due to an inappropriate allocation of the economy's resources. But he concluded that neither effect would be large.[24]

Price controls on agricultural products have not been frequent. At times they have undoubtedly made given items less profitable than they would otherwise have been, mostly to the detriment of large producers who sell in the bigger city markets.[25]

Basing our conclusions partly on recorded experience in other countries and partly on an impressionistic interpretation of the Colombian scene, it seems likely that price policy, like so many of the other instruments already mentioned, has had a negative effect on distribution. However, this is an area where much research remains to be done.

Land Policy and Agrarian Reform

As remarked in the introduction to this chapter, one type of policy that has received attention because it was expected to significantly improve income distribution is land policy, beginning with President Alfonso Lopez's Law 200 of 1936 and extending through the Agrarian Reform Law of 1961 and subsequent amendments. But the

---

potatoes regardless of the price. The group of farmers whom one might call marginal because of their low income is frequently the opposite of the group who are marginal in the relevant economic sense of having the highest opportunity cost.

23. Wayne Thirsk, "Income Distribution Consequences of Agricultural Price Supports in Colombia," Houston, Texas: Rice University Program of Development Studies, mimeo, Fall 1973.

24. Certainly less than 0.5 percent of national income would be transferred from low-income groups (less than 1,000 pesos income per month of family income). His best estimate would imply a transfer of 0.2 percent of national income (ibid., p. 19).

25. If one takes into account the other side of this market (the consumers), the price controls may well worsen income distribution if, as one might expect, they especially decrease the supply to the unfavored marginal or poor buyer. There is some evidence of this in the case of controlled price for milk in Bogota over the last decade; but this issue remains largely to be studied.

actual effects of such policy steps as have been taken is an open question. Land Law 200 of 1936 required landowners to pay tenants for improvements they made during their status as tenants, ruled that unutilized land would revert to the state after a period of ten years, and established rules that left most squatters in possession of the lands they were on. Many observers feel that it actually backfired. They argue that subsequent to its passage a sizable number of tenants were dispossessed because of the landlords' fear of litigation over improvements made and that considerable welfare loss was the result. The fact that real wages fell in the latter part of the 1930s has also been noted, and there is some possibility that this legislation may have been one causal factor. Fear has been expressed again with respect to a 1968 amendment to Law 135 of 1961; the amendment stipulated that all tenants be registered, with the presumed purpose of turning them eventually into owners. The fear, again, is that it induced farmers to evict their renters and sharecroppers. In both cases there are wide differences of opinion as to the extent of the phenomenon in question.[26]

Land redistribution is at first sight the most obvious policy to improve income distribution in an agricultural sector with a highly unequal distribution of income traceable mainly to the maldistribution of land. At the same time, given the greater output per hectare characterizing small farms, a strong argument can be made that transferring land from large to small producers will raise output. As of about 1960 value added per effective hectare[27] was more than twice as high on farms of less than 5 hectares as on those greater than 200 hectares (see table 10.2). (The differential in value added per hectare was much greater.) The source of the higher land productivity of small farms is the greater intensity of use (see col. 9); small farms dedicate a much greater share of their resources to the production of crops (vs. livestock) than do large farms.[28] Unfortunately, major obstacles usually arise to frustrate such a policy.

26. The historian Malcolm Dees, for one, has indicated to the authors that he has not found any evidence of ejection of tenants due to Law 200 of 1936 in the hacienda records he has worked with.
27. Where effective hectare is defined as an amount of land with a given productive potential. One hectare of fertile land is defined as equivalent to 2 hectares of land that is only half as fertile.
28. For a fuller discussion of these issues see A. Berry, "Land Distribution."

Table 10.2
Factor Productivity and Farm Size in Colombia, 1960
(Value figures in thousands of 1960 pesos)

Farm Size (Hectares)	Value of Output per Worker (1)	Value Added per Worker (2)	Value Added/ Effective Hectare (3)	Value Added/ Hectare (4)	Value Added/ Value of Land and Capital (5)	Overall Yield Index[a] (6)	Yield Index of Cultivated and Fallow Land (7)	Value of Crop Output/ Hectare of Cropped Fallow Land (8)	Percentage of Arable and Pasture Land in Crops (9)
0–3	1.83	1.67	.75	1.37	.35	94.2[b]	80.5[b]	1.05[b]	.87[b]
3–5	2.37	2.08	.79	.86	.36	96.8[c]	81.6[c]	1.03[c]	.77[c]
5–10	3.15	2.71	.73	.73	.33	96.7	79.4	1.04	.66
10–50	4.15	3.47	.57	.44	.25	98.4	72.3	.96	.47
50–200	6.65	5.35	.38	.25	.17	117.8	68.8	.87	.28
200–500	10.76	8.61	.35	.21	.15	140.3	70.7	.90	.18
>500	17.16	15.07	.35	.13	.14	147.4	67.3	.89	.06
All farms	4.44	3.71	.46	.28	.20				

Sources and Methodology: Figures in the first five columns are best estimates (Berry, "Land Distribution"). Alternative estimates and the methodology of the various calculations are presented in tables A-4, A-5, and A-7 of the cited study.
[a] Index of value of product per cultivated hectare assuming for each size category the distribution of land among crops characterizing the crop sector as a whole.
[b] 0–2 hectares rather than 0–3.
[c] 2–5 hectares rather than 3–5.

The most obvious is the opposition of the large-scale landowners to giving up land at below market values. This attitude is manifested in opposition to new legislation, efforts to pick loopholes in the legislation and to hamstring the policy via legal delays, attempts to bribe officials, and so on. Where landed interests are strong enough, these pressures themselves may be adequate to indefinitely delay land reform, especially if the government is lukewarm—a natural reflection of the political power of the landed groups—and gives little budgetary support to the reform.

Less obvious but possibly equally problematic obstacles also arise. They include technical misinformation about the nature of the agricultural sector, which typically afflicts technicians as well as politicians, and built-in habits in the public service institutions dealing with the agricultural sector. These agencies, such as the credit and research institutions, traditionally focus on the large-scale farmer and are neither accustomed to nor convinced of the value of having much to do with the small producer. Much of the problem involves the idea, intuitively obvious to many people, that large-scale, modern capital-intensive production is more efficient than small-scale traditional (or at least less modern) and labor-intensive production. The confusion involves the assumption that the labor productivity of an activity is an indicator of its efficiency. Whereas this assumption obviously holds for the economy as a whole at a point in time (maximizing productivity of any one factor implies maximizing average productivity of all the others too), from an analytical point of view maximization of labor productivity is a less helpful way of defining the objective of the system than is maximization of capital productivity, assuming the latter factor is the one in short supply. Because capital productivity and labor productivity tend to be inversely correlated across different productive units (especially across size units), high labor productivity is very likely to be associated with low capital productivity and therefore low efficiency. Unfortunately, this point seems counterintuitive to most people. An agrarian reform agency afflicted with the preconception that high labor productivity signals efficiency is likely to find itself in the strange dilemma of trying to help producers in whose inherent efficiency it has little confidence and of trying to push them toward a modernity that may not in fact imply greater economic efficiency.

The idea that farms should not be less than a minimum size is another manifestation of this syndrome. Actually, in Colombia as in most other countries land productivity is higher the smaller the farm (see table 10.2). INCORA's concentration on capital-intensive projects in irrigated areas and its use of modern technology help to lower political opposition. Such a policy puts a financial ceiling on land reform and implicitly reinforces the position of the large agro-industries, which claim that only large-scale capitalistic agricultural production will be viable in the last two decades of the twentieth century. When in the early 1970s INCORA started to move toward a more redistributive strategy, opposition from traditional agricultural interests managed to block any further progress in this direction.

Statistics bearing on INCORA's record through 1969 are presented in table 10.3. As of mid-1969 only 7,000 families had received farms on land not previously in the public domain. The great majority of the 81,000 who had received title to previously government-owned land had already been on it.

The business of transferring land and aiding the small farmer to expand his operations successfully in a short time is a difficult and complicated task at best, even with clear ideas as to what constitutes economic efficiency and why some productive units are more efficient than others. But when misinformation is abundant and when preconceptions weigh against any confidence in the program, difficulties are multiplied. It is a serious question whether in a reasonable period of time (say five or ten years) the understanding and efficiency of the public service sector, including the land reform agency, could be so improved as to permit a well-executed policy to help the small-scale farmers, including the transfer of land to this group. Technically the undertaking, on the surface an "obvious" policy to improve distribution, would be much more arduous than some other agricultural policies, such as changes in interest rates, prices of capital goods, credit distribution, and tax policy. Therefore, in the present political and institutional context the policy of a heavy presumptive income tax on land seems to have many advantages over land redistribution through agrarian reform, both as a redistributive and as a production technique.

At the same time it must be recognized that, *if land reform can be*

Table 10.3
Land and Credit Achievements of INCORA

		Way Land Was Distributed by INCORA					Land Acquired by INCORA in Given Years (Hectares)			Credit[d]			
	Families Receiving Titles to Land (1)	Hectares Distributed to These Families (2)	Government Lands[b]		Purchase, Expropriation, or Extinction of Private Domain		Purchases (7)	Expropriation (8)	Extinction of Private Domain and Cession (9)	Number of Families Receiving Loans in Given Year (10)	New Loans (Thousands of pesos) (11)	Loans Outstanding (Thousands of pesos) (12)	Number of New Loans (13)
			Number of Farms (3)	Area (4)	Number of Farms (5)	Area (6)							
1962	4,377	211,924	4,324	211,112			617	154	18,136				
1963	6,550	321,427	6,109	316,865			12,422	1,483	263,427				
1964	8,813	405,888					17,045	7,651	1,044,102				
1965	12,213	383,548					23,655	9,453	384,249	2,556	27.5	26.0	
1966	16,160	458,241					11,611	11,699	95,352	7,621	82.7	90.0	
1967	18,388	455,723					35,047	13,305	393,712	11,993	46.0	189.0	
1968	16,972	362,073						15,130	41,949	19,269	247.2	350.0	
Jan.-June 30, 1969 (process completed)	8,727	152,477						4,769		26,482	279.1	517.0	
Jan.-April 1969										17,849	440.8	289.4	39,094
Total (including all processes initiated as of June 30, 1969)[a]	92,200	2,751,301	81,188	2,638,531	7,012	112,770	145,632	64,333	3,174,166[c]	26,500	778.5		

[a]Data from DANE, *Boletin Mensual de Estadistica*, Jan. 1970, p. 119.
[b]Of the public lands distributed under the overall program of INCORA, some are distributed directly by INCORA and others by delegations in the departmental governments. The figures have included both.
[c]As of Dec. 1967 this total was 2,209,553 and included extinction of private domain and cession (1,944,910 and 264,643, respectively).
[d]The credit program began in Feb. 1964.
[e]As of Dec. 1967.
[f]As of Dec. 1968.

carried out efficiently, no other policy can be as effective in terms of swift income redistribution. From a technical point of view land reform is definitely riskier and costlier than, say, a presumptive income tax on land, but the potential benefits are also greater. From a political perspective, although generalizations are difficult, a vigorous land reform would seem to be one of the most troublesome policies to pursue.

Education

Chapter 8 discusses in more detail the relationship between educational levels and income levels for the Colombian economy as a whole and concludes that much of the dispersion in labor income—which is, to say the least, substantial—is a consequence of differences in educational attainment. Clearly the people on the bottom of the educational totem pole are the rural dwellers. In many regions only two years of part-time education (because of alternation between boys and girls) has been available, and until quite recently a significant share of the rural population did not attend school at all. The situation has been improving gradually in recent years, but this group, also very low in the country's income distribution, is disadvantaged compared to everyone else. At the same time the first serious study of the benefits to rural education suggests that they may be substantial when farmers are required to choose among a number of alternative input combinations. For the most part such situations are characterized by substantial technological change.[29] These results suggest that primary education could have valuable benefits at the national level if technological change were to become more rapid and widespread. It is also clear that more inclusive rural primary

---

29. Thomas Haller, "Education and Rural Development in Colombia" (Ph. D. diss., Purdue University, 1972). Haller used production-function and rate-of-return-to-schooling analyses. Data were collected in four regions of the country, regions selected so that they would differ in tendency to monoculture and in degree of technological change. In three of the four regions Haller concluded that primary schooling did not generally lead to higher farm family incomes (ibid., p. 112). He also concluded that schooling did not have a discernible worker effect (i.e., direct effect of education on production) but did have an allocation effect vis-à-vis certain inputs in certain regions. In the region with modern technology and multiple enterprises (Espinal) the rate of return at all grade levels was estimated at greater than 15 percent (ibid., p. 114).

education up to the fifth year (to permit access to secondary) could have a considerable impact on income distribution in the nation as a whole by equalizing opportunities. Inequality of access to education has been an important source of income inequality in the past.

Desirable Policy Steps from a Redistribution Point of View: Summary

Few steps that would have a significant impact on income distribution via increases in the incomes of the rural poor within agriculture are either simple to design or easy to carry out. But it is very probable that with better information and analysis a policy package could be evolved over time (partly, admittedly, by trial and error) that would substantially improve income distribution. At present, guesses as to which components of such a package might be most productive must remain somewhat speculative, but some do appear to have much more promise than others. In our judgment the most promising short-run possibilities include better distribution of credit (i.e., readier access for the smaller farmers though not necessarily at subsidized rates),[30] a more effective price support program for certain crops, greater emphasis on feeder roads, and a better tax structure, with particular emphasis on a stronger presumptive income tax on land. All these policies would be expected to produce benefits rather quickly if they were feasible to apply. The institutional infrastructure for distributing credit in a reasonably efficient fashion to smaller farmers already exists to some extent, so credit policy can be used to achieve fairly rapid results if those responsible for the official agricultural banks become convinced of the desirability of providing credit to these farmers. The other goals mentioned can surely be achieved in substantial degree under existing institutional constraints (if we except the political constraints that always weigh

---

30. Enforcing subsidized rates on credit to small farmers can easily be counterproductive. If the only action taken is to put an interest rate ceiling on small farmer credit, it may well dry up. (See the discussion of the Brazilian case in Dale Adams, Richard L. Meyer, Norman Rask, and Paulo F. Cidade de Aranjo, "Brazil," in Agency for International Development, *Small Farmer Credit Country Surveys*, vol. 17, June 1973.) Given high payoff investments, small farmers can be expected to borrow at moderate real rates; in the informal credit markets they borrow at very high rates.

against tax increases or closing of tax loopholes). The most promising policy of all, in our judgment, would be a high presumptive income tax on land. It would have the effect not only of decreasing land values and putting them within the reach of more individuals, but also of pushing inefficient producers out of the industry and transferring the land to the hands of more capable entrepreneurs, of increasing tax revenues and the horizontal equity of the tax system, and in short, of inducing by a market mechanism a land transfer from inefficient large-scale producers (this scheme penalizes both inefficiency per se and large size per se) toward more efficient smaller producers. Where feasible, it is an efficient way to achieve an agrarian reform. Administrative difficulties are not great, since the important thing is to have taxes assessed well on the few thousand large farms in the country.

However, the political constraints on passing such a land tax are formidable. The Colombian Congress, which today is really powerful only in the area of tax legislation, is dominated by landed interests. No recent tax reform (there has been some significant legislation in this area between 1967 and 1972) has managed to increase the tax burden of agricultural landowners. The fact that the agricultural tax burden has not increased in the last decade while that of most other groups has illustrates the political constraints on agricultural tax reform.

Policies to spread the effects of research and extension more widely among farmers and to improve education might be expected to have substantial payoffs, but only after a gestation period; this distinguishes them from the policies just cited above. But clearly the scope of the problem is such that all avenues should be explored. Also, these are areas where the political opposition to change may be weakest.

A policy designed to reduce mechanization's labor-displacing effects, if they exist, and an agrarian reform program are both more complex and therefore less obvious components of a desirable package. In the case of mechanization it will be necessary to undertake further studies in order to ascertain its overall impact on labor utilization, and especially to formulate policy instruments that could diminish the negative effects of this phenomenon without erasing also its positive contributions. In the case of agrarian reform, preconditions for expecting very favorable results would seem to include a more balanced political situation with less power to obstruct on the part of the large landowners and much better understanding of the agricultural sector by many of the individuals and technicians applying the agrarian reform. In the absence of these conditions it is difficult to view massive land redistribution programs with much confidence.[31]

31. Doubts about the feasibility of massive programs should not be construed as a reason not to undertake smaller programs. There is much to be said for more gradual redistribution, especially in terms of the learning experience it may permit. But there are problems too, particularly those related to the expectations of large owners not yet expropriated but who may be candidates in the future.

11

An Overview: Looking Ahead

Income distribution is now an important policy question in Colombia and will almost certainly become more so. Income differentials are becoming more widely recognized by the poorer members of the population as urbanization proceeds and education and communications improve. Inequality is at a high absolute level compared to other countries. Under these circumstances it is not surprising that increasing attention is being given in Colombia to the problem of inequality in income distribution.

In this study we have tried to present more detailed information on the structure of income distribution in Colombia, focusing our attention on the year 1964. We have also attempted to trace some recent trends in income distribution for the economy as a whole, by region, and for the agricultural sector. In explaining income distribution and its trends, we have attempted to pinpoint some of the determinants of inequality with a view to laying a better foundation for the analysis of income distribution policy.

Perhaps the most important component of this volume is the empirical work described in chapters 2-4. Before the data presented in these chapters became available in Colombia in 1969, there was limited awareness among professional economists and policymakers of the distributional dimension of economic growth. For example, it was commonly believed that Colombia had less economic inequity than other Latin American countries. Furthermore, observing the growing significance and wealth of a prosperous middle class, politicians and technicians involved in policymaking had been led to the conclusion that income distribution was improving and that economic growth benefited people in all social classes. However, the data in chapter 2 show fairly conclusively that the distribution problem is as serious in Colombia as in neighboring nations, and the data in chapter 4 show that it was precisely this so-called middle class, which can be placed in the eighth and ninth deciles of the distribution, that has benefited most from the development achieved so far. But overall distribution has probably not improved over the last thirty to forty years. In the face of new evidence on the distribution problem the response of Colombian planners and policymakers has been encouraging. There has been an increasing tendency to take this dimension into consideration when evaluating alternative development strategies and projects. Even at the political level, real interest has been shown in the issues posed by the problem of income distribution. Although there is probably a substantial lag between awareness of the issues and concrete action in the field of policy, there is a chance that some poverty groups will benefit from the introduction of distribution objectives in the evaluation of certain policy decisions.

Increased information on the agricultural sector has been helpful recently in the formulation of criteria for some lending institutions trying to reach the small farmer. The weight of budget expenditures in the areas of health and education has also been growing. It is unlikely that all such developments would have taken place without a statistical description of the distribution problem. Further research on the distributional impact of different policies may ultimately have a positive impact on other disadvantaged groups in the population.

At a more detailed level, several main conclusions emerge from the study. First, as of the mid-1960s the distribution of personal income in Colombia was highly unequal. In our estimated distribution for 1964 the Gini coefficient was 0.57, ranking Colombia among the countries with the most unequal distributions if available studies from other countries may be taken as reasonably accurate. (This is not necessarily a valid assumption, and it may well be that some of the less detailed studies in other countries tend to underestimate the degree of inequality.) Our estimates suggest that distribution in 1964 was highly unequal in both agricultural and nonagricultural sectors or, when a different division is used, in both rural and urban sectors. The Gini coefficient of the urban nonagricultural distribution was 0.55, and that of the rural and agricultural distribution was 0.57.

Evidence bearing on income distribution trends over time (see chaps. 3–5) suggests that since some time in the 1930s there has been, if anything, a slight worsening, but there appear to have been different trends in different periods. A period of relatively clear-cut worsening begins (with the start of our usable information) in the 1930s and continues to about the mid-1950s. Not only does overall distribution seem to have worsened during this period but so did the rural and urban distributions separately. From then until about the mid-1960s (beyond which information is too scanty to give us a clear picture of what has been happening) the evidence suggests an improvement in urban distribution, a continued worsening of the distribution in agriculture, and a moderate improvement overall. Clearly, one must lay aside any naïve notion either that distribution has continuously worsened in Colombia or that it has systematically improved; the truth seems much more complicated.

What factors have been important in the high degree of inequality observed at each point in time and in the trends just mentioned? A principal element, certainly, is the extremely unequal distribution of wealth or physical capital. Although the share of national income accruing to physical capital appears to be only in the range of 35–40 percent, this does constitute the bulk of the income of many if not most people in the top income decile (which received about 48 percent of income in 1964). The fact that we were unable to include capital gains income in our calculations forces us to underestimate the significance of concentration of this wealth. The share of all personal income including capital gains that comes from physical capital is definitely greater than the 35 or 40 percent just mentioned, and gains from asset appreciation are probably at least as concentrated as overall income from capital. Another major source of inequality (this is perhaps less to be expected) is a wide variance in labor incomes. Given the fact that labor now receives the bulk of national income in Colombia, if this huge wage bill were fairly evenly distributed, overall inequality would not be nearly so dramatic as it now is. Underlying the inequality of labor incomes is inequality of the distribution of human capital, much of it acquired through formal education (see the discussion in chap. 8).

Other sources of inequality in distribution are much more difficult to appraise and quantify. Nevertheless, we feel that monopoly power in certain sectors has contributed to high capital incomes and to substantial inequality in those incomes. Furthermore, it seems quite clear that the structure and functioning of the capital market and the financial sector have the same effect. Imperfections in this market tend to work strongly in favor of wealthier persons (see chap. 9).

The observation that distribution worsened from the mid-1930s to approximately the mid-1950s and improved from then to the mid-1960s (although agricultural distribution continued to worsen) raises the fascinating question of "what changed" between the two periods. One definite possibility (see chap. 4) is that distribution tends to worsen during periods of rapid growth (the first period cited tended for the most part to be so characterized and included the accelerated growth of the late 1940s and early 1950s, whereas periods of slow growth are characterized by improved distribution, at least in the urban sector. But there are other possibilities. The late 1940s and early 1950s were a period of rapid industrialization and creation of new industries under substantial protection. This situation would be expected not only to lead to monopoly profits but also to decrease the income of labor relative to capital, assuming that the protected industries were more capital intensive than the typical activity in the economy. This period also witnessed very rapid rural-to-urban migration. In Professor Kuznets's scheme the early stages of the shift of the labor force from agriculture to nonagriculture, when the latter sector is still relatively small but has substantially higher income per capita, are associated with worsening distribution. In the Colombian case the shift to the cities, which may have been accelerated by the violence in the late 1940s and early 1950s, may have played a role in holding down blue-collar salaries during that period. The burst of industrialization seems to have created a strong demand for more-skilled workers and for white-collar workers, whose incomes rose dramatically in the industrial sector between 1945 and 1953; blue-collar salaries generally rose much less. In agriculture the advent of mechanization may have helped keep the relative income of labor down, but in these early years of commercial agriculture (referring particularly to the beginning of the postwar period), the widening dispersion may more appropriately be related to the rapid increase in high incomes from commercial farming and to the continued gradual increase in the high incomes from cattle farming.

The impression is that during this period the import-substitution policy—with extensive use of administered prices—between the late 1930s and early 1950s had a significant role in the worsening of the income distribution. Although the Kuznets model suggests that some deterioration was to be expected, it would appear that industrial policy, combined with political action that might have facilitated the stagnation of real urban wages and with the disorganization of some of the poorest rural production units through the violencia, helped to make this deterioration very serious.

In the second period (mid-1950s to mid-1960s) wages of most categories of workers rose, dramatically for blue-collar workers in factory manufacturing, substantially for construction workers and some other groups. Agricultural wages climbed gradually but less quickly than average incomes in agriculture. Just why the urban distribution should have improved in this period is not clear. One hypothesis is that with the relative stagnation of the economy and the tightness of the balance of payments, the rapid advance of large-scale industry characteristic of the previous period did not continue and that small-scale establishments, less dependent on imports and new technology embodied in capital, were relatively more successful. The growth of small firms normally implies a better distribution of income than that of large ones. It is true also that primary education began expanding rapidly in the early 1950s and may have begun to contribute positively toward equality by the mid-1960s. This period saw some increase in the total labor share of national income.

Information on the regional distribution of income is less solid than distribution by factor or by occupational group. Nevertheless, the analysis reported in chapter 5 does suggest rather strongly that there has been no overall worsening of distribution by regions since the 1930s, contrary to the frequently stated position that the concentration of industrialization in the four or five largest cities must have worsened the regional distribution. There is some evidence of increasing regional disparities during the period when overall distribution was worsening, but improvement seems to have taken place between the mid-1950s and the mid-1960s, when the same trend characterized overall distribution. It is evident that some of the traditionally poor departments have benefited from the opportunity to emigrate to booming areas. Most notable is the case of Boyaca,

An Overview: Looking Ahead

from which a high share of persons has emigrated to Bogota. There has also been some industrialization in Boyaca, but probably the major factor in the considerable increase in wages has been emigration. Other areas (Nariño is the prime example) are apparently too far from or too weakly linked to expanding urban employment opportunities (Cali would be the main one for Nariño) to have benefited greatly from these spillovers. As a result Nariño seems to have slipped back through time in terms of some income and welfare indicators. Overall, the picture is mixed; perhaps the most striking conclusion is that even though specific types of economic activity have become increasingly concentrated, there is no evidence of widening income differentials among regions, either on the average or for specific occupations. Clearly, information is incomplete, and much research will be required to paint an adequate picture.

Some of the theoretical discussion of chapter 1 and the historical data in chapter 4 suggest that at Colombia's present stage of development important forces are working toward greater equity. For example, rural–urban migration may now help to diminish income dispersion, given the fact that the country is quickly becoming more urban than rural. Such migration may also begin to raise rural labor income in some areas as relative labor scarcities develop. Buoyant international demand for some rural products, such as meat and certain basic foodstuffs, may also facilitate the improvement of low rural incomes. We believe (see the end of chap. 4) that there are no unalterable forces for increasing income inequalities at the present time, given the mixed structure of the Colombian economy. However, there is some indication that unless the right kinds of policies are followed, a period of rapid economic growth could produce a greater variance of incomes. There is some tentative evidence that the latest episode of fast growth, between 1967 and 1973, may have been characterized by a deterioration at least in the position of the urban employed workers. Some of this effect may have been compensated by the decrease in unemployment, but the key point is that the rapid rates of growth have not been exploited to achieve a direct decrease in income dispersion.

The challenge that now faces the country is how to avoid a future increase in inequality as economic growth accelerates. The analysis of some policy instruments in part II of this volume is an attempt to evaluate the effectiveness of several types of government action in avoiding this outcome. Four areas are considered and an attempt is made to evaluate the income-distribution impact of past policies in these particular areas and to judge their potential future effects. In the case of overall fiscal policy (government taxation, transfers, and expenditure patterns), we conclude that it has been comparatively neutral as to the overall distribution. The tax and transfer side is positive although it is more or less neutral over most of the income range, taking a substantially higher share of income only for the top decile. The distributional implications of expenditure patterns are notoriously difficult to measure. Subject to such problems, our best guess is that the expenditure pattern is mildly redistributive in a positive direction, but that, even under the most optimistic assumptions, these expenditures do not significantly improve the level of consumption of goods and services by the poor. However, this does not mean that the government budget cannot be used to increase the welfare of poverty groups. It would appear that even without increasing the proportion of government expenditure in gross national product, a greater emphasis on the financing of a minimum per capita level of some services such as health and the lower levels of education and less emphasis on investment for infrastructure might produce a substantial improvement in the welfare of the poorer sectors of the population. Chapter 8 tries to show that government provision of services such as education can not only foster a more equitable distribution of current consumption but may also contribute directly to a decrease in income dispersion in the future.

When the possibility of increasing the tax burden (measured by the relationship between tax revenues and GNP) through progressive taxes is considered, the prospects that fiscal policy could help to create a more egalitarian society are much improved. Better administration of taxes has already helped to improve the equity of the system and could certainly do much more. Overall, fiscal policy can undoubtedly contribute substantially more than it now does, but it would have to contribute *much more* to make a large dent in the extreme inequality from which Colombia now suffers.

Chapter 8 cites the clear positive correlation between education and income in Colombia, implying that the very unequal distribution of education probably explains a significant part of the dispersion in labor incomes. A large effort on the part of the state to guarantee full primary education to all children would probably diminish markedly the dispersion of labor incomes in the future. A switch from higher toward primary education would also have a positive effect on both equity and economic growth, given the higher social rates of return found for investment in primary education.

As for the argument that an expansion of education will not improve the income of the lower deciles of the distribution because of its low quality and the poor adaptation of the present curriculum to the needs of the system, some evidence from other countries suggests that the quality of education as conventionally measured is often a less important determinant of future economic performance than is the learning environment created by the schooling. Furthermore, in the case of Colombia there is no clear evidence that the classical curriculum is less well adapted to the needs of the economy than are vocational types of education. All these considerations reinforce the recommendation of expanding primary education without waiting for widespread changes in the quality of that education.

A major emphasis in this study has been placed on the negative distributional impact of many aspects of the financial and exchange rate systems and policy. The imperfections in the capital markets tend to prevent the small-scale investor from achieving the high real rate of return available to the large-scale investor, who may operate in stocks, real capital, and so on. Small savers are further penalized by inflation since the assets in which they can invest usually do not maintain their real value over time—as in the case of cash and saving deposits. Low interest rate policies, often defended as a distribution-improving policy, have almost surely had the opposite effect, as well as leading to misallocation of resources and (less directly) decreased incentives to savings. Inflation itself has probably been a cause of the rapid increase in the real value of certain types of physical assets, with most of the capital gains accruing to the rich. Financial systems generally favor large borrowers because of their better guarantees, but this discrimination tends to become stronger under the disequilibrium conditions created by inflation and interest rate ceilings. In short, the functioning of the capital market seems to be a virtual disaster from the distribution point of view. Making this market more perfect (i.e., giving more equal access to different participants) would be an important first step toward improving distribution of income in both the short and the long run. Market prices might promote a greater growth in the demand for labor, whereas government control of key prices such as the exchange rate and certain interest rates has in the past implied substantial net transfers of income from the poor to the rich.

The agricultural sector is of special interest to the overall question of distribution because many of the poorest members of the Colombian population are located there. Worse, for many if not most of them, real incomes have been rising less rapidly than for the population as a whole; this group includes the landless farmers and many of the small-scale operators. Both agricultural policy, which has in general favored modernization via the mechanization or labor-saving route, and partially exogenous events such as the transfer of technology from more developed countries seem to have contributed to the systematically worsening distribution within this sector. Agrarian reform, unquestionably the most highly touted policy intended to offset such trends, has clearly been unsuccessful; it is not even obvious that its effect on distribution has been positive at all. The institutions, both private and public, dealing with agriculture are basically inclined to service the larger-scale farmers and to neglect the smaller ones. In the private sector this is a natural result of the greater difficulties and probably smaller profits of doing business with small farmers. In the public sector it reflects the implicit assumption that the way of the future lies with the larger farm and that the small farmer has little potential. Correspondingly, credit policy tends not to reach the very small farmer, research is directed at crops grown primarily on the large farms, and so on. None of this is exogenously fixed but rather a reflection of conscious and unconscious policy.

The indications that government policy has been biased against labor-intensive technologies and methods of production suggest that the country has not exploited the great potential implicit in the fact that small farms have higher levels of production per hectare than large enterprises. Moreover, it is the small farms that produce the basic foods that have low supply elasticities and whose prices have been increasing rapidly in the latest period of rapid economic growth. Both these conditions would seem to suggest that land reform in Colombia could have a positive impact on production. Since the redistribution effect of such reform is clearly desirable, the slow progress made in the last decade seems at first sight completely unjustified. But it must be recognized that there are very important nonpolitical constraints on effective land reform.

One of the major problems is the difficulty of convincing agricultural technicians trained in developed countries that in Colombia small farms using intermediate technologies are more efficient (from an overall point of view) than large capital-intensive enterprises. This difficulty has been a barrier to efficient production on expropriated land. Instead of giving the land to the peasants, land reform administrators have started experimenting with all kinds of cooperative systems that have made inefficient state farms out of inefficient farms managed by absentee landlords. These experiments have not been spectacularly successful production-wise and they have decreased the interest for land reform among the peasantry.

Little is said concerning the political constraints on land reform, but it is probably a valid generalization that opposition is minimized if the land reform institute concentrates on capital-intensive projects in irrigated areas and if it uses the most modern technology. Such a policy puts a financial ceiling on land reform and implicitly reinforces the position of the large agroindustries, which claim that only large-scale capitalistic agricultural production will be viable in the last two decades of the twentieth century. The tragedy is that this is almost certainly the wrong policy to follow. But when in the early 1970s INCORA started to move toward a more redistributive strategy, opposition from traditional agricultural interests managed to block any further progress in this direction.

It is perhaps not surprising, given that an improved income distribution did not even enter into the discussions of economic policy until quite recently, that policy measures taken over the last few decades have not tended to support it. On balance they have probably worsened it. There is no evidence to date that this is in any sense a result of a natural conflict between growth policies and distribution policies although many policymakers have probably viewed the issue in these terms. It is much more likely due primarily to a playing-out of the relative political power of different groups in the population, the wealthier having the power and manipulating the instruments either deliberately or subconsciously to favor their own interests. The inclination to assume that the technologies and ways of doing things in developed countries are necessarily appropriate tends to decrease the demand for labor and worsen distribution. Some foreign policy advice has probably contributed to this inclination.

In summary, there are three broad types of policies that can improve the welfare of the poorest sectors of society. One involves changes in government policy to affect consumption differentials directly, for example, changes in the means of financing the budget and changes in the distribution of government expenditure. This strategy implies higher tax burdens and a redirection of expenditure toward social services such as education and health.

A second strategy consists of redistributing assets. This includes the government transfer of assets such as land to groups who are usually considered disadvantaged and who with such complementary assets can increase the productivity of their labor. An improved distribution of education also implies a shift of assets, in this case human capital, to the poorer sectors of the population.

A third route involves improving the functioning of markets, partly by market regulation. The capital market in particular is in need of the kind of reorganization discussed above. We believe that benefits will stand a much greater chance of being achieved by removal of imperfections (moving the system toward perfect markets) than by imposition of controls designed to improve on competitive markets (price controls sometimes fall in this category).

Asset redistribution, redirection of public economic policy toward transferal of consumption power to the poor, and better regulation of markets are all probably essential to ensure that the lowest deciles of the income distribution benefit substantially from the process of economic growth in the future. Yet each strategy will be difficult to achieve in a society with the institutions and the distribution of power of Colombia. However, the sociopolitical structure of the country probably makes it easier to implement economic policy shifts of the type discussed than to effect direct redistribution of physical assets. Societies that seem to have been dominated by groups as conservative as the Colombian elite have nevertheless achieved free universal primary education and progressive fiscal systems. The question is whether such modest but apparently viable policy shifts will take place and whether such reforms would be sufficient to produce a greater degree of equity as economic development proceeds.

APPENDIX TABLES

Table A1
Income Trends by Occupation
(1958 pesos per year)

	Agricultural Laborers (1)	Blue-Collar Manufacturing Workers (2)	Bogota Unskilled Construction Workers (3)	White Collar Manufacturing Workers (4)	Government Employees (5)	Total Labor Force (6)	Median Income of Total Labor Force (7)
1935	1,443 }	2,280–2,365	(1,511) }	4,348–4,822			
1936	1,289		(1,320)				
1937	1,400		1,659				
1938	1,260		1,488				
1939	1,166		1,456				
1940	1,345		1,488				
1941	1,297		1,493		3,677		
1942	1,058		1,345		3,662		
1943	880				3,668		
1944	945				3,645		
1945	1,010	2,561		6,391	3,585	2,564	1,272
1946	1,050				3,598	2,802	1,390
1947	1,106				3,699	2,936	1,456
1948	1,186				3,743	2,993	1,485
1949	1,113				3,741	3,276	1,625
1950	1,115		1,091		3,895	3,472	1,722
1951	1,137		1,048		3,930	3,414	1,693
1952	1,212		1,122		3,938	3,565	1,768
1953	1,164	3,193	1,067	9,600	4,041	3,823	1,896
1954	1,164		1,075		4,178	4,147	2,057
1955	1,289	3,462	1,138	9,510	4,157	4,027	1,997
1956	1,191	3,792	1,463	9,666	4,235	4,123	2,045
1957	1,063	3,906	1,353	9,303	4,294	3,977	1,973
1958	1,125	4,030	1,378	9,839	4,387	3,856	1,913
1959	1,195	4,147	1,540	10,357	4,489	4,014	1,991
1960	1,262	4,396	1,606	10,937	4,702	4,102	2,035

Table A1 (continued)

1961	1,270	4,572	1,727	11,575	4,929	4,205	2,086
1962	1,415	5,294	1,884	12,560	5,073	4,332	2,149
1963	1,380	5,839	1,713	12,630	5,180	4,351	2,158
1964	1,230	5,680	1,793	12,500	5,256	4,663	2,313
1965	1,401	5,931	2,071	13,020	5,248	4,671	2,317
1966	1,332	5,889	1,843	12,993		4,812	2,387
1967	1,379	6,012	1,810	13,638		4,840	2,401
1968	1,282	6,174	1,810	14,160			
1969		6,324	1,735	14,944			
1970			1,708				

Sources and Methodology: Column (1) is based on data compiled in Berry, *Development of Agricultural Sector*, statistical appendix. Columns (2) and (4) are from A. Berry, "A Review of Development in Colombia Since World War II," mimeo, 1971. Column (5) is from the sources cited in table 4.1. Column (6) is from Berry, ibid., table A-1. Column (8) is simply col. (7) times 0.496, a coefficient based on the observed relationship between the median and the mean in 1964, when estimates of both were available. Clearly this ratio is not constant over time so this column gives only a rough estimate of the true median. Column (3)'s sources are cited in table 4.3.

Note: Figures in parentheses [col. (3), 1935 and 1936] are rough estimates.

Table A2
Departmental Income (or Output) Distribution in 1953
(Monetary values expressed in millions of 1953 pesos, except where indicated)

Department	Agriculture Labor Force	Agriculture Output	Factory Labor Force	Manufacturing Factory Output	Artisan Labor Force	Manufacturing Artisan Output	Commerce Labor Force	Commerce Output	Labor Force in Sectors Listed	Output of Sectors Listed	Output per Worker (1953 pesos)	Share of Total Labor Force in Sectors Listed (1951 population census)
	(1)	(2)	(3)	(4)	(5)	(6)	(7)	(8)	(9)	(10)	(11)	(12)
Antioquia	263.17	386.16	47,278	342.514	26,772	78.228	23,639	144.44	360,859	951.342	2,636	.7013
Atlantico	28.44	32.55	18,334	109.934	14,626	29.603	17,911	68.24	79,321	240.327	3,030	.5653
Bolivar and Coroba	191.85	386.43	6,852	39.860	19,899	45.191	17,324	49.60	235,925	521.081	2,209	.7720
Bolivar	122.18	192.97					11,209	37.63				
Boyaca	188.22	176.57	3,340	11.826	14,554	17.960	7,000	16.15	213,114	222.506	1,044	.8151
Caldas	213.80	452.39	12,134	84.307	22,084	97.633	19,334	195.57	267,352	829.900	3,104	.7575
Cauca	103.72	154.44	1,550	9.850	7,497	22.963	4,821	12.60	117,588	199.853	1,700	.8039
Cordoba	69.67[a]	193.46					6,115	11.97				
Cundinamarca (and Bogota)	226.07	323.25	47,859	320.862	47,915	103.161	45,000	281.08	366,844	1028.353	2,803	.5154
Huila	70.47	92.27	1,010	7.238	7,448	32.481	4,300	16.20	83,228	148.189	1,780	.7494
Magdalena	97.34[b]	207.00	1,390	11.421	11,169	43.961	9,500	26.00	119,399	288.382	2,415	.7722

Table A2 (continued)

	(1)	(2)	(3)	(4)	(5)	(6)	(7)	(8)	(9)	(10)	(11)	(12)
Nariño	126.06	123.84	2,772	12.993	41,431	76.357	7,000	12.92	177,263	226.110	1,276	.8273
Norte de Santander	82.06	108.83	3,451	19.874	7,995	21.027	7,900	27.58	101,406	177.311	1,748	.7096
Santander	173.43	154.84	12,471	61.642	17,596	33.098	11,500	45.14	214,997	294.720	1,371	.7345
Tolima	146.22	324.08	5,181	27.624	12,462	42.470	9,701	55.09	173,564	449.264	2,588	.7761
Valle	190.26	313.13	34,729	226.476	34,295	97.501	30,224	185.00	289,508	822.107	2,840	.6951
Other			765	5.867	4,891	34.476	3,070	25.82				
Total	2,101.110	3235.78	199,126	1,292.288	290,634	776.110	218,224	1161.43	2,800,368	6,465.608	2,302	.6929

Sources and Methodology: The agricultural labor force estimate was based (1) on the upward adjustment to the labor force reported in the 1951 population census used in Berry, *Development of Agricultural Sector*, for the male labor force and (2) on a 1951–53 growth rate based on the 1951–64 growth rate calculated in the same source for the male labor force.

Figures for factory manufacturing correspond to net value added based on an adjustment to DANE's 1953 industrial census value-added estimates. The adjustment involves subtraction of specific inputs not subtracted by DANE but routinely subtracted by the Central Bank in its value added estimates. The figures come from Miguel Urrutia and Clara Elsa Villalba, "El Sector Artesanal en el Desarrollo Colombiano," *Revista de Planeacion y Desarrollo* 1, no. 3 (Oct. 1969), 43–78, table 2a, the same source used for the artisan manufacturing output figures shown here.

Commerce labor force estimates for 1953 were based primarily on interpolation between the 1951 and 1964 population census figures but also taking into account the 1954 commerce census figures, which suggested some underenumeration for a few departments in the 1951 population census (especially Boyaca and Huila and possibly Cundinamarca, Santander, and Norte de Santander) and which in general give reasonable guidelines. The 1953 commerce labor force estimated here (218,224), together with the estimate for 1954 of 240,000, would imply a growth rate of about 10 percent between the two years. This is probably a little high but not so high as to imply that the 1953 figures are seriously out of line.

Estimation of commerce incomes for 1953 was more difficult than in 1967 due to lack of figures (in the 1954 commerce census) on purchases and inventory changes by commerce establishments to go with the sales figures. Here we have assumed that income generated in commerce was .177 percent of sales for retail and wholesale except for food and beverages (this corresponds to the 1967 percentages). For an amount of wholesale in each department equal to the amount of retail we assume a 10 percent ratio and for the excess a 25 percent ratio. The 1954 census appears to have captured coffee exports in the wholesale figures, and we believe that the national accounts has assumed a 25 percent commerce margin in this category. The importance of coffee is seen clearly in Caldas's very high figure. In 1967 the ratio of food and beverage retail sales to wholesale sales was only about 1:2, but it seems plausible that in 1954 it would have been greater than this, owing to the probably smaller degree of vertical integration. A noncomparability between the two years does appear to exist in that the 1967 figures do not capture coffee sales and must accordingly be assumed to be incomplete. To effect the 1953 estimate, we have scaled down the 1954 values by assuming a 1 percent increase in real income in each department, taking account of inflation.

Information on percentage distribution of value of agricultural output among departments is available for 1965; this 1965 distribution was then applied to the national 1967 value-added estimate of the national accounts. In other words we assume the same distribution of value added in 1967 that was found for value of output in 1965. As of 1967 the ratio of purchased inputs to value of output in agriculture as a whole was assumed by the Central Bank in its national accounts calculations to be about 12 percent. This figure would be substantially higher in the departments with more commercial farms than in more traditional ones, so our data overestimate the concentration of agricultural output by department. (The 1965 estimate of agricultural output by department did not include Choco, the Guajira, or the territories, and it was assumed that in 1967 they had 2 percent of total value of output.

The 1967 labor force estimate was calculated by extrapolating the 1951–64 labor force growth rate through 1967 and then subtracting for each department the percentage by which the estimated total 1967 agricultural labor force is less than that obtained by this simple extrapolation. (The total agricultural labor force in 1967 can be estimated with reasonable accuracy because a 1970 figure is available, but no post-1964 figures are available at the departmental level.) The total 1964 labor force is estimated on the assumption that underenumeration was the same for females as for males; male underenumeration ratios were calculated in Berry, *Development of Agricultural Sector.* It is implicitly assumed that the departmental joint male and female growth rate of the labor force (1964–67) will be the same as for the male labor force in the previous intercensal period. This might constitute an upward bias, but since our department figures are corrected to match a reasonably accurate national labor force figure, it should not create too much of a problem.

The figures for factory manufacturing come from DANE, *Industria Manufacturero: 1967* (Bogota, n.d.). DANE's value added figures are substantially above those of the Central Bank, the latter institution subtracting out more costs in making the calculation than does DANE. In 1967 the Central Bank estimate for value added at market prices was 13,182.0 million pesos as opposed to the DANE estimate of 15,406.4 million pesos; the difference is about 14.5 percent. Probably DANE's overestimation is greater in the larger centers such as Bogota and Medellin since some of the difference has to do with advertising expenditures and the like. But because of lack of information in this regard, we here simply reduce the DANE estimate for each department by 10 percent.

Table A2 (continued)

Incomplete and somewhat contradictory sources of information on the number of artisans by department leave a considerable range of error in the estimates for 1967, which are based on data for 1964 and 1970. The basic 1964 estimate (made by Urrutia and Villalba, "Sector Artesanal," p. 49) provided our estimate for 1964 for all departments except Cundinamarca, where our comparison of the 1964 Bogota population census and 1964 DANE survey data suggested a larger number of artisans than reported by Urrutia-Villalba for total urban Cundinamarca. We assumed that Cundinamarca excluding Bogota had 4,000 urban artisans, and as a result our total estimate of artisans is about 10,000 higher than that of Urrutia-Villalba in 1964. Figures for 1970 come from DANE's 1970 household survey; we have used here the estimate of occupied persons (859,000 for the nation) as presented in *Boletin Mensual de Estadistica*, No. 238, p. 79. DANE's estimate of the total labor force (all sectors) is reasonable for 1970, but it may have overestimated the nonagricultural sectors, so this figure could be somewhat upward biased. On the other hand it excludes all the unemployed persons normally attached to this sector; DANE's own figures indicate a total labor force (employed and unemployed) in manufacturing of 950,000. Hence, on balance our estimate seems conservative. For each of the five major regions into which it divided the country the household survey presented figures on the percentage of the labor force in each sector. From these data we derived estimates of total occupied manufacturing labor force in rural and urban regions. These estimates matched the total of 859,000. (DANE appears to have made errors in its calculations of percentage distribution of the occupied labor force for each region as a whole. As a result, using the percentage distribution given for the regions, our estimate of occupied manufacturing labor force in each region was higher than the sum of the rural and urban labor forces in that region. Since this latter figure produced the correct national when summed across the five regions, we assume that the error was in estimating the percentage distribution by activity in the region as a whole.) Our estimate of 1970 factory employment was a simple extrapolation of DANE's published figures for 1966 (*Boletin Mensual de Estadistica*, no. 224, p. 187) and 1968 (DANE, *Industria Manufacturera Nacional: 1968*, p. 14). There was little change between these two years and we assumed a comparably small change up to 1970. As discussed elsewhere, DANE has substantial underenumeration of the factory labor force, so that our factory employment figures are on the low side, as noted earlier; there is a corresponding upward bias in the artisan category. Since little information is available with which to quantify this underenumeration of the factory labor force by department, we have not tried to correct for this problem. The underenumeration occurs for the smaller plants, which are relatively more frequent in the departments with smaller cities, so there may be some relative overestimation of artisanry in the departments with smaller cities, which are normally the poorer departments. This situation would imply some tendency to overestimate the regional skewness of income distribution. To ascertain the artisan labor force by department, we have extrapolated from 1964 to 1967 using the growth rates calculated for the five regions between 1964 and 1970. Therefore, each department within a region is assumed to have the same artisan labor force growth rate as the region as a whole. This assumption is obviously invalid, but any alternative seemed too arbitrary. Unfortunately, for three of the regions the implicit growth rate of artisanry was extremely fast over this period, so a not insignificant error could be introduced. For example, it seems highly probable that Nariño, which seemed to be losing artisans between 1953 and 1964, did not gain many or might even have continued to lose in the succeeding years, so that the number for that region is overestimated whereas perhaps that in Valle is underestimated. Altantico may be underestimated and some other regions of the north coast overestimated, and so on.

For artisan output figures we again relied primarily on the Urrutia-Villalba estimates of income by department in 1964. Value added per person in the artisan sector is taken from Urrutia and Villalba, "Sector Artesanal," table 5b, as expressed in 1964 pesos. The assumption was then made that productivity per person rose at 2 percent a year over 1964–67 (about equal to the growth during 1953–64 taking the average across the country). Values in 1964 prices were converted to 1967 pesos by the GDP deflator.

For the commerce sector it was important to make corrections to the 1967 commerce census (the basic source of information) because there was evidence of considerable labor force underenumeration. A guide to the degree of underenumeration was provided by the 1964 population census. (Detailed methodology is presented in another study, from which the labor force and income data were taken, A. Berry, "Urban Labor Surplus and the Commerce Section: Colombia," Yale Economic Growth Center Discussion Paper no. 178, 1973).

The estimate of commerce income is based on wages paid according to the 1967 commerce census and on an estimate of proprietory income for those proprietors listed in that census (see Berry, ibid., table A-22). Since a substantial and widely varying share of the commerce labor force appears to have been missed in this census, an estimate was made of the number of missed workers (see same study, table A-22.5). When this estimate was less than 10 percent, it was assumed that the average income of the missed persons was equal to the average wage rate in food and beverage retailing, which was somewhat below that in all retail commerce or all commerce in general. (Figures were not available on wages by size of establishment at the departmental level.) When higher shares of the labor force were missed it seems plausible to assume that the average size of the establishments missed was probably greater, or at least greater relative to the departmental universe. In general there seems to be some tendency for departments with apparently severe underreporting to wind up with high estimates of proprietory income per unpaid worker (table A-22) consistent with the idea that a good number of establishments were missed and that they were relatively small. The only exception to this rule appears to be Magdalena establishments, which nevertheless wound up with a low estimate of proprietory income per unpaid worker. When the share of missed persons reaches 50 percent we assumed an average income of missed persons double the reported food and beverage retailing salary; for 30 percent we raised that salary by 50 percent, and so on.

*a*Assuming a distribution between Cordoba and post-1952 Bolivar calculated by the authors on the basis of the municipal census figures. Subject to considerable error.

*b*This is a guess because the 1951 population census estimate is particularly open to question.

Table A3
Total Income or Output by Department, 1967
(Monetary values expressed in millions of current pesos, except where indicated)

Department	Agriculture		Factory Manufacturing			Cottage-Shop Manufacturing		Commerce		Agriculture, Manufacturing, and Commerce					
	Labor Force	Output	Labor Force	Value Added		Labor Force	Output	Labor Force	Income	Labor Force	Percentage of Total Departmental Labor Force in 1964	Income (or Output)	Average Income (or Output) (pesos)	Percentage of Total Income (or Output)	Relative Income (or Output)
	(1)	(2)	(3)	(4)		(5)	(6)	(7)	(8)	(9)	(10)	(11)	(12)	(13)	(14)
Antioquia	312,685	2,181.44	74,259	3,590.7		39,726	326.64	51,769	1,164.79	478,439	61.95	7,263.57	15,182	14.07	1.103
Atlantico	34,190	142.17	26,809	1,258.43		20,333	237.36	28,300	704.69	109,632	40.46	2,342.70	21,369	4.54	1.560
Bolivar	163,300	1,711.12	6,083	560.70		21,762	226.26	22,751	439.10	218,896	65.47	2,937.18	13,418	5.69	.980
Boyaca	211,170	1,658.91	4,908	383.26		20,889	91.96	13,537	190.96	230,324	77.17	2,325.09	9,281	4.50	.675
Caldas	215,200	2,320.61	14,292	691.92		35,997	493.62	39,008	945.08	304,497	63.74	4,451.23	14,618	8.62	1.067
Cauca	148,570	926.82	2,350	119.48		10,109	71.44	8,124	65.09	169,153	79.72	1,182.83	6,993	2.29	.511
Cordoba	125,030	1,716.83	556	30.66		9,408	535.05	9,737	151.73	144,731	74.40	2,434.26	16,819	4.71	1.223
Bogota	—	—	75,368	3,231.67		79,418	781.76	99,895	2,462.45	254,681	27.37	6,475.88	25,427	12.54	1.857
Cundinamarca	237,290	1,560.94	13,493	677.01		16,578	58.28	17,188	132.42	284,549	72.36	2,428.65	8,535	4.70	.623
Choco	—*	—*	80	.65		2,174	20.28	—	—						
Guajira	—	—	123	2.63		—	—	—	—						
Huila	79,650	915.82	1,055	57.44		10,461	141.25	6,532	112.09	97,698	68.53	1,226.60	12,555	2.38	.917
Magdalena	150,650	3,069.01	1,664	151.83		15,047	193.36	16,885	306.07	184,246	68.90	3,720.27	20,192	7.20	1.474
Meta	—	627.48	706	56.20		—	—	—	—						
Nariño	149,060	820.43	3,311	94.17		42,888	170.96	9,025	139.51	204,284	78.43	1,225.07	5,997	2.37	.435
Norte de Santander	80,300	504.30	2,799	135.79		15,749	114.18	13,669	228.11	112,517	61.93	982.38	8,731	1.90	.637
Santander	162,420	1,243.07	12,121	839.44		31,125	260.68	23,990	697.48	229,656	65.64	3,040.67	13,240	5.89	.967
Tolima	155,730	1,813.56	2,946	172.12		19,380	225.75	17,183	305.00	195,239	68.27	2,516.43	12,850	4.87	.941
Valle	168,620	2,223.34	50,597	3,076.07		62,300	577.94	61,256	1,209.85	342,773	52.68	7,087.20	20,676	13.72	1.510
Other	172,580	—	305	—		—	—	16,131	—						
Colombia	2,371,395	23,435.85	293,825	15,130.23		453,344	4,526.73	455,000	9,254.42	3,770,481	61.37	51,640.01	13,696	100.00	1.000

Sources and Methodology: See table A2.

Note: Column totals are the sum of the departmental figures presented in the column. Since there are different information gaps according to the sector, these totals are not comparable.

*Dash indicates data not available.

Table A4
Distribution of Education in 1951 for
the 20–24-Year Age Group

Years of Schooling	Number of Persons	Years of Education	Percentage of Persons	Percentage of Education	Accumulated Percentage of Persons	Accumulated Percentage of Education
0	338,529	—	33.4	—	33.4	—
1	75,231	75,272	7.4	2.9	40.8	2.9
2	140,231	280,462	13.8	10.8	54.6	13.7
3	144,583	433,749	14.2	16.7	68.8	30.4
4	136,072	544,288	13.4	21.0	82.2	51.4
5	77,440	387,200	7.6	14.9	89.8	66.3
6	18,573	111,438	1.8	4.3	91.6	70.6
7	23,618	165,326	2.3	6.4	93.9	77.0
8	19,210	153,680	1.9	5.9	95.8	82.9
9	14,496	130,464	1.4	5.0	97.2	87.9
10	7,951	79,510	0.8	3.1	98.0	91.0
11	9,642	106,062	0.9	4.1	98.9	95.1
12	2,213	26,556	0.2	1.0	99.1	96.1
13	2,456	31,928	0.3	1.2	99.4	97.3
14	1,877	26,278	0.2	1.0	99.6	98.3
15	1,368	20,520	0.1	0.8	99.7	99.1
16	888	14,208	0.1	0.5	99.8	99.6
17	625	10,625	0.1	0.4	99.9	100.0
	1,015,044	2,593,566	99.9	100.0		

Sources: From tables A-1 and A-3 in Miguel Urrutia and Clara Elsa de Sandoval, "Distribucion de la Educacion y Distribucion de Ingreso," *Revista del Banco de la Republica* 44, no. 519 (Jan. 1971): 12–25. The data come from the 1951 census. The information on education used covered 25,638 fewer people than in the age group according to the census.

Table A5
Distribution of Education in 1964 for
the 20–24-Year Age Group

Years of Schooling	Number of Persons	Years of Education	Percentage of Persons	Percentage of Education	Accumulated Percentage of Persons	Accumulated Percentage of Education
0	284,223	—	21.2	—	21.2	—
1	92,425	92,425	6.9	2.1	28.1	2.1
2	210,620	421,240	15.7	9.6	43.8	11.7
3	225,668	677,004	16.9	15.4	60.7	27.1
4	165,933	663,732	12.4	15.1	73.1	42.2
5	169,758	848,790	12.7	19.3	85.8	61.5
6	35,620	213,720	2.7	4.9	88.5	66.4
7	34,012	238,084	2.5	5.4	91.0	71.8
8	27,647	221,176	2.1	5.0	93.1	76.8
9	23,840	214,560	1.8	4.9	94.9	81.7
10	13,322	133,220	1.0	3.0	95.9	84.7
11	28,814	316,954	2.2	7.2	98.1	91.9
12	6,556	78,672	0.5	1.8	98.6	93.7
13	6,569	85,397	0.5	1.9	99.1	95.6
14	5,214	72,996	0.4	1.7	99.5	97.3
15	3,888	58,320	0.3	1.3	99.8	98.6
16	2,206	35,296	0.2	0.8	100.0	99.4
17	1,318	22,406	0.1	0.5	100.1	99.9
	1,337,633	4,393,992	100.1	99.9		

Sources: From tables A-2 and A-4 of Urrutia and Sandoval, "Distribucion de Educacion y Ingresos." The data are from the 1964 census. For the reason explained in the footnote to table A4, only 94 percent of the population in the age group is included.

Index

Abilities, distribution of, 178–81
Absentee landlords, 29
Adams, Dale, 249 n
Adelman, Irma, 25 n
Agrarian reform. See Agriculture; Land reform
Agricultural income distribution, 53–86, 230–32; changes over time, 64–72; in development, *1930s–1960s*, 90–95; labor and capital, 60–64; nonagriculture compared with, 16–20, 31–35, 71–72, 107 n–108 n; personal, 54–57
Agricultural labor force: and crops, 80–85; and farm size, 73; increase, 74 n; minimum wage, 152; real wages by department and climate, 66–67; shift to nonagricultural sector, 16–20, 255; surplus, 13, 53, 69 n; unpaid family workers, 31, 94 n; wages, 59–72, 74–77, 90–95, 99–108, 115, 118, 133, 145 n, 256
Agriculture, 230–51, 253, 255, 260–61; agrarian reform, 230, 242–43, 250–51, 260; credit policy, 232–36, 249; crops, changing, 74, 76, 231, 237–38; crops, labor share in, 80, 82–95; factor proportions, changing, 73, 77, 80–85; farm size, 53–54, 57–59, 73–74, 77, 80, 84, 85, 233–35, 244, 246; government policy on, 230–51; income distribution (*see* Agricultural income distribution); and inflation, 227–28; land policy, 242–48 (*see also* Land reform); large commercial farms, 229, 238, 241, 245, 246, 260, 261; output per capita, 132, 134; prices, 75, 76; price supports and controls, 241–42; product composition of demand, 74–77, 231; public expenditures in, 165–66; research and extension, 237–38, 250; taxes 238–40, 249–50; technological change (mechanization), 73–79, 231, 236–37, 250, 261; tractors, 76, 78–79, 236
Ahluwalia, Montek, 40 n, 118 n
Alianza Nacional Popular (ANAPO), 221
Allende, Salvador, 200
Antioquia, 138 n
Argentina, 40, 41, 43
Arrubla, Mario, 110 n
Asociacion Colombiana de Facultades de Medicina (ASCOFAME), 24 n, 130
Atlantico, 131, 138 n , 223
Automobiles. See Motor vehicles

Ballentine, Gregory, 3 n
Banco de la Republica, 122 n
Banco Internacional de Reconstruccion y Fomento. See World Bank
Banking, 200–01, 205; and agriculture, 233; gross assets, classification, 210, 211; loans, 208, 209, 221, 233. See also Interest rates; Savings
Barley, 76, 82, 83
Beans, 82, 83
Bell, Clive, 40 n, 118 n
Berry, Albert, 11 n, 27 n, 49–52, 65 n, 70 n, 71 n, 72 n, 75 n, 76 n, 94 n, 95 n, 104 n, 107 n, 108 n, 110 n, 115 n, 125 n, 195 n, 233, 236 n, 237, 238 n, 239 n, 243 n
Birth rate: and education, 198 n; and income, 24 n
Black market, 204
Blaug, Mark, 195 n, 196
Bogota, 37, 49, 122, 130, 136, 154, 164, 190, 257; labor income, 181–83; population growth, 144; public utility rates, 169; wages, 71 n, 97 n, 99, 103 n, 104, 105, 109, 110
Bonds: government, 214; Mortgage Bank, 218, 222 n; tax-exempt, 218, 222, 227

Boyaca, 103 n, 131, 133, 138 n, 256–57
Brazil, 124, 188; financial policy, 204 n, income distribution, 40, 41
Budd, Edward C., 228 n
Burt, C., 180

Caja Agraria, 232–36
Caldas, 131, 134 n, 136
Cali, 104 n, 144, 257
Calvo, Guillermo, 6 n
Capital: agricultural income, 60–64, 75; and asset appreciation, 116–17; human (see Human capital); income distribution, 8–10, 22–26, 95, 96, 105–06, 110–11, 115, 116–17, 254–55; and labor surplus, 13; and price changes, 10; regional inequality, 125; return on, 7, 23–24, 205
Capital gains: in agriculture, 56; income, 45
Capital-intensive production, 10, 206, 213; agricultural, 245, 246, 261
Capital/labor ration, 6–7, 9–10
Capital market, 201–03, 259–60; political power in, 228–29; tax incentives in, 218–20
Cattle, 75, 76, 80, 82–83, 85
Cauca, 131, 138 n, 139, 238
Central Bank, 203, 231 n, 218, 219, 220, 228, 229
Centro de Estudios sobre Desarrollo Economico (CEDE), 28, 49, 111 n, 122n, 219 n
Centro Interamericana para la Agricultura Tropical (CIAT), 238
CEPAL (Comision Economica para America Latina), 47 n
Chenery, Hollis, 40 n, 118 n
Child mortality, 149
Chile: banking system, 200; income distribution, 40, 41
Chu, David, 106
Cidade de Aranjo, Paulo F., 249 n
Cities. See Urban areas
Cline, William F., 3 n
Cobb–Douglas production function, 9–10
Coffee, 231; prices, 90, 207 n, 239 n, 241; production, labor in, 74, 76, 82; tax on exports, 156, 238
Comision Economica para America Latina (CEPAL), 47 n
Commerce: output per capita, 132; wages, 104, 105, 109, 118
Construction: wages, 71, 99–105, 109–10, 119, 256
Contraloria General de la Republica, 111
Cordoba, Polibio, 49–50, 219 n
Corn, 76, 82, 83, 238, 241
Costa Rica, 40
Cottage-shop workers, 143
Cotton, 74, 82, 83, 86, 231
Credit, 208, 210, 213, 215, 221; in agriculture, 232–36, 249; foreign, 215–18; regulation of, 202
Cultural services, expenditures for, 164
Cundinamarca, 131, 136, 138 n, 139; wages, 99 n, 103

Daly, Herman, 8 n
DANE. See Departamento Administrativo Nacional de Estadistica
Debt, external, 215–18
Dees, Malcolm, 243 n
Departamento Administrativo Nacional de Estadistica (DANE, National Statistical Institute), 29, 31 n, 41, 49–51, 77, 95, 96, 111 n, 122 n, 130, 143 n
Departamento Nacional de Planeacion. See National Planning Department
Depression, 75, 76, 90
Development expenditures, 168
Duloy, John, 40 n, 118 n

ECIEL (Estudios Conjuntos de Integracion Economica Latinoamericana), 51, 62 n
ECLA. See United Nations Economic Commission for Latin America
Economic growth rate and lower-income groups, 117–21
Eddison, John, 208 n
Education, 150, 175–99, 256; and

Index

capital distribution, 8, 95, 175–76; countries compared, 189, 191, 193; distribution for, 20–24-year age group, 273, 274; and income distribution, 181, 182, 183–99; lack of, 149; public expenditures for, 162–64, 175, 258–59; rate of return on investment in, 189–92, 195, 198; and regional income distribution, 136, 137; in rural areas, 248–49; of women, 190
El Salvador, 40
Engels, Friedrich, 201 n
Estudios Conjuntos de Integracion Economica Latinoamericana (ECIEL), 51, 62 n
Exchange, control of, 202, 203, 204, 206–07
Exchange Control Office, 203

Family income, 43–44
Family size and income level, 8, 24
Farming. See Agriculture
Fei, John C. H., 11 n, 14 n
Felstehausen, Hermann, 240 n
Financial sector, 151, 200–29, 259–60
Fiscal policy, 150, 153–74, 258–59. See also Public expenditures; Taxation
Foreign debt, 215–18
Foreign exchange. See Exchange
Foreign trade, 206–07, 229
France: banking system, 200, 201
Fried, I., 23 n
Fuller, Varden, 241 n

Gillespie, W. Irwin, 159 n, 166 n, 167 n
Gillis, Malcolm, 48 n, 170 n, 239 n
Gini coefficient, 18 n–19 n, 34 n, 41, 44, 50, 52, 57, 61–62, 105 n, 107 n, 116, 170, 192 n–193 n, 253; concentration ratio, 37–39
Goering, T., 241 n
Goldsmith, Raymond, 202 n
Government employees: wages, 97–99, 133
Government expenditures. See Public expenditures
Great Britain. See United Kingdom

Gross domestic product (GDP), 128–29, 130, 142
Gross national product (GNP), 202, 203
Guillen Martinez, Fernando, 195 n

Haller, Thomas, 248 n
Hanneson, Bill, 57 n
Hansen, W. Lee, 194
Harberger, Arnold C., 125 n, 186, 192
Heckscher, Eli F., 21 n
Hicks, John, 10
Housing: regional distribution of improvements, 134–36, 145 n; rents and inflation, 227; in rural areas, 35; subsidies, 168
Huila, 90 n
Human capital, 150, 175, 183; in agriculture, 60, 63 n, 95; definition of, 22 n–23 n

ICSS. See Social Security Institute
Import controls, 206, 228
Import licensing, 203, 206
Import substitution, 21, 256
Income distribution: agricultural and nonagricultural compared, 16–20, 31–35, 71–72, 107 n–108 n (see also Agricultural income distribution; Rural areas); of capital and labor, 8–10; changes, determinants of, 3–17, 21; conclusions on, 252–63; in development, 1930s–1960s, 24–25, 87–123; and education, 175–99; and finance, 200–29; individual and family, 43–44; international comparisons, 39–43; of labor (see Labor income distribution); of lower-income groups, 117–21; in 1960s, 27–52; by occupation, 265–66; and output per capita, 90; regional (see Regional income distribution); and taxation, 153–58; urban (see Urban areas)
Income tax. See Taxation
INCORA. See Instituto Colombiano de Reforma Agraria
Industries, 22, 255; large and small,

Industries (*continued*)
208, 213; loans to, 208. *See also*
Manufacturing
Inflation, 220–29, 259; and
agriculture, 227–28; and economic
growth, 118 *n*; and income
distribution, 220–23; and interest
rates, 213 *n*, 221–22; and land
prices, 224; and pensions, 226–27;
and rents, 227; wages and
salaries affected by, 223–28
Infrastructure projects, 216–18
Instituto Colombiano de Reforma
Agraria (INCORA), 165, 230,
246, 247, 261
Instituto de Mercadeo Agropecurario
(IDEMA), 241
Instituto Nacional de
Abasteciemientos (INA), 241
Intelligence: inheritance of, 178–79;
racial differences, 180 *n*
Interamerican Development Bank
(IDB), 236 *n*
Interest rates, 186, 202, 205, 207–08,
212, 213–15, 259; on agricultural
loans, 229, 234; ceilings on,
221 *n*; and inflation, 213 *n*,
221–22; subsidies, 213
International Labor Organization
(ILO), 203 *n*
Isaza, Rafael, 111 *n*

Jackson, Andrew, 200
Japan, 65 *n*, 94 *n*
Jensen, Arthur R., 178 *n*, 179, 180 *n*
Jimenez, Gustavo, 3 *n*
Johnson, Harry G., 5 *n*
Jolly, Richard, 40 *n*, 118 *n*
Junguito, Roberto, 222, 239 *n*
Junta, Monetaria, 203, 204

Kaldor, N., 5 *n*
Kalecki, M., 5 *n*
Kravis, Irving, 23 *n*
Kuznets, Simon, 16, 23 *n*, 24, 107 *n*,
116, 255, 256
Kuznets ratio, 39

Labor, public expenditures for, 166
Labor force, 255; job security, 195;
occupational structure change,
139–42; and regional inequality,
125, 138–44; sectoral distribution
changes, 15–21; unskilled, 90–91,
95; women in, 181, 183. *See also*
Agricultural labor force; Wages
Labor income distribution, 8–26,
90–105, 176–77, 255–56; and
abilities, 178–81; age and sex in,
181–83; by departments, 267–72
(*see also* Regional income
distribution); and education, 181,
182, 183–99; in England and
Colombia, 176, 177; and inflation,
223–28; by occupation, 265–66;
total labor force, 36, 37, 45
Labor surplus: in agriculture, 13,
53, 69 *n*; income distribution
changes with, 10–15; modern and
traditional sectors, 11–15; and
wages, 14–15
Labor unions, 151–52, 223, 226, 228
Land: and agricultural income, 60,
68, 75; distribution, 53, 57–58,
76 *n*; government policy on,
242–48; prices compared with
cost-of-living increases, 244;
taxes on, 239–40, 249–50
Land Law 200 of 1936, 75, 230,
242–43
Landlords, 75; absentee, 29
Land reform, 150, 151, 242–48,
260–61; public expenditures for,
165–66
Lebret, C. J.: mission, 27 *n*, 47
Lewis, W. Arthur, 10 *n*, 11 *n*,
15 *n*, 24
Livestock, 82–83, 85. *See also*
Cattle
Loans, 208, 209, 221; in agriculture,
233–36; Mortgage Bank, 218–19
Locke, John, 160
Lopez, Alfonso, 105 *n*, 230, 242
Lorenz curves, 18 *n*, 34 *n*, and
concentration ratio, 37–39; for
labor income and education, 186,
187, 188; for personal income
distribution, 57, 58; for wage/
salary income of Colombia and
England, 177
Louisiana: road construction, 166
Lydall, Harold, 180 *n*

Index

McGreevey, William P., 118 n
McLure, Charles E., Jr., 48–51, 154, 156
Magdalena, 134, 136
Maids: wages, 104, 105, 109, 119
Malnutrition, 149, 171
Manizales, 44
Manufacturing: cottage-shop, 143; output per capita, 132; wages, 71, 95–97, 108–10, 119, 133, 226, 256
Marabelli, Francesco, 127, 130, 131 n, 138 n
Marginal productivities, 4–6
Marginal propensity to save, 118 n
Marketing system: imperfections in, 4–9, 21–22; perfect, 4–5, 9
Marx, Karl, 201
Meade, James E., 8 n, 23 n, 193
Medellin, 44, 71 n, 144
Mental health, 149
Mexico, 188, 195; financial policy, 204 n; income distribution, 34 n, 40, 41; inflation, 228 n
Meyer, Richard L., 249 n
Minami, Ryoshin, 94 n
Mincer, Jacob, 184, 187
Minifundia, 53, 70
Ministry of Agriculture, 232
Ministry of Public Health, 24 n, 49, 130
Monetary policy, 203–08, 213–15, 229
Monopoly, 254, 255; in foreign trade, 229; and inflation, 228; and technological change, 6, 22
Morris, Cynthia Taft, 25 n
Mortgage Bank, 213 n; bonds, 218, 222 n; loans, 218–19
Motor vehicles: gasoline consumption, 167; and road expenditures, 166, 167; taxation, 156
Musalem, Alberto, 220 n, 221 n
Musgrave, Richard, 48 n, 170 n, 239 n; commission, 27 n, 48, 158, 240 n
Myrdal, Gunnar, 25, 125 n

Nariño, 131, 133, 138 n, 139, 257
National Planning Department, 47, 203 n, 232
National Statistical Institute. *See*
Departamento Administrativo Nacional de Estadistica
Navarrete, I. M. de, 228 n
Nelson, R. R., 198 n
Neoclassical economic system, 4–10, 21, 201, 204

Ohlin, Bertil, 21 n
Old people, inflation effects on, 226, 227
Ortega, Francisco, 111 n
Output per capita, 90

Padilla, Alfonso, 27 n
Panela, 82, 83
Payan Lopez, Genaro, 208 n
Pensions and inflation, 226–27
Perlman, R., 223, 225 n
Personalism, 22
Philippines, 124
Plantains, 238
Polk, James K., 200
Pombo, Joaquin de, 214 n
Populist movements, 221
Potatoes, 82, 83, 238
Poverty, 149, 150, 171, 174
Price indices: income classes compared, 121–23
Prices, 260; agricultural, 75, 76, 241–42; relative, of goods, 9, 10; in rural and urban areas, 35; and wages, 76
Prieto, Rafael, 51–52, 57 n
Public expenditures, 150, 158–74; distribution among users of services, 162–69; effect summarized, 169–74, 258–59; on goods and services, 159–62; individual and group benefits from, 158–60; local, 170; transfers, 159, 258
Public health, expenditures for, 164–65
Public utilities, expenditures for, 168–69
Public works, expenditures for, 166–68
Puerto Rico, 34 n, 40, 195

Ranis, Gustav, 11 n, 14 n
Rask, Norman, 249 n

Rationing, 205
Real estate: value, 22–23, 227
Real income, definition of, 9 n
Regional income distribution,
  124–45, 256–57; Colombia
  compared with other countries,
  124–27; by departments, 127–30,
  132–34, 267–72; and education,
  136, 137; and housing, 134–36,
  145 n; and labor force, 125, 138–44
Reyes, Marco, 57 n
Rice, 74, 76, 82, 83, 86, 231, 241
Road construction, 166–67, 240–41
Rodriguez, Mario L., 50 n
Ross, William D., 166 n
Rural areas: education, 248–49;
  housing, 35, 134 n; income
  distribution, 131; labor force,
  income, 31–35 (see also
  Agricultural labor force);
  minimum wage, 152; prices, 35
Rural–urban migration, 255, 257;
  and income changes, 16, 20–21,
  90, 138–39, 144; and
  unemployment, 35, 37

Samper D., Felipe, 130 n
Sandoval, Clara Elsa de, 27 n,
  50 n, 226 n
Santander del Norte, 223
Sarmiento, Eduardo, 125 n, 192 n
Savings, 201–02; deposits, 114–15,
  222; interest on, 212, 213–15;
  rate of, 7, 23, 213; tax exemption
  for income, 218, 220
Schlesinger, Arthur M., Jr., 200 n
Schultz, T. Paul, 164 n, 190, 192,
  198 n
Schumpeter, Joseph A., 6
Sectoral policy, 149–52
Seiders, David, 228 n
Selowsky, Marcelo, 164 n, 189,
  190, 192
Service sector, 22
Sesame, 74, 76, 82, 83, 231
Slighton, R., 198 n–199 n
Social classes, 252–53; and abilities,
  178–79; and inflation, 223, 226–28
Social mobility, 177, 195
Social security, 150, 166, 176
Social Security Institute (ICSS),
  150, 166 n, 176
Solis, Leopoldo, 228 n
Sorghum, 83
Soybeans, 83
Stiglitz, Joseph, 6 n
Stocks: rate of return, 222, 226–27
Sugar production, 76, 82, 83, 85,
  231

Taxation, 150, 153–58, 258; in
  agriculture, 238–40, 249–50;
  alcohol, beer, and tobacco, 156;
  and capital income, 111–12;
  corporation income, 156;
  exemptions on investments,
  218–20, 222, 227; income, 154,
  156, 158, 239, 249–50; income
  distribution before and after
  taxes, 154, 155, 172–73; land,
  239–40, 249–50; motor vehicle,
  156; property, 156, 158, 239
Taylor, Milton C.: mission, 27 n,
  48, 50, 51, 52
Teachers: wages, 97
Technological change: in
  agriculture, 73–79, 231, 236–37,
  250, 261; capital-saving, 14–15;
  and economic growth, 118 n;
  labor-saving, 7, 118 n; and
  monopoly, 6, 22; neutral, 10
Thirsk, Wayne, 236 n, 242
Tobacco, 82, 83; taxes on, 156
Tolima, 90 n, 134, 136
Tourism, 168
Tractors, 76, 78–79, 236

Udall, Alan, 90 n, 97 n, 99 n,
  103 n, 104, 105, 109, 110
Unemployment, 206; rural, 77; and
  rural–urban migration, 35, 37;
  and unions, 28 n, 31
United Kingdom: income
  distribution, 40, 42–43; wage/
  salary income, 176, 177
United Nations Economic
  Commission for Latin America
  (ECLA), 27 n, 39, 47, 82 n, 110
United States: aid from, 216;
  education, 194; income
  distribution, 40, 228 n; labor,
  195–96

United States Bank, 200
Urban areas: housing, 134 n, 136; income distribution, 28–31, 34–35, 37, 44, 104–05, 108–10, 131, 144; labor force, 29; minimum wage, 152
Urrutia, Miguel, 27 n, 49–52, 88 n, 110, 123 n, 152, 223 n, 226 n

Valle, 131, 138 n, 139
Veblen, Thorstein, 201
Venezuela, 40, 41
Vernon, P. E., 197, 198 n
Victaliano, Izquierdo B., 82 n
Violencia (1940s and 1950s), 76 n, 90, 103, 121 n, 255

Wages, 90–105, 255–56; of agricultural laborers, 59–72, 74–77, 90–95, 99–108, 115, 118, 133, 145 n, 256; in commerce, 104, 105, 109, 118; in construction, 71, 99–105, 109–10, 119, 256; and depression, 75, 76; of government employees, 97–99, 133; and inflation, 223–28; and labor surplus, 12, 14–15; of low-income groups, 117–21; in manufacturing, 71, 95–97, 108–10, 119, 133, 226, 256; minimum wage policy, 151–52; and prices, 76; real, selected series, 112–13; regional distribution, 133–34; rises and capital falls, 10; and unions, 152, 223, 226, 228; of white-collar group, 95–96, 105 n, 109, 225. See also Labor income distribution
Wealth, distribution of, 6, 22–24; and inflation, 221–23
Weisbrod, Burton A., 194
Weisskoff, Richard, 25, 34 n
Wheat, 76, 83, 241
Women: education, 190; in labor force, 181, 183
World Bank (Banco Internacional de Reconstruccion y Fomento), 40 n, 47, 236 n, 240 n

Yucca, 82, 83, 238

Economic Growth Center Book Publications

Werner Baer, *Industrialization and Economic Development in Brazil* (1965).

Werner Baer and Isaac Kerstenetsky, eds., *Inflation and Growth in Latin America* (1964).

Bela A. Balassa, *Trade Prospects for Developing Countries* (1964). Out of print.

Albert Berry and Miguel Urrutia, *Income Distribution in Colombia* (1976).

Thomas B. Birnberg and Stephen A. Resnick, *Colonial Development: An Econometric Study* (1975).

Benjamin I. Cohen, *Multinational Firms and Asian Exports* (1975).

Carlos F. Díaz Alejandro, *Essays on the Economic History of the Argentine Republic* (1970).

Robert Evenson and Yoav Kislev, *Agricultural Research and Productivity* (1975).

John C. H. Fei and Gustav Ranis, *Development of Labor Surplus Economy: Theory and Policy* (1964).

Gerald K. Helleiner, *Peasant Agriculture, Government, and Economic Growth in Nigeria* (1966)

Lawrence R. Klein and Kazushi Ohkawa, eds., *Economic Growth: The Japanese Experience since the Meiji Era* (1968).

A. Lamfalussy, *The United Kingdom and the Six* (1963). Out of print.

Markos J. Mamalakis, *The Growth and Structure of the Chilean Economy: From Independence to Allende* (1976).

Markos J. Mamalakis and Clark W. Reynolds, *Essays on the Chilean Economy* (1965).

Donald C. Mead, *Growth and Structural Change in the Egyptian Economy* (1967).

Richard Moorsteen and Raymond P. Powell, *The Soviet Capital Stock* (1966).

Douglas S. Paauw and John C. H. Fei, *The Transition in Open Dualistic Economies: Theory and Southeast Asian Experience* (1973).

Howard Pack, *Structural Change and Economic Policy in Israel* (1971).

Frederick L. Pryor, *Public Expenditures in Communist and Capitalist Nations* (1968).

Gustav Ranis, ed., *Government and Economic Development* (1971).

Clark W. Reynolds, *The Mexican Economy: Twentieth-Century Structure and Growth* (1970).

Lloyd G. Reynolds, ed., *Agriculture in Development Theory* (1975).

Lloyd G. Reynolds and Peter Gregory, *Wages, Productivity, and Industrialization in Puerto Rico* (1965).

Donald R. Snodgrass, *Ceylon: An Export Economy in Transition* (1966.)

Soc
HC
200
I5
B47

DATE DUE	
NOV 20 1975	CT NOV 04 1986
JUN 13 1977	NOV 07 1990
DEC 25 1978	
JUN 23 1980	
CT DEC 29 1981	
CT JAN 19 1982	OCT 2 0 1984
GR OCT 13 1982	
LS OCT 13 1984	
1984	
LR NOV 27 1984	
LR DEC 19 1984	